ESSAYS OF JOHN DRYDEN

W. P. KER

ESSAYS

OF

JOHN DRYDEN

SELECTED AND EDITED

BY

W. P. KER

VOLUME II

New York
RUSSELL & RUSSELL
1961

PR
3417
A1
1961
V. 2

CONTENTS

EXAMEN POETICUM:

BEING THE THIRD PART OF MISCELLANY POEMS

[1693]

DEDICATION

TO THE RIGHT HONOURABLE MY

LORD RADCLIFFE

My Lord,

THESE Miscellany Poems are by many titles yours. The first they claim, from your acceptance of my promise to present them to you, before some of them were yet in being. The rest are derived from your own merit, the exactness of your judgment in Poetry, and 5 the candour of your nature, easy to forgive some trivial faults, when they come accompanied with countervailing beauties. But, after all, though these are your equitable claims to a dedication from other poets, yet I must acknowledge a bribe in the case, which is your par- 10 ticular liking of my verses. 'Tis a vanity common to all writers, to overvalue their own productions ; and 'tis better for me to own this failing in myself, than the world to do it for me. For what other reason have I spent my life in so unprofitable a study ? why am 15 I grown old, in seeking so barren a reward as fame ?

The same parts and application which have made me
a poet might have raised me to any honours of the
gown, which are often given to men of as little learning
and less honesty than myself. No Government has
5 ever been, or ever can be, wherein timeservers and
blockheads will not be uppermost. The persons are
only changed, but the same jugglings in State, the same
hypocrisy in religion, the same self-interest and mis-
management, will remain for ever. Blood and money
10 will be lavished in all ages, only for the preferment of
new faces, with old consciences. There is too often
a jaundice in the eyes of great men ; they see not those
whom they raise in the same colours with other men.
All whom they affect look golden to them, when the
15 gilding is only in their own distempered sight. These
considerations have given me a kind of contempt for
those who have risen by unworthy ways. I am not
ashamed to be little, when I see them so infamously
great ; neither do I know why the name of poet should
20 be dishonourable to me, if I am truly one, as I hope
I am ; for I will never do anything that shall dishonour
it. The notions of morality are known to all men ;
none can pretend ignorance of those ideas which are
inborn in mankind ; and if I see one thing, and practise
25 the contrary, I must be disingenuous not to acknowledge a clear truth, and base to act against the light of
my own conscience. For the reputation of my honesty,
no man can question it, who has any of his own ; for
that of my poetry, it shall either stand by its own
30 merit, or fall for want of it. Ill writers are usually
the sharpest censors ; for they, as the best poet and the
best patron said,

> When in the full perfection of decay,
> Turn vinegar, and come again in play.

35 Thus the corruption of a poet is the generation of

a critic ; I mean of a critic in the general acceptation
of this age ; for formerly they were quite another species
of men. They were defenders of poets, and commentators on their works ; to illustrate obscure beauties ;
to place some passages in a better light ; to redeem 5
others from malicious interpretations ; to help out an
author's modesty, who is not ostentatious of his wit ;
and, in short, to shield him from the ill-nature of those
fellows, who were then called *Zoili* and *Momi*, and now
take upon themselves the venerable name of censors. 10
But neither Zoilus, nor he who endeavoured to defame
Virgil, were ever adopted into the name of critics by the
Ancients ; what their reputation was then, we know ;
and their successors in this age deserve no better. Are
our auxiliary forces turned our enemies ? are they, 15
who at best are but wits of the second order, and
whose only credit amongst readers is what they
obtained by being subservient to the fame of writers,
are these become rebels, of slaves, and usurpers, of
subjects ? or, to speak in the most honourable terms 20
of them, are they from our seconds become principals
against us ? Does the ivy undermine the oak which
supports its weakness ? What labour would it cost
them to put in a better line, than the worst of those
which they expunge in a true poet ? Petronius, the 25
greatest wit perhaps of all the Romans, yet when his
envy prevailed upon his judgment to fall on Lucan, he
fell himself in his attempt ; he performed worse in his
Essay of the Civil War than the author of the *Pharsalia ;*
and, avoiding his errors, has made greater of his own. 30
Julius Scaliger would needs turn down Homer, and
abdicate him after the possession of three thousand
years : has he succeeded in his attempt ? He has indeed
shown us some of those imperfections in him, which are
incident to humankind ; but who had not rather be that 35

Homer than this Scaliger ?   You see the same hypercritic, when he endeavours to mend the beginning of
Claudian, (a faulty poet, and living in a barbarous age,)
yet how short he comes of him, and substitutes such
5 verses of his own as deserve the ferula.   What a censure
has he made of Lucan, that " he rather seems to bark
than sing " !   Would any but a dog have made so
snarling a comparison ?   one would have thought he
had learned Latin as late as they tell us he did Greek.
10 Yet he came off, with a *pace tuâ,* " by your good leave,
Lucan " ;   he called him not by those outrageous names,
of *fool, booby,* and *blockhead :* he had somewhat more of
good manners than his successors, as he had much
more knowledge.   We have two sorts of those gentle-
15 men in our nation ;   some of them, proceeding with
a seeming moderation and pretence of respect to the
dramatic writers of the last age, only scorn and vilify
the present poets, to set up their predecessors.   But
this is only in appearance ;   for their real design is
20 nothing less than to do honour to any man, besides
themselves.   Horace took notice of such men in his
age—

> *Non ingeniis favet ille sepultis,*
> *Nostra sed impugnat ; nos nostraque lividus odit.*

25   'Tis not with an ultimate intention to pay reverence
to the *Manes* of Shakespeare, Fletcher, and Ben
Johnson, that they commend their writings, but to
throw dirt on the writers of this age : their declara-
tion is one thing, and their practice is another.   By
30 a seeming veneration to our fathers, they would thrust
out us, their lawful issue, and govern us themselves,
under a specious pretence of reformation.   If they
could compass their intent, what would wit and learning get by such a change ?   If we are bad poets, they
35 are worse ;   and when any of their woful pieces come

abroad, the difference is so great betwixt them and good
writers, that there need no criticisms on our part to
decide it. When they describe the writers of this age,
they draw such monstrous figures of them, as resemble
none of us ; our pretended pictures are so unlike, that 5
'tis evident we never sat to them : they are all grotesque ;
the products of their wild imaginations, things out of
nature ; so far from being copied from us, that they
resemble nothing that ever was, or ever can be. But
there is another sort of insects, more venomous than 10
the former ; those who manifestly aim at the destruction
of our poetical church and state ; who allow nothing to
their countrymen, either of this or of the former age.
These attack the living by raking up the ashes of the
dead ; well knowing that if they can subvert their 15
original title to the stage, we who claim under them
must fall of course. Peace be to the venerable shades
of Shakespeare and Ben Johnson ! none of the living
will presume to have any competition with them ; as
they were our predecessors, so they were our masters. 20
We trail our plays under them ; but as at the funerals
of a Turkish emperor, our ensigns are furled or dragged
upon the ground, in honour to the dead, so we may
lawfully advance our own afterwards, to show that we
succeed ; if less in dignity, yet on the same foot and 25
title, which we think too we can maintain against the
insolence of our own Janizaries. If I am the man, as
I have reason to believe, who am seemingly courted,
and secretly undermined ; I think I shall be able to
defend myself, when I am openly attacked ; and to 30
show, besides, that the Greek writers only gave us the
rudiments of a stage which they never finished ; that
many of the tragedies in the former age amongst us
were without comparison beyond those of Sophocles
and Euripides. But at present I have neither the 35

leisure, nor the means, for such an undertaking. 'Tis
ill going to law for an estate, with him who is in possession of it, and enjoys the present profits, to feed his
cause. But the *quantum mutatus* may be remembered
5 in due time. In the meanwhile, 1 leave the world to
judge, who gave the provocation.

   This, my Lord, is, I confess, a long digression, from
Miscellany Poems to *Modern Tragedies ;* but I have the
ordinary excuse of an injured man, who will be telling
10 his tale unseasonably to his betters ; though, at the
same time, I am certain you are so good a friend, as
to take a concern in all things which belong to one who
so truly honours you. And besides, being yourself
a critic of the genuine sort, who have read the best
15 authors in their own languages, who perfectly distinguish
of their several merits, and in general prefer them to the
Moderns, yet, I know, you judge for the English
tragedies, against Greek and Latin, as well as against
the French, Italian, and Spanish, of these latter ages.
20 Indeed, there is a vast difference betwixt arguing like
Perrault, in behalf of the French poets, against Homer
and Virgil, and betwixt giving the English poets their
undoubted due, of excelling Æschylus, Euripides, and
Sophocles. For if we, or our greater fathers, have not
25 yet brought the drama to an absolute perfection, yet at
least we have carried it much further than those ancient
Greeks ; who, beginning from a Chorus, could never
totally exclude it, as we have done ; who find it an unprofitable encumbrance, without any necessity of enter-
30 taining it amongst us, and without the possibility of
establishing it here, unless it were supported by a public
charge. Neither can we accept of those Lay-Bishops,
as some call them, who, under pretence of reforming
the stage, would intrude themselves upon us, as our
35 superiors ; being indeed incompetent judges of what

is manners, what religion, and, least of all, what is
poetry and good sense. I can tell them, in behalf of
all my fellows, that when they come to exercise a juris-
diction over us, they shall have the stage to themselves,
as they have the laurel. As little can I grant, that the 5
French dramatic writers excel the English. Our authors
as far surpass them in genius, as our soldiers excel
theirs in courage. 'Tis true, in conduct they surpass
us either way ; yet that proceeds not so much from
their greater knowledge, as from the difference of 10
tastes in the two nations. They content themselves
with a thin design, without episodes, and managed by
few persons. Our audience will not be pleased, but
with variety of accidents, an underplot, and many
actors. They follow the ancients too servilely in the 15
mechanic rules, and we assume too much licence to
ourselves, in keeping them only in view at too great
a distance. But if our audience had their tastes, our
poets could more easily comply with them, than the
French writers could come up to the sublimity of our 20
thoughts, or to the difficult variety of our designs.
However it be, I dare establish it for a rule of practice
on the stage, that we are bound to please those whom
we pretend to entertain ; and that at any price, religion
and good manners only excepted. And I care not 25
much if I give this handle to our bad illiterate
poetasters, for the defence of their *scriptions*, as they
call them. There is a sort of merit in delighting the
spectators, which is a name more proper for them, than
that of auditors ; or else Horace is in the wrong, when 30
he commends Lucilius for it. But these common-places
I mean to treat at greater leisure ; in the meantime
submitting that little I have said to your Lordship's
approbation, or your censure, and choosing rather to
entertain you this way, as you are a judge of writing, 35

than to oppress your modesty with other commendations ; which, though they are your due, yet would
not be equally received in this satirical and censorious
age. That which cannot, without injury, be denied to
5 you, is the easiness of your conversation, far from
affectation or pride ; not denying even to enemies their
just praises. And this, if I would dwell on any theme
of this nature, is no vulgar commendation to your
Lordship. Without flattery, my Lord, you have it in
10 your nature to be a patron and encourager of good
poets ; but your fortune has not yet put into your
hands the opportunity of expressing it. What you
will be hereafter, may be more than guessed by what
you are at present. You maintain the character of
15 a nobleman, without that haughtiness which generally
attends too many of the nobility ; and when you converse with gentlemen, you forget not that you have
been of their order. You are married to the daughter
of a King, who, amongst her other high perfections,
20 has derived from him a charming behaviour, a winning
goodness, and a majestic person. The Muses and the
Graces are the ornaments of your family ; while the
Muse sings, the Grace accompanies her voice : even the
servants of the Muses have sometimes had the happiness
25 to hear her, and to receive their inspirations from her.

I will not give myself the liberty of going further ;
for 'tis so sweet to wander in a pleasing way, that
I should never arrive at my journey's end. To keep
myself from being belated in my letter, and tiring
30 your attention, I must return to the place where I was
setting out. I humbly dedicate to your Lordship my
own labours in this *Miscellany ;* at the same time not
arrogating to myself the privilege, of inscribing to you
the works of others who are joined with me in this
35 undertaking, over which I can pretend no right. Your

Lady and you have done me the favour to hear me
read my translations of Ovid ; and you both seemed
not to be displeased with them. Whether it be the
partiality of an old man to his youngest child, I know
not ; but they appear to me the best of all my endeavours 5
in this kind. Perhaps this poet is more easy to be
translated than some others whom I have lately
attempted ; perhaps, too, he was more according to my
genius. He is certainly more palatable to the reader,
than any of the Roman wits ; though some of them are 10
more lofty, some more instructive, and others more
correct. He had learning enough to make him equal
to the best ; but, as his verse came easily, he wanted
the toil of application to amend it. He is often luxuriant
both in his fancy and expressions, and, as it has lately 15
been observed, not always natural. If wit be pleasantry,
he has it to excess ; but if it be propriety, Lucretius,
Horace, and, above all, Virgil, are his superiors.
I have said so much of him already in my Preface to
his *Heroical Epistles*, that there remains little to be 20
added in this place. For my own part, I have endeavoured to copy his character, what I could, in this
translation ; even, perhaps, further than I should have
done ; to his very faults. Mr. Chapman, in his *Translation of Homer*, professes to have done it somewhat 25
paraphrastically, and that on set purpose ; his opinion
being that a good poet is to be translated in that
manner. I remember not the reason which he gives
for it ; but I suppose it is for fear of omitting any of
his excellencies. Sure I am, that if it be a fault, 'tis 30
much more pardonable than that of those, who run into
the other extreme of a literal and close translation,
where the poet is confined so straitly to his author's
words, that he wants elbow-room to express his elegancies. He leaves him obscure ; he leaves him prose, 35

where he found him verse ; and no better than thus
has Ovid been served by the so-much-admired Sandys.
This is at least the idea which I have remaining of his
translation ; for I never read him since I was a boy.
5 They who take him upon content, from the praises
which their fathers gave him, may inform their judgment by reading him again, and see (if they understand
the original) what is become of Ovid's poetry in his
version ; whether it be not all, or the greatest part of
10 it, evaporated.   But this proceeded from the wrong
judgment of the age in which he lived.   They neither
knew good verse, nor loved it ; they were scholars, 'tis
true, but they were pedants ; and for a just reward of
their pedantic pains, all their translations want to be
15 translated into English.

If I flatter not myself, or if my friends have not
flattered me, I have given my author's sense for the
most part truly ; for, to mistake sometimes is incident
to all men ; and not to follow the Dutch commentators
20 always, may be forgiven to a man who thinks them, in
the general, heavy gross-witted fellows, fit only to gloss
on their own dull poets.   But I leave a further satire
on their wit, till I have a better opportunity to show
how much I love and honour them.   I have likewise
25 attempted to restore Ovid to his native sweetness,
easiness, and smoothness ; and to give my poetry
a kind of cadence, and, as we call it, a run of verse,
as like the original, as the English can come up to the
Latin.   As he seldom uses any synalœphas, so I have
30 endeavoured to avoid them as often as I could.   I have
likewise given him his own turns, both on the words
and on the thought ; which I cannot say are inimitable,
because I have copied them, and so may others, if they
use the same diligence ; but certainly they are wonder-
35 fully graceful in this poet.   Since I have named the

synalœpha, which is the cutting off one vowel immediately before another, I will give an example of it from
Chapman's *Homer*, which lies before me, for the benefit
of those who understand not the Latin *prosodia*. 'Tis
in the first line of the argument to the first *Iliad*—   5
    Apollo's priest to th' Argive fleet doth bring, &c.

There we see he makes it not *the Argive*, but *th'Argive*,
to shun the shock of the two vowels, immediately
following each other. But in his second argument, in
the same page, he gives a bad example of the quite 10
contrary kind—

    Alpha the pray'r of Chryses sings :
    The army's plague, the strife of kings.

In these words, *the army's*, *the* ending with a vowel,
and *army's* beginning with another vowel, without 15
cutting off the first, which by it had been *th' army's*,
there remains a most horrible ill-sounding gap betwixt
those words. I cannot say that I have everywhere
observed the rule of the synalœpha in my translation ;
but wheresoever I have not, 'tis a fault in sound. The 20
French and the Italians have made it an inviolable
precept in their versification ; therein following the
severe example of the Latin poets. Our countrymen
have not yet reformed their poetry so far, but content
themselves with following the licentious practice of the 25
Greeks ; who, though they sometimes use synalœphas,
yet make no difficulty, very often, to sound one vowel
upon another ; as Homer does, in the very first line
of *Alpha*—

    Μῆνιν ἄειδε, θεά, Πηληϊάδεω Ἀχιλῆος   30

It is true, indeed, that, in the second line, in these
words, μυρί᾽ Ἀχαιοῖς, and ἄλγε᾽ ἔθηκε, the synalœpha, in
revenge, is twice observed. But it becomes us, for the
sake of euphony, rather *Musas colere severiores*, with the
Romans, than to give into the looseness of the Grecians. 35

I have tired myself, and have been summoned by the press to send away this *Dedication ;* otherwise I had exposed some other faults, which are daily committed by our English poets ; which, with care and observa-
5 tion, might be amended. For after all, our language is both copious, significant, and majestical, and might be reduced into a more harmonious sound. But for want of public encouragement, in this Iron Age, we are so far from making any progress in the improvement
10 of our tongue, that in few years we shall speak and write as barbarously as our neighbours.

Notwithstanding my haste, I cannot forbear to tell your Lordship, that there are two fragments of Homer translated in this *Miscellany ;* one by Mr. Congreve,
15 (whom I cannot mention without the honour which is due to his excellent parts, and that entire affection which I bear him,) and the other by myself. Both the subjects are pathetical ; and I am sure my friend has added to the tenderness which he found in the original,
20 and without flattery, surpassed his author. Yet I must needs say this in reference to Homer, that he is much more capable of exciting the manly passions than those of grief and pity. To cause admiration is, indeed, the proper and adequate design of an Epic Poem ; and in
25 that he has excelled even Virgil. Yet, without presum- ing to arraign our master, I may venture to affirm, that he is somewhat too talkative, and more than somewhat too digressive. This is so manifest, that it cannot be denied in that little parcel which I have translated,
30 perhaps too literally : there Andromache, in the midst of her concernment and fright for Hector, runs off her bias, to tell him a story of her pedigree, and of the lamentable death of her father, her mother, and her seven brothers. The devil was in Hector if he knew
35 not all this matter, as well as she who told it him ; for

she had been his bedfellow for many years together :
and if he knew it, then it must be confessed, that
Homer, in this long digression, has rather given us
his own character, than that of the fair lady whom he
paints. His dear friends the commentators, who never 5
fail him at a pinch, will needs excuse him, by making
the present sorrow of Andromache to occasion the
remembrance of all the past ; but others think, that
she had enough to do with that grief which now
oppressed her, without running for assistance to her 10
family. Virgil, I am confident, would have omitted
such a work of supererogation. But Virgil had the
gift of expressing much in little, and sometimes in
silence ; for, though he yielded much to Homer in
invention, he more excelled him in his admirable judg- 15
ment. He drew the passion of Dido for Æneas, in
the most lively and most natural colours that are
imaginable. Homer was ambitious enough of moving
pity, for he has attempted twice on the same subject of
Hector's death ; first, when Priam and Hecuba beheld 20
his corpse, which was dragged after the chariot of
Achilles ; and then in the lamentation which was made
over him, when his body was redeemed by Priam ; and
the same persons again bewail his death, with a chorus
of others to help the cry. But if this last excite com- 25
passion in you, as I doubt not but it will, you are more
obliged to the translator than the poet ; for Homer,
as I observed before, can move rage better than he
can pity. He stirs up the irascible appetite, as our
philosophers call it ; he provokes to murder, and the 30
destruction of God's images ; he forms and equips
those ungodly man-killers, whom we poets, when we
flatter them, call heroes ; a race of men who can never
enjoy quiet in themselves, till they have taken it from
all the world. This is Homer's commendation ; and, 35

such as it is, the lovers of peace, or at least of more
moderate heroism, will never envy him. But let Homer
and Virgil contend for the prize of honour betwixt
themselves ; I am satisfied they will never have a third
5 concurrent. I wish Mr. Congreve had the leisure to
translate him, and the world the good nature and
justice to encourage him in that noble design, of which
he is more capable than any man I know. The Earl
of Mulgrave and Mr. Waller, two of the best judges of
10 our age, have assured me, that they could never read
over the translation of Chapman without incredible
pleasure and extreme transport. This admiration of
theirs must needs proceed from the author himself ;
for the translator has thrown him down as low as harsh
15 numbers, improper English, and a monstrous length of
verse could carry him. What then would he appear
in the harmonious version of one of the best writers,
living in a much better age than was the last ? I mean
for versification, and the art of numbers ; for in the
20 drama we have not arrived to the pitch of Shakespeare
and Ben Johnson. But here, my Lord, I am forced
to break off abruptly, without endeavouring at a compliment in the close. This *Miscellany* is, without dispute,
one of the best of the kind which has hitherto been
25 extant in our tongue. At least, as Sir Samuel Tuke
has said before me, a modest man may praise what is
not his own. My fellows have no need of any protection ; but I humbly recommend my part of it, as much
as it deserves, to your patronage and acceptance, and
30 all the rest to your forgiveness.

I am,

My Lord,

Your Lordship's most obedient servant,

John Dryden.

A DISCOURSE CONCERNING THE
ORIGINAL AND PROGRESS OF SATIRE:

DEDICATED TO

THE RIGHT HONOURABLE

CHARLES, EARL OF DORSET AND MIDDLESEX

LORD CHAMBERLAIN OF THEIR MAJESTIES' HOUSEHOLD; KNIGHT
OF THE MOST NOBLE ORDER OF THE GARTER, ETC.

MY LORD,

THE wishes and desires of all good men, which have attended your Lordship from your first appearance in the world, are at length accomplished, in your obtaining those honours and dignities which you have so long 5 deserved. There are no factions, though irreconcilable to one another, that are not united in their affection to you, and the respect they pay you. They are equally pleased in your prosperity, and would be equally concerned in your afflictions. Titus Vespasian was not 10 more the delight of human-kind. The universal Empire made him only more known, and more powerful, but could not make him more beloved. He had greater ability of doing good, but your inclination to it is not less ; and though you could not extend your beneficence 15 to so many persons, yet you have lost as few days as that excellent Emperor ; and never had his complaint

to make when you went to bed, that the sun had shone
upon you in vain, when you had the opportunity of
relieving some unhappy man. This, my Lord, has
justly acquired you as many friends as there are persons
5 who have the honour to be known to you.   Mere
acquaintance you have none ; you have drawn them all
into a nearer line ; and they who have conversed with
you are for ever after inviolably yours. This is a truth
so generally acknowledged, that it needs no proof : 'tis
10 of the nature of a first principle, which is received as
soon as it is proposed ; and needs not the reformation
which Descartes used to his ; for we doubt not, neither
can we properly say, we think we admire and love you
above all other men ; there is a certainty in the proposi-
15 tion, and we know it. With the same assurance I can
say, you neither have enemies, nor can scarce have any ;
for they who have never heard of you, can neither love
or hate you ; and they who have, can have no other
notion of you, than that which they receive from the
20 public, that you are the best of men. After this, my
testimony can be of no further use, than to declare
it to be daylight at high-noon ; and all who have the
benefit of sight, can look up as well, and see the sun.

'Tis true, I have one privilege which is almost par-
25 ticular to myself, that I saw you in the east at your first
arising above the hemisphere : I was as soon sensible
as any man of that light, when it was but just shooting
out, and beginning to travel upwards to the meridian.
I made my early addresses to your Lordship, in my
30 *Essay of Dramatic Poetry ;* and therein bespoke you
to the world, wherein I have the right of a first dis-
coverer. When I was myself in the rudiments of my
poetry, without name or reputation in the world, having
rather the ambition of a writer, than the skill ; when
35 I was drawing the outlines of an art, without any living

master to instruct me in it ; an art which had been better
praised than studied here in England, wherein Shakespeare, who created the stage among us, had rather
written happily, than knowingly and justly, and Johnson, who, by studying Horace, had been acquainted 5
with the rules, yet seemed to envy to posterity that
knowledge, and, like an inventor of some useful art,
to make a monopoly of his learning ; when thus, as
I may say, before the use of the loadstone, or knowledge of the compass, I was sailing in a vast ocean, 10
without other help than the pole-star of the Ancients,
and the rules of the French stage amongst the Moderns,
which are extremely different from ours, by reason of
their opposite taste ; yet even then, I had the presumption to dedicate to your Lordship : a very unfinished 15
piece, I must confess, and which only can be excused
by the little experience of the author, and the modesty
of the title *An Essay.*   Yet I was stronger in prophecy
than I was in criticism ; I was inspired to foretell you
to mankind, as the restorer of poetry, the greatest 20
genius, the truest judge, and the best patron.

  Good sense and good nature are never separated,
though the ignorant world has thought otherwise.
Good nature, by which I mean beneficence and candour,
is the product of right reason ; which of necessity will 25
give allowance to the failings of others, by considering
that there is nothing perfect in mankind ; and by distinguishing that which comes nearest to excellency, though
not absolutely free from faults, will certainly produce
a candour in the judge.   'Tis incident to an elevated 30
understanding, like your Lordship's, to find out the
errors of other men ; but it is your prerogative to pardon
them ; to look with pleasure on those things, which are
somewhat congenial, and of a remote kindred to your
own conceptions ; and to forgive the many failings of 35

those, who, with their wretched art, cannot arrive to
those heights that you possess, from a happy, abundant,
and native genius : which are as inborn to you, as they
were to Shakespeare ; and, for aught I know, to Homer ;
5 in either of whom we find all arts and sciences, all moral
and natural philosophy, without knowing that they ever
studied them.

There is not an English writer this day living, who is
not perfectly convinced that your Lordship excels all
10 others in all the several parts of poetry which you have
undertaken to adorn. The most vain, and the most
ambitious of our age, have not dared to assume so
much, as the competitors of Themistocles : they have
yielded the first place without dispute ; and have been
15 arrogantly content to be esteemed as second to your
Lordship ; and even that also, with a *longo, sed proximi
intervallo*. If there have been, or are any, who go further in their self-conceit, they must be very singular in
their opinion ; they must be like the officer in a play,
20 who was called Captain, Lieutenant, and Company. The
world will easily conclude, whether such unattended
generals can ever be capable of making a revolution in
Parnassus.

I will not attempt, in this place, to say anything par-
25 ticular of your lyric poems, though they are the delight
and wonder of this age, and will be the envy of the
next. The subject of this book confines me to Satire ;
and in that, an author of your own quality, (whose ashes
I will not disturb,) has given you all the commendation
30 which his self-sufficiency could afford to any man : *The
best good man, with the worst-natur'd Muse*. In that
character, methinks, I am reading Johnson's verses to
the memory of Shakespeare ; an insolent, sparing, and
invidious panegyric : where good nature, the most god-
35 like commendation of a man, is only attributed to your

person, and denied to your writings ; for they are everywhere so full of candour, that, like Horace, you only
expose the follies of men, without arraigning their vices ;
and in this excel him, that you add that pointedness of
thought, which is visibly wanting in our great Roman. 5
There is more of salt in all your verses, than I have
seen in any of the Moderns, or even of the Ancients ;
but you have been sparing of the gall, by which means
you have pleased all readers, and offended none.
Donne alone, of all our countrymen, had your talent ; 10
but was not happy enough to arrive at your versification ; and were he translated into numbers, and English,
he would yet be wanting in the dignity of expression.
That which is the prime virtue, and chief ornament, of
Virgil, which distinguishes him from the rest of writers, 15
is so conspicuous in your verses, that it casts a shadow
on all your contemporaries ; we cannot be seen, or but
obscurely, while you are present. You equal Donne in
the variety, multiplicity, and choice of thoughts ; you
excel him in the manner and the words. I read you 20
both with the same admiration, but not with the same
delight. He affects the metaphysics, not only in his
satires, but in his amorous verses, where nature only
should reign ; and perplexes the minds of the fair sex
with nice speculations of philosophy, when he should 25
engage their hearts, and entertain them with the soft-
nesses of love. In this (if I may be pardoned for so bold
a truth) Mr. Cowley has copied him to a fault ; so
great a one, in my opinion, that it throws his *Mistress*
infinitely below his Pindarics and his latter composi- 30
tions, which are undoubtedly the best of his poems, and
the most correct. For my own part, I must avow it
freely to the world, that I never attempted anything in
satire, wherein I have not studied your writings as the
most perfect model. I have continually laid them before 35

me ; and the greatest commendation, which my own
partiality can give to my productions, is, that they are
copies, and no further to be allowed, than as they have
something more or less of the original.   Some few
5 touches of your Lordship, some secret graces which
I have endeavoured to express after your manner, have
made whole poems of mine to pass with approbation ;
but take your verses altogether, and they are inimitable.
If therefore I have not written better, it is because
10 you have not written more.   You have not set me sufficient copy to transcribe ; and I cannot add one letter
of my own invention, of which I have not the example
there.

'Tis a general complaint against your Lordship, and
15 I must have leave to upbraid you with it, that, because
you need not write, you will not.   Mankind, that wishes
you so well in all things that relate to your prosperity,
have their intervals of wishing for themselves, and are
within a little of grudging you the fulness of your for-
20 tune :   they would be more malicious if you used it not
so well, and with so much generosity.

Fame is in itself a real good, if we may believe Cicero,
who was perhaps too fond of it.   But even fame, as
Virgil tells us, acquires strength by going forward.   Let
25 Epicurus give indolency as an attribute to his gods, and
place in it the happiness of the blest ; the Divinity which
we worship has given us not only a precept against
it, but his own example to the contrary.   The world,
my Lord, would be content to allow you a seventh day
30 for rest ; or if you thought that hard upon you, we
would not refuse you half your time : if you came out,
like some great monarch, to take a town but once a
year, as it were for your diversion, though you had no
need to extend your territories.   In short, if you were
35 a bad, or, which is worse, an indifferent poet, we would

thank you for our own quiet, and not expose you to the
want of yours.   But when you are so great and so
successful, and when we have that necessity of your
writing, that we cannot subsist entirely without it, any
more (I may almost say) than the world without the 5
daily course of ordinary providence, methinks this
argument might prevail with you, my Lord, to forego
a little of your repose for the public benefit. 'Tis not
that you are under any force of working daily miracles,
to prove your being ; but now and then somewhat of 10
extraordinary, that is, anything of your production, is
requisite to refresh your character.

   This, I think, my Lord, is a sufficient reproach to
you ; and should I carry it as far as mankind would
authorise me, would be little less than satire.   And, 15
indeed, a provocation is almost necessary, in behalf of
the world, that you might be induced sometimes to
write ; and in relation to a multitude of scribblers, who
daily pester the world with their insufferable stuff, that
they might be discouraged from writing any more. 20
I complain not of their lampoons and libels, though
I have been the public mark for many years.   I am
vindictive enough to have repelled force by force, if
I could imagine that any of them had ever reached me ;
but they either shot at rovers, and therefore missed, or 25
their powder was so weak, that I might safely stand
them, at the nearest distance.   I answered not *The
Rehearsal*, because I knew the author sat to himself
when he drew the picture, and was the very Bayes of
his own farce : because also I knew, that my betters 30
were more concerned than I was in that satire : and,
lastly, because Mr. Smith and Mr. Johnson, the main
pillars of it, were two such languishing gentlemen in
their conversation, that I could liken them to nothing
but to their own relations, those noble characters of 35

• men of wit and pleasure about the town. The like
considerations have hindered me from dealing with the
lamentable companions of their prose and doggerel.
I am so far from defending my poetry against them,
5 that I will not so much as expose theirs. And for my
morals, if they are not proof against their attacks, let
me be thought by posterity, what those authors would
be thought, if any memory of them, or of their writings,
could endure so long as to another age. But these dull
10 makers of lampoons, as harmless as they have been to
me, are yet of dangerous example to the public. Some
witty men may perhaps succeed to their designs, and,
mixing sense with malice, blast the reputation of the
most innocent amongst men, and the most virtuous
15 amongst women.

Heaven be praised, our common libellers are as free
from the imputation of wit as of morality ; and therefore
whatever mischief they have designed, they have performed but little of it. Yet these ill-writers, in all
20 justice, ought themselves to be exposed ; as Persius
has given us a fair example in his First Satire, which is
levelled particularly at them ; and none is so fit to
correct their faults, as he who is not only clear from
any in his own writings, but is also so just, that he will
25 never defame the good ; and is armed with the power
of verse, to punish and make examples of the bad.
But of this I shall have occasion to speak further, when
I come to give the definition and character of true
satires.

30 In the mean time, as a counsellor bred up in the
knowledge of the municipal and statute laws may
honestly inform a just prince how far his prerogative
extends ; so I may be allowed to tell your Lordship,
who, by an undisputed title, are the king of poets, what
35 an extent of power you have, and how lawfully you may

exercise it, over the petulant scribblers of this age. As
Lord Chamberlain, I know, you are absolute by your
office, in all that belongs to the decency and good
manners of the stage. You can banish from thence
scurrility and profaneness, and restrain the licentious 5
insolence of poets, and their actors, in all things that
shock the public quiet, or the reputation of private
persons, under the notion of humour. But I mean not
the authority, which is annexed to your office ; I speak
of that only which is inborn and inherent to your 10
person ; what is produced in you by an excellent wit,
a masterly and commanding genius over all writers :
whereby you are empowered, when you please, to give
the final decision of wit ; to put your stamp on all that
ought to pass for current ; and set a brand of repro- 15
bation on clipt poetry, and false coin. A shilling dipped
in the bath may go for gold amongst the ignorant, but
the sceptres on the guineas show the difference. That
your Lordship is formed by nature for this supremacy,
I could easily prove, (were it not already granted by 20
the world,) from the distinguishing character of your
writing : which is so visible to me, that I never could
be imposed on to receive for yours, what was written by
any others ; or to mistake your genuine poetry for their
spurious productions. I can further add, with truth, 25
(though not without some vanity in saying it,) that in
the same paper, written by divers hands, whereof your
Lordship's was only part, I could separate your gold
from their copper ; and though I could not give back to
every author his own brass, (for there is not the same 30
rule for distinguishing betwixt bad and bad, as betwixt
ill and excellently good,) yet I never failed of knowing
what was yours, and what was not ; and was absolutely
certain, that this, or the other part, was positively yours,
and could not possibly be written by any other. 35

True it is, that some bad poems, though not all, carry
their owners' marks about them. There is some peculiar awkwardness, false grammar, imperfect sense, or,
at the least, obscurity ; some brand or other on this
5 buttock, or that ear, that 'tis notorious who are the
owners of the cattle, though 'they should not sign it
with their names. But your Lordship, on the contrary,
is distinguished, not only by the excellency of your
thoughts, but by your style and manner of expressing
10 them. A painter, judging of some admirable piece,
may affirm, with certainty, that it was of Holbein, or
Vandyck ; but vulgar designs, and common draughts,
are easily mistaken, and misapplied. Thus, by my
long study of your Lordship, I am arrived at the know-
15 ledge of your particular manner. In the good poems
of other men, like those artists, I can only say, this is
like the draught of such a one, or like the colouring of
another. In short, I can only be sure, that 'tis the
hand of a good master ; but in your performances, it is
20 scarcely possible for me to be deceived. If you write
in your strength, you stand revealed at the first view ;
and should you write under it, you cannot avoid some
peculiar graces, which only cost me a second consideration to discover you : for I may say it, with all the
25 severity of truth, that every line of yours is precious.
Your Lordship's only fault is, that you have not written
more ; unless I could add another, and that yet greater,
but I fear for the public the accusation would not be
true, that you have written, and out of a vicious modesty
30 will not publish.

Virgil has confined his works within the compass of
eighteen thousand lines, and has not treated many
subjects ; yet he ever had, and ever will have, the
reputation of the best poet. Martial says of him, that
35 he could have excelled Varius in tragedy, and Horace

in lyric poetry, but out of deference to his friends, he attempted neither.

The same prevalence of genius is in your Lordship, but the world cannot pardon your concealing it on the same consideration ; because, we have neither a living 5 Varius, nor a Horace in whose excellencies, both of poems, odes, and satires, you had equalled them, if our language had not yielded to the Roman majesty, and length of time had not added a reverence to the works of Horace. For good sense is the same in all or most 10 ages ; and course of time rather improves Nature, than impairs her. What has been, may be again : another Homer, and another Virgil, may possibly arise from those very causes which produced the first ; though it would be impudence to affirm, that any such have yet 15 appeared.

It is manifest, that some particular ages have been more happy than others in the production of great men, in all sorts of arts and sciences ; as that of Eurip- ides, Sophocles, Aristophanes, and the rest, for stage 20 poetry amongst the Greeks ; that of Augustus, for heroic, lyric, dramatic, elegiac, and indeed all sorts of poetry, in the persons of Virgil, Horace, Varius, Ovid, and many others ; especially if we take into that cen- tury the latter end of the commonwealth, wherein we 25 find Varro, Lucretius, and Catullus ; and at the same time lived Cicero, Sallust, and Cæsar. A famous age in modern times, for learning in every kind, was that of Lorenzo de Medici, and his son Leo the Tenth ; wherein painting was revived, and poetry flourished, 30 and the Greek language was restored.

Examples in all these are obvious : but what I would infer is this ; that in such an age, it is possible some great genius may arise, to equal any of the ancients ; abating only for the language. For great contem- 35 poraries whet and cultivate each other ; and mutual borrowing, and commerce, makes the common riches of learning, as it does of the civil government.

But suppose that Homer and Virgil were the only of
5 their species, and that Nature was so much worn out in producing them, that she is never able to bear the like again, yet the example only holds in Heroic Poetry : in Tragedy and Satire, I offer myself to maintain against some of our modern critics, that this age and the last,
10 particularly in England, have excelled the ancients in both those kinds ; and I would instance in Shakespeare of the former, in your Lordship of the latter sort [1].

Thus I might safely confine myself to my native country ; but if I would only cross the seas, I might
15 find in France a living Horace and a Juvenal, in the person of the admirable Boileau ; whose numbers are excellent, whose expressions are noble, whose thoughts are just, whose language is pure, whose satire is pointed, and whose sense is close ; what he borrows from the
20 Ancients, he repays with usury of his own, in coin as good, and almost as universally valuable : for, setting prejudice and partiality apart, though he is our enemy, the stamp of a Louis, the patron of all arts, is not much inferior to the medal of an Augustus Cæsar.
25 Let this be said without entering into the interests of factions and parties, and relating only to the bounty of that king to men of learning and merit ; a praise so just, that even we, who are his enemies, cannot refuse it to him.

3 ⟨ Now if it may be permitted me to go back again to the consideration of Epic Poetry, I have confessed, that no man hitherto has reached, or so much as approached, to the excellencies of Homer, or of Virgil ; I must further add, that Statius, the best versificator next to

[1] Of your Lordship in the latter sort. Ed. 1693.

Virgil, knew not how to design after him, though he
had the model in his eye ; that Lucan is wanting both
in design and subject, and is besides too full of heat and
affectation ; that amongst the Moderns, Ariosto neither
designed justly, nor observed any unity of action, or 5
compass of time, or moderation in the vastness of his
draught ; his style is luxurious, without majesty or
decency, and his adventures without the compass of
nature and possibility.   Tasso, whose design was
regular, and who observed the rules of unity in time 10
and place more closely than Virgil, yet was not so
happy in his action ; he confesses himself to have been
too lyrical, that is, to have written beneath the dignity
of heroic verse, in his episodes of Sophronia, Erminia,
and Armida ; his story is not so pleasing as Ariosto's ; 15
he is too flatulent sometimes, and sometimes too dry ;
many times unequal, and almost always forced ; and,
besides, is full of conceits, points of epigram, and witti-
cisms ; all which are not only below the dignity of
heroic verse, but contrary to its nature : Virgil and 20
Homer have not one of them.   And those who are
guilty of so boyish an ambition in so grave a subject,
are so far from being considered as heroic poets, that
they ought to be turned down from Homer to the
Anthologia, from Virgil to Martial and Owen's Epi- 25
grams, and from Spenser to Fleckno ; that is, from
the top to the bottom of all poetry.   But to return to
Tasso : he borrows from the invention of Boiardo, and
in his alteration of his poem, which is infinitely for the
worse, imitates Homer so very servilely, that (for 30
example) he gives the King of Jerusalem fifty sons,
only because Homer had bestowed the like number on
King Priam ; he kills the youngest in the same manner,
and has provided his hero with a Patroclus, under
another name, only to bring him back to the wars, when 35

his friend was killed. The French have performed nothing in this kind which is not far below those two Italians, and subject to a thousand more reflections, without examining their *St. Lewis*, their *Pucelle*, or 5 their *Alaric*. The English have only to boast of Spenser and Milton, who neither of them wanted either genius or learning to have been perfect poets, and yet both of them are liable to many censures. For there is no uniformity in the design of Spenser : he aims 10 at the accomplishment of no one action ; he raises up a hero for every one of his adventures ; and endows each of them with some particular moral virtue, which renders them all equal, without subordination, or preference. Every one is most valiant in his own legend : 15 only we must do him that justice to observe, that magnanimity, which is the character of Prince Arthur, shines throughout the whole poem ; and succours the rest, when they are in distress. The original of every knight was then living in the court of Queen Elizabeth ; 20 and he attributed to each of them that virtue, which he thought was most conspicuous in them ; an ingenious piece of flattery, though it turned not much to his account. Had he lived to finish his poem, in the six remaining legends, it had certainly been more of a 25 piece ; but could not have been perfect, because the model was not true. But Prince Arthur, or his chief patron Sir Philip Sidney, whom he intended to make happy by the marriage of his Gloriana, dying before him, deprived the poet both of means and spirit to 30 accomplish his design : for the rest, his obsolete language, and the ill choice of his stanza, are faults but of the second magnitude ; for, notwithstanding the first, he is still intelligible, at least after a little practice ; and for the last, he is the more to be admired, that, labour- 35 ing under such a difficulty, his verses are so numerous,

so various, and so harmonious, that only Virgil, whom
he profestly imitated, has surpassed him among the
Romans ; and only Mr. Waller among the English.

As for Mr. Milton, whom we all admire with so
much justice, his subject is not that of an Heroic Poem, 5
properly so called.   His design is the losing of our
happiness ; his event is not prosperous, like that of
all other epic works ; his heavenly machines are many,
and his human persons are but two.   But I will not
take Mr. Rymer's work out of his hands.   He has 10
promised the world a critique on that author ; wherein,
though he will not allow his poem for heroic, I hope he
will grant us, that his thoughts are elevated, his words
sounding, and that no man has so happily copied the
manner of Homer, or so copiously translated his Gre- 15
cisms, and the Latin elegancies of Virgil.   'Tis true,
he runs into a flat of thought, sometimes for a hundred lines together, but it is when he is got into a track
of Scripture.   His antiquated words were his choice,
not his necessity ; for therein he imitated Spenser, as 20
Spenser did Chaucer.   And though, perhaps, the love
of their masters may have transported both too far, in
the frequent use of them, yet, in my opinion, obsolete
words may then be laudably revived, when either they
are more sounding, or more significant, than those in 25
practice ; and when their obscurity is taken away, by
joining other words to them, which clear the sense ;
according to the rule of Horace, for the admission of
new words.   But in both cases a moderation is to be
observed in the use of them : for unnecessary coinage, 30
as well as unnecessary revival, runs into affectation ;
a fault to be avoided on either hand.   Neither will
I justify Milton for his blank verse, though I may
excuse him, by the example of Hannibal Caro, and
other Italians, who have used it ; for whatever causes 35

he alleges for the abolishing of rhyme, (which I have not now the leisure to examine,) his own particular reason is plainly this, that rhyme was not his talent ; he had neither the ease of doing it, nor the graces of it ;
5 which is manifest in his *Juvenilia,* or verses written in his youth, where his rhyme is always constrained and forced, and comes hardly from him, at an age when the soul is most pliant, and the passion of love makes almost every man a rhymer, though not a poet.

10   By this time, my Lord, I doubt not but that you wonder, why I have run off from my bias so long together, and made so tedious a digression from satire to heroic poetry. But if you will not excuse it by the tattling quality of age, which, as Sir William D'Avenant
15 says, is always narrative, yet I hope the usefulness of what I have to say on this subject will qualify the remoteness of it ; and this is the last time I will commit the crime of prefaces, or trouble the world with my notions of anything that relates to verse. I have then,
20 as you see, observed the failings of many great wits amongst the Moderns, who have attempted to write an epic poem. Besides these, or the like animadversions of them by other men, there is yet a further reason given, why they cannot possibly succeed so well as the
25 Ancients, even though we could allow them not to be inferior, either in genius or learning, or the tongue in which they write, or all those other wonderful qualifications which are necessary to the forming of a true accomplished heroic poet. The fault is laid on our
30 religion ; they say, that Christianity is not capable of those embellishments which are afforded in the belief of those ancient heathens.

And 'tis true, that, in the severe notions of our faith, the fortitude of a Christian consists in patience, and
35 suffering, for the love of God, whatever hardships can

befall him in the world ; not in any great attempt, or in
performance of those enterprises which the poets call
heroic, and which are commonly the effects of interest,
ostentation, pride, and worldly honour : that humility
and resignation are our prime virtues ; and that these 5
include no action, but that of the soul ; when as, on
the contrary, an heroic poem requires to its necessary
design, and as its last perfection, some great action of
war, the accomplishment of some extraordinary undertaking ; which requires the strength and vigour of the 10
body, the duty of a soldier, the capacity and prudence
of a general, and, in short, as much, or more, of the
active virtue, than the suffering. But to this the answer
is very obvious. God has placed us in our several
stations ; the virtues of a private Christian are patience, 15
obedience, submission, and the like ; but those of a magistrate, or general, or a king, are prudence, counsel, active
fortitude, coercive power, awful command, and the exercise of magnanimity, as well as justice. So that this objection hinders not, but that an Epic Poem, or the heroic 20
action of some great commander, enterprised for the
common good, and honour of the Christian cause, and
executed happily, may be as well written now, as it was
of old by the heathens ; provided the poet be endued
with the same talents ; and the language, though not 25
of equal dignity, yet as near approaching to it, as our
modern barbarism will allow, which is all that can be
expected from our own, or any other now extant, though
more refined ; and therefore we are to rest contented
with that only inferiority, which is not possible to be 30
remedied.

I wish I could as easily remove that other difficulty
which yet remains. 'Tis objected by a great French
critic, as well as an admirable poet, yet living, and whom
I have mentioned with that honour which his merit 35

exacts from me, I mean Boileau, that the machines of
our Christian religion, in heroic poetry, are much more
feeble to support that weight than those of heathenism.
Their doctrine, grounded as it was on ridiculous fables,
5 was yet the belief of the two victorious Monarchies, the
Grecian and Roman. Their gods did not only interest
themselves in the event of wars, (which is the effect of
a superior providence,) but also espoused the several
parties in a visible corporeal descent, managed their
10 intrigues, and fought their battles sometimes in opposition to each other : though Virgil (more discreet than
Homer in that last particular)has contented himself with
the partiality of his deities, their favours, their counsels
or commands, to those whose cause they had espoused,
15 without bringing them to the outrageousness of blows.
Now, our religion (says he) is deprived of the greatest
part of those machines ; at least the most shining in
epic poetry. Though St. Michael, in Ariosto, seeks out
Discord, to send her among the Pagans, and finds her
20 in a convent of friars, where peace should reign, which
indeed is fine satire ; and Satan, in Tasso, excites Soly-
man to an attempt by night on the Christian camp, and
brings an host of devils to his assistance ; yet the archangel, in the former example, when Discord was restive,
25 and would not be drawn from her beloved monastery
with fair words, has the whip-hand of her, drags her out
with many stripes, sets her, on God's name, about her
business, and makes her know the difference of strength
betwixt a nuncio of Heaven, and a minister of Hell.
30 The same angel, in the latter instance from Tasso, (as
if God had never another messenger belonging to the
court, but was confined like Jupiter to Mercury, and
Juno to Iris,) when he sees his time, that is, when half
of the Christians are already killed, and all the rest are
35 in a fair way to be routed, stickles betwixt the remainders

of God's host, and the race of fiends ; pulls the devils
backward by the tails, and drives them from the quarry ;
or otherwise the whole business had miscarried, and
Jerusalem remained untaken.   This, says Boileau, is
a very unequal match for the poor devils, who are sure 5
to come by the worst of it in the combat ; for nothing is
more easy, than for an Almighty Power to bring his old
rebels to reason when he pleases.   Consequently, what
pleasure, what entertainment, can be raised from so
pitiful a machine, where we see the success of the battle 10
from the very beginning of it ; unless that, as we are
Christians, we are glad that we have gotten God on our
side, to maul our enemies, when we cannot do the work
ourselves ?   For if the poet had given the faithful more
courage, which had cost him nothing, or at least have 15
made them exceed the Turks in number, he might have
gained the victory for us Christians, without interessing
Heaven in the quarrel ; and that with as much ease, and
as little credit to the conqueror, as when a party of
a hundred soldiers defeats another which consists only 20
of fifty.

This, my Lord, I confess, is such an argument against
our modern poetry, as cannot be answered by those
mediums which have been used.   We cannot hitherto
boast, that our religion has furnished us with any such 25
machines, as have made the strength and beauty of the
ancient buildings.

But what if I venture to advance an invention of my
own, to supply the manifest defect of our new writers ?
I am sufficiently sensible of my weakness ; and it is not 30
very probable that I should succeed in such a project,
whereof I have not had the least hint from any of my
predecessors, the poets, or any of their seconds and
coadjutors, the critics.   Yet we see the art of war is
improved in sieges, and new instruments of death are 35

invented daily ; something new in philosophy and the
mechanics is discovered almost every year ; and the
science of former ages is improved by the succeeding.
I will not detain you with a long preamble to that,
5 which better judges will, perhaps, conclude to be little
worth.

It is this, in short, that Christian poets have not
hitherto been acquainted with their own strength. If
they had searched the Old Testament as they ought,
10 they might there have found the machines which are
proper for their work ; and those more certain in their
effect, than it may be the New Testament is, in the
rules sufficient for salvation. The perusing of one
chapter in the prophecy of Daniel, and accommodating
15 what there they find with the principles of Platonic
philosophy, as it is now Christianised, would have made
the ministry of angels as strong an engine, for the working up heroic poetry, in our religion, as that of the
Ancients has been to raise theirs by all the fables of
20 their gods, which were only received for truths by the
most ignorant and weakest of the people.

'Tis a doctrine almost universally received by Christians, as well Protestants as Catholics, that there are
guardian angels, appointed by God Almighty, as his
25 vicegerents, for the protection and government of cities,
provinces, kingdoms, and monarchies ; and those as well
of heathens, as of true believers. All this is so plainly
proved from those texts of Daniel, that it admits of no
further controversy. The prince of the Persians, and
30 that other of the Grecians, are granted to be the guardians
and protecting ministers of those empires. It cannot be
denied, that they were opposite, and resisted one another.
St. Michael is mentioned by his name as the patron of
the Jews, and is now taken by the Christians, as the
35 protector-general of our religion. These tutelar genii,

who presided over the several people and regions committed to their charge, were watchful over them for good,
as far as their commissions could possibly extend. The
general purpose and design of all was certainly the
service of their Great Creator. But 'tis an undoubted 5
truth, that, for ends best known to the Almighty Majesty
of Heaven, his providential designs for the benefit of
his creatures, for the debasing and punishing of some
nations, and the exaltation and temporal reward of
others, were not wholly known to these his ministers ; 10
else why those factious quarrels, controversies, and
battles amongst themselves, when they were all united
in the same design, the service and honour of their
common Master ? But being instructed only in the
general, and zealous of the main design ; and, as infinite 15
beings, not admitted into the secrets of government, the
last resorts of providence, or capable of discovering
the final purposes of God, who can work good out of
evil as he pleases, and irresistibly sways all manner of
events on earth, directing them finally for the best, to 20
his creation in general, and to the ultimate end of his
own glory in particular ; they must, of necessity, be
sometimes ignorant of the means conducing to those
ends, in which alone they can jar and oppose each other.
One angel, as we may suppose the Prince of Persia, as 25
he is called, judging, that it would be more for God's
honour, and the benefit of his people, that the Median
and Persian Monarchy, which delivered them from the
Babylonish captivity, should still be uppermost ; and
the patron of the Grecians, to whom the will of God 30
might be more particularly revealed, contending, on the
other side, for the rise of Alexander and his successors,
who were appointed to punish the backsliding Jews, and
thereby to put them in mind of their offences, that they
might repent, and become more virtuous, and more 35

observant of the law revealed. But how far these
controversies and appearing enmities of those glorious
creatures may be carried ; how these oppositions may
best be managed, and by what means conducted, is not
5 my business to show or determine ; these things must
be left to the invention and judgment of the poet ; if
any of so happy a genius be now living, or any future
age can produce a man, who, being conversant in the
philosophy of Plato, as it is now accommodated to
10 Christian use, (for, as Virgil gives us to understand by
his example, that is the only proper, of all others, for
an epic poem,) who,to his natural endowments, of a large
invention, a ripe judgment, and a strong memory, has
joined the knowledge of the liberal arts and sciences,
15 and particularly moral philosophy, the mathematics,
geography, and history, and with all these qualifications
is born a poet ; knows, and can practise the variety of
numbers, and is master of the language in which he
writes ;—if such a man, I say, be now arisen, or shall
20 arise, I am vain enough to think, that I have proposed
a model to him, by which he may build a nobler, a more
beautiful and more perfect poem, than any yet extant
since the Ancients.

There is another part of these machines yet wanting ;
25 but, by what I have said, it would have been easily supplied by a judicious writer. He could not have failed
to add the opposition of ill spirits to the good ; they
have also their design, ever opposite to that of Heaven ;
and this alone has hitherto been the practice of the
30 Moderns : but this imperfect system, if I may call it
such, which I have given, will infinitely advance and
carry further that hypothesis of the evil spirits contending with the good. For, being so much weaker, since
their fall, than those blessed beings, they are yet sup-
35 posed to have a permitted power from God of acting ill,

as, from their own depraved nature, they have always
the will of designing it. A great testimony of which we
find in holy writ, when God Almighty suffered Satan
to appear in the holy synod of the angels, (a thing not
hitherto drawn into example by any of the poets,) and 5
also gave him power over all things belonging to his
servant Job, excepting only life.

Now, what these wicked spirits cannot compass, by
the vast disproportion of their forces to those of the
superior beings, they may by their fraud and cunning 10
carry farther, in a seeming league, confederacy, or sub-
serviency to the designs of some good angel, as far as
consists with his purity to suffer such an aid, the end
of which may possibly be disguised, and concealed from
his finite knowledge. This is, indeed, to suppose a great 15
error in such a being ; yet since a devil can appear like
an angel of light ; since craft and malice may sometimes
blind for a while a more perfect understanding ; and,
lastly, since Milton has given us an example of the like
nature, when Satan, appearing like a cherub to Uriel, 20
the Intelligence of the Sun, circumvented him even in
his own province, and passed only for a curious traveller
through those new-created regions, that he might observe
therein the workmanship of God, and praise him in his
works ; I know not why, upon the same supposition, or 25
some other, a fiend may not deceive a creature of more
excellency than himself, but yet a creature ; at least, by
the connivance, or tacit permission, of the Omniscient
Being.

Thus, my Lord, I have, as briefly as I could, given 30
your Lordship, and by you the world, a rude draught
of what I have been long labouring in my imagination,
and what I had intended to have put in practice, (though
far unable for the attempt of such a poem,) and to have
left the stage, (to which my genius never much inclined 35

me,) for a work which would have taken up my life in
the performance of it. This, too, I had intended chiefly
for the honour of my native country, to which a poet is
particularly obliged. Of two subjects, both relating to
5 it, I was doubtful whether I should choose that of King
Arthur conquering the Saxons, which, being farther
distant in time, gives the greater scope to my invention ;
or that of Edward, the Black Prince, in subduing Spain,
and restoring it to the lawful prince, though a great
10 tyrant, Don Pedro the Cruel : which, for the compass
of time, including only the expedition of one year ; for
the greatness of the action, and its answerable event ;
for the magnanimity of the English hero, opposed to
the ingratitude of the person whom he restored ; and
15 for the many beautiful episodes, which I had interwoven
with the principal design, together with the characters
of the chiefest English persons ; wherein, after Virgil
and Spenser, I would have taken occasion to represent
my living friends and patrons of the noblest families,
20 and also shadowed the events of future ages, in the
succession of our imperial line ; with these helps, and
those of the machines, which I have mentioned, I might
perhaps have done as well as some of my predecessors,
or at least chalked out a way for others to amend my
25 errors in a like design. But being encouraged only
with fair words by King Charles II, my little salary ill
paid, and no prospect of a future subsistence, I was then
discouraged in the beginning of my attempt ; and now
age has overtaken me, and want, a more insufferable
30 evil, through the change of the times, has wholly dis-
enabled me. Though I must ever acknowledge, to the
honour of your Lordship, and the eternal memory of
your charity, that, since this revolution, wherein I have
patiently suffered the ruin of my small fortune, and the
35 loss of that poor subsistence which I had from two

kings, whom I had served more faithfully than profit-
ably to myself ; then your Lordship was pleased, out
of no other motive but your own nobleness, without any
desert of mine, or the least solicitation from me, to make
me a most bountiful present, which at that time, when 5
I was most in want of it, came most seasonably and unexpectedly to my relief.   That favour, my Lord, is of
itself sufficient to bind any grateful man to a perpetual
acknowledgment, and to all the future service which
one of my mean condition can ever be able to perform. 10
May the Almighty God return it for me, both in blessing
you here, and rewarding you hereafter !   I must not
presume to defend the cause for which I now suffer,
because your Lordship is engaged against it ; but the
more you are so, the greater is my obligation to you, 15
for your laying aside all the considerations of factions
and parties, to do an action of pure disinteress'd charity.
This is one amongst many of your shining qualities,
which distinguish you from others of your rank.   But
let me add a farther truth, that, without these ties of 20
gratitude, and abstracting from them all, I have a most
particular inclination to honour you ; and, if it were not
too bold an expression, to say, I love you.   'Tis no
shame to be a poet, though 'tis to be a bad one.
Augustus Cæsar of old, and Cardinal Richelieu of late, 25
would willingly have been such ; and David and Solomon
were such.   You who, without flattery, are the best of
the present age in England, and would have been so,
had you been born in any other country, will receive
more honour in future ages by that one excellency, than 30
by all those honours to which your birth has entitled
you, or your merits have acquired you.

Ne, forte, pudori
Sit tibi Musa lyræ solers, et cantor Apollo.

I have formerly said in this Epistle, that I could dis- 35

tinguish your writings from those of any others ; 'tis
now time to clear myself from any imputation of self-
conceit on that subject. I assume not to myself any
particular lights in this discovery ; they are such only
5 as are obvious to every man of sense and judgment,
who loves poetry, and understands it. Your thoughts
are always so remote from the common way of thinking,
that they are, as I may say, of another species than the
conceptions of other poets ; yet you go not out of nature
10 for any of them. Gold is never bred upon the surface
of the ground, but lies so hidden, and so deep, that the
mines of it are seldom found ; but the force of waters
casts it out from the bowels of mountains, and exposes
it amongst the sands of rivers ; giving us of her bounty
15 what we could not hope for by our search. This success attends your Lordship's thoughts, which would look
like chance, if it were not perpetual, and always of the
same tenour. If I grant that there is care in it, 'tis
such a care as would be ineffectual and fruitless in other
20 men. 'Tis the *curiosa felicitas* which Petronius ascribes
to Horace in his Odes. We have not wherewithal to
imagine so strongly, so justly, and so pleasantly ; in
short, if we have the same knowledge, we cannot draw
out of it the same quintessence ; we cannot give it such
25 a turn, such a propriety, and such a beauty ; something
is deficient in the manner, or the words, but more in
the nobleness of our conception. Yet when you have
finished all, and it appears in its full lustre, when the
diamond is not only found, but the roughness smoothed,
30 when it is cut into a form, and set in gold, then we cannot
but acknowledge, that it is the perfect work of art and
nature ; and every one will be so vain, to think he himself could have performed the like, till he attempts it.
It is just the description that Horace makes of such
35 a finished piece : it appears so easy,

. . . Ut sibi quivis
Speret idem, sudet multum, frustraque laboret,
Ausus idem.

And, besides all this, 'tis your Lordship's particular
talent to lay your thoughts so close together, that, were 5
they closer, they would be crowded, and even a due
connexion would be wanting. We are not kept in
expectation of two good lines, which are to come after
a long parenthesis of twenty bad ; which is the April
poetry of other writers, a mixture of rain and sunshine 10
by fits : you are always bright, even almost to a fault,
by reason of the excess. There is a continual abundance,
a magazine of thought, and yet a perpetual variety of
entertainment ; which creates such an appetite in your
reader, that he is not cloyed with anything, but satisfied 15
with all. 'Tis that which the Romans call *cæna dubia ;*
where there is such plenty, yet withal so much diversity,
and so good order, that the choice is difficult betwixt
one excellency and another ; and yet the conclusion, by
a due climax, is evermore the best ; that is, as a con- 20
clusion ought to be, ever the most proper for its place.
See, my Lord, whether I have not studied your Lordship with some application ; and, since you are so
modest, that you will not be judge and party, I appeal
to the whole world, if I have not drawn your picture 25
to a great degree of likeness, though it is but in miniature, and that some of the best features are yet wanting.
Yet what I have done is enough to distinguish you from
any other, which is the proposition that I took upon me
to demonstrate.   30

And now, my Lord, to apply what I have said to my
present business : the *Satires* of Juvenal and Persius
appearing in this new English dress cannot so
properly be inscribed to any man as to your Lordship, who are the first of the age in that way of writing. 35

Your Lordship, amongst many other favours, has given
me your permission for this address ; and you have
particularly encouraged me by your perusal and approbation of the *Sixth* and *Tenth Satires* of Juvenal, as
5 I have translated them. My fellow-labourers have likewise commissioned me to perform, in their behalf, this
office of a Dedication to you ; and will acknowledge,
with all possible respect and gratitude, your acceptance
of their work. Some of them have the honour to be
10 known to your Lordship already ; and they who have
not yet that happiness desire it now. Be pleased to
receive our common endeavours with your wonted
candour, without intitling you to the protection of our
common failings in so difficult an undertaking. And
15 allow me your patience, if it be not already tired with
this long epistle, to give you, from the best authors, the
origin, the antiquity, the growth, the change, and the
completement of Satire among the Romans ; to describe,
if not define, the nature of that poem, with its several
20 qualifications and virtues, together with the several
sorts of it ; to compare the excellencies of Horace,
Persius, and Juvenal, and show the particular manners
of their satires ; and, lastly, to give an account of this
new way of version, which is attempted in our perform-
25 ance. All which, according to the weakness of my
ability, and the best lights which I can get from others,
shall be the subject of my following discourse.

The most perfect work of Poetry, says our master
Aristotle, is Tragedy. His reason is, because it is the
30 most united ; being more severely confined within the
rules of action, time, and place. The action is entire,
of a piece, and one, without episodes ; the time limited
to a natural day ; and the place circumscribed at least
within the compass of one town, or city. Being exactly
35 proportioned thus, and uniform in all its parts, the mind

is more capable of comprehending the whole beauty of
it without distraction.

But after all these advantages, an Heroic Poem is
certainly the greatest work of human nature. The
beauties and perfections of the other are but mechanical ; 5
those of the Epic are more noble : though Homer has
limited his place to Troy, and the fields about it ; his
actions to forty-eight natural days, whereof twelve are
holidays, or cessation from business, during the funeral
of Patroclus. To proceed ; the action of the Epic is 10
greater ; the extension of time enlarges the pleasure of
the reader, and the episodes give it more ornament,
and more variety. The instruction is equal ; but the
first is only instructive, the latter forms a hero, and a
prince. 15

If it signifies anything which of them is of the more
ancient family, the best and most absolute Heroic
Poem was written by Homer long before Tragedy was
invented. But if we consider the natural endowments
and acquired parts which are necessary to make an 20
accomplished writer in either kind, Tragedy requires
a less and more confined knowledge ; moderate learning,
and observation of the rules, is sufficient, if a genius be
not wanting. But in an epic poet, one who is worthy
of that name, besides an universal genius, is required 25
universal learning, together with all those qualities and
acquisitions which I have named above, and as many
more as I have, through haste or negligence, omitted.
And, after all, he must have exactly studied Homer and
Virgil as his patterns ; Aristotle and Horace as his 30
guides ; and Vida and Bossu as their commentators ;
with many others, both Italian and French critics,
which I want leisure here to recommend.

In a word, what I have to say in relation to this
subject, which does not particularly concern Satire, is, 35

that the greatness of an heroic poem, beyond that of
a tragedy, may easily be discovered, by observing how
few have attempted that work in comparison to those
who have written dramas ; and, of those few, how small
5 a number have succeeded. But leaving the critics, on
either side, to contend about the preference due to this
or that sort of poetry, I will hasten to my present
business, which is the antiquity and origin of Satire,
according to those informations which I have received
10 from the learned Casaubon, Heinsius, Rigaltius, Dacier,
and the Dauphin's *Juvenal ;* to which I shall add some
observations of my own.

There has been a long dispute among the modern
critics, whether the Romans derived their Satire from
15 the Grecians, or first invented it themselves.   Julius
Scaliger, and Heinsius, are of the first opinion ;
Casaubon, Rigaltius, Dacier, and the publisher of the
Dauphin's *Juvenal*, maintain the latter. If we take
Satire in the general signification of the word, as it
20 is used in all modern languages, for an invective, it is
certain that it is almost as old as verse ; and though
hymns, which are praises of God, may be allowed to
have been before it, yet the defamation of others was
not long after it.   After God had cursed Adam and Eve
25 in Paradise, the husband and wife excused themselves, by laying the blame on one another ; and gave
a beginning to those conjugal dialogues in prose, which
the poets have perfected in verse.   The third chapter
of Job is one of the first instances of this poem in holy
30 Scripture ; unless we will take it higher, from the latter
end of the second, where his wife advises him to curse
his Maker.

This original, I confess, is not much to the honour of
satire ; but here it was nature, and that depraved : when
35 it became an art, it bore better fruit.   Only we have

learnt thus much already, that scoffs and revilings are
of the growth of all nations ; and, consequently, that
neither the Greek poets borrowed from other people
their art of railing, neither needed the Romans to take
it from them.   But, considering Satire as a species of 5
poetry,   here   the   war   begins   amongst   the critics.
Scaliger, the father, will have it descend from Greece
to Rome ; and derives the word Satire from *Satyrus*,
that mixed kind of animal, or, as the ancients thought
him, rural god, made up betwixt a man and a goat ; 10
with a human head, hooked nose, pouting lips, a bunch,
or struma, under the chin, pricked ears, and upright
horns ; the body shagged with hair, especially from the
waist, and ending in a goat, with the legs and feet of
that creature.   But Casaubon, and his followers, with 15
reason, condemn this derivation ; and prove, that from
Satyrus, the word *satira*, as it signifies a poem, cannot
possibly descend.   For *satira* is not properly a substantive, but an adjective ; to which the word *lanx* (in
English, a charger, or large platter) is understood ; so 20
that the Greek poem, made according to the manners
of a Satyr, and expressing his qualities, must properly
be called satyrical, and not Satire.   And thus far 'tis
allowed that the Grecians had such poems ; but that
they were wholly different *in specie* from that to which 25
the Romans gave the name of Satire.

Aristotle divides all Poetry, in relation to the progress
of it, into nature, without art, art begun, and art completed.   Mankind, even the most barbarous, have the
seeds of poetry implanted in them.   The first specimen 30
of it was certainly shown in the praises of the Deity,
and prayers to him ; and as they are of natural obligation, so they are likewise of divine institution : which
Milton observing, introduces Adam and Eve every
morning adoring God in hymns and prayers.   The first 35

poetry was thus begun, in the wild notes of natural
poetry, before the invention of feet, and measures.
The Grecians and Romans had no other original of
their poetry. Festivals and holidays soon succeeded to
5 private worship, and we need not doubt but they were
enjoined by the true God to his own people, as they
were afterwards imitated by the heathens ; who, by the
light of reason, knew they were to invoke some superior
Being in their necessities, and to thank him for his
10 benefits. Thus, the Grecian holidays were celebrated
with offerings to Bacchus, and Ceres, and other deities,
to whose bounty they supposed they were owing for
their corn and wine, and other helps of life. And
the ancient Romans, as Horace tells us, paid their
15 thanks to mother Earth, or Vesta, to Silvanus, and
their Genius, in the same manner. But as all festivals
have a double reason of their institution, the first of
religion, the other of recreation, for the unbending of
our minds, so both the Grecians and Romans agreed,
20 after their sacrifices were performed, to spend the
remainder of the day in sports and merriments ; amongst
which, songs and dances, and that which they called
wit, (for want of knowing better,) were the chiefest entertainments. The Grecians had a notion of Satyrs, whom
25 I have already described ; and taking them, and the
Sileni, that is, the young Satyrs and the old, for the
tutors, attendants, and humble companions of their
Bacchus, habited themselves like those rural deities,
and imitated them in their rustic dances, to which they
30 joined songs, with some sort of rude harmony, but
without certain numbers ; and to these they added
a kind of chorus.

The Romans, also, (as Nature is the same in all
places,) though they knew nothing of those Grecian
35 demi-gods, nor had any communication with Greece,

yet had certain young men, who, at their festivals,
danced and sung, after their uncouth manner, to a
certain kind of verse, which they called Saturnian.
What it was, we have no certain light from antiquity to
discover ; but we may conclude, that, like the Grecian, 5
it was void of art, or, at least, with very feeble beginnings of it. Those ancient Romans, at these holidays,
which were a mixture of devotion and debauchery, had
a custom of reproaching each other with their faults, in
a sort of *ex tempore* poetry, or rather of tunable hobbling 10
verse ; and they answered in the same kind of gross
raillery ; their wit and their music being of a piece.
The Grecians, says Casaubon, had formerly done the
same, in the persons of their petulant Satyrs : but I am
afraid he mistakes the matter, and confounds the sing- 15
ing and dancing of the Satyrs with the rustical entertainments of the first Romans. The reason of my
opinion is this : that Casaubon, finding little light from
antiquity of these beginnings of Poetry amongst the
Grecians, but only these representations of Satyrs, who 20
carried canisters and cornucopias full of several fruits
in their hands, and danced with them at their public
feasts ; and afterwards reading Horace, who makes
mention of his homely Romans jesting at one another
in the same kind of solemnities, might suppose those 25
wanton Satyrs did the same ; and especially because
Horace possibly might seem to him to have shown the
original of all Poetry in general, including the Grecians
as well as Romans ; though it is plainly otherwise, that
he only described the beginning and first rudiments of 30
Poetry in his own country. The verses are these,
which he cites from the First Epistle of the Second
Book, which was written to Augustus—

> *Agricolæ prisci, fortes, parvoque beati,*
> *Condita post frumenta, levantes tempore festo*   35

Corpus, et ipsum animum spe finis dura ferentem,
Cum sociis operum, et pueris, et conjuge fida,
Tellurem porco, Silvanum lacte piabant ;
Floribus et vino Genium memorem brevis ævi :
5   *Fescennina per hunc inventa licentia morem*
Versibus alternis opprobria rustica fudit.

Our brawny clowns, of old, who turn'd the soil,
Content with little, and inur'd to toil,
At harvest-home, with mirth and country cheer,
10   Restor'd their bodies for another year ;
Refresh'd their spirits, and renew'd their hope
Of such a future feast, and future crop.
Then, with their fellow-joggers of the ploughs,
Their little children, and their faithful spouse,
15   A sow they slew to *Vesta's* deity,
And kindly milk, *Silvanus,* pour'd to thee ;
With flow'rs, and wine, their Genius they adored
A short life, and a merry, was the word.
From flowing cups, defaming rhymes ensue,
20   And at each other homely taunts they threw.

Yet since it is a hard conjecture, that so great a man
as Casaubon should misapply what Horace writ concerning ancient Rome, to the ceremonies and manners
of ancient Greece, I will not insist on this opinion, but
25 rather judge in general, that since all Poetry had its
original from religion, that of the Grecians and Rome
had the same beginning : both were invented at festivals
of thanksgiving, and both were prosecuted with mirth
and raillery, and rudiments of verses : amongst the
30 Greeks, by those who represented Satyrs ; and amongst
the Romans, by real clowns.

For, indeed, when I am reading Casaubon on these
two subjects, methinks I hear the same story told twice
over with very little alteration. Of which Dacier taking
35 notice, in his interpretation of the Latin verses which
I have translated, says plainly, that the beginning of
Poetry was the same, with a small variety, in both
countries ; and that the mother of it, in all nations,

was devotion. But, what is yet more wonderful, that most learned critic takes notice also, in his illustrations on the First Epistle of the Second Book, that as the poetry of the Romans, and that of the Grecians, had the same beginning, (at feasts and thanksgiving, as it 5 has been observed,) and the Old Comedy of the Greeks, which was invective, and the Satire of the Romans, which was of the same nature, were begun on the very same occasion, so the fortune of both, in process of time, was just the same ; the Old Comedy of the Grecians 10 was forbidden, for its too much licence in exposing of particular persons ; and the rude Satire of the Romans was also punished by a law of the Decemviri, as Horace tells us, in these words—

Libertasque recurrentes accepta per annos 15
Lusit amabiliter ; donec jam sævus apertam
In rabiem verti cœpit jocus, et per honestas
Ire domos impune minax : doluere cruento
Dente lacessiti ; fuit intactis quoque cura
Conditione super communi : quinetiam lex, 20
Pœnaque lata, malo quæ nollet carmine quenquam
Describi : vertere modum, formidine fustis
Ad benedicendum delectandumque redacti.

The law of the Decemviri was this : *Siquis occentassit malum carmen, sive condidisit, quod infamiam faxit, flagi-* 25 *tiumve alteri, capital esto.* A strange likeness, and barely possible ; but the critics being all of the same opinion, it becomes me to be silent, and to submit to better judgments than my own.

But, to return to the Grecians, from whose satyric 30 dramas the elder Scaliger and Heinsius will have the Roman Satire to proceed, I am to take a view of them first, and to see if there be any such descent from them as those authors have pretended.

Thespis, or whoever he were that invented Tragedy, 35 (for authors differ,) mingled with them a chorus and

dances of Satyrs, which had before been used in the
celebration of their festivals ; and there they were ever
afterwards retained. The character of them was also
kept, which was mirth and wantonness ; and this was
5 given, I suppose, to the folly of the common audience,
who soon grow weary of good sense, and, as we daily
see in our own age and country, are apt to forsake
poetry, and still ready to return to buffoonry and farce.
From hence it came, that, in the Olympic games, where
10 the poets contended for four prizes, the satyric tragedy
was the last of them ; for, in the rest, the Satyrs were
excluded from the chorus. Among the plays of Euripides which are yet remaining, there is one of these
Satyrics, which is called the *Cyclops ;* in which we may
15 see the nature of those poems, and from thence conclude what likeness they have to the Roman satire.

The story of this Cyclops, whose name was Polyphemus, so famous in the Grecian fables, was, that
Ulysses, who, with his company, was driven on that
20 coast of Sicily, where those Cyclops inhabited, coming
to ask relief from Silenus, and the Satyrs, who were
herdsmen to that one-eyed giant, was kindly received
by them, and entertained ; till, being perceived by
Polyphemus, they were made prisoners against the
25 rites of hospitality, (for which Ulysses eloquently
pleaded,) were afterwards put down into the den, and
some of them devoured ; after which Ulysses, having
made him drunk, when he was asleep, thrust a great
firebrand into his eye, and so, revenging his dead
30 followers, escaped with the remaining party of the
living ; and Silenus and the Satyrs were freed from
their servitude under Polyphemus, and remitted to
their first liberty of attending and accompanying their
patron, Bacchus.

35   This was the subject of the tragedy ; which, being

one of those that end with a happy event, is therefore,
by Aristotle, judged below the other sort, whose success
is unfortunate. Notwithstanding which, the Satyrs, who
were part of the *dramatis personæ*, as well as the whole
chorus, were properly introduced into the nature of the 5
poem, which is mixed of farce and tragedy. The adventure of Ulysses was to entertain the judging part of the
audience ; and the uncouth persons of Silenus, and
the Satyrs, to divert the common people with their
gross railleries.   10

Your Lordship has perceived by this time, that this
satyric tragedy, and the Roman Satire, have little resemblance in any of their features. The very kinds are
different ; for what has a pastoral tragedy to do with
a paper of verses satirically written ? The character 15
and raillery of the Satyrs is the only thing that could
pretend to a likeness, were Scaliger and Heinsius alive
to maintain their opinion. And the first farces of the
Romans, which were the rudiments of their poetry,
were written before they had any communication with 20
the Greeks, or indeed any knowledge of that people.

And here it will be proper to give the definition of
the Greek satyric poem from Casaubon, before I leave
this subject. " The Satyric," says he, " is a dramatic
poem, annexed to a tragedy, having a chorus, which 25
consists of Satyrs. The persons represented in it are
illustrious men ; the action of it is great ; the style
is partly serious, and partly jocular ; and the event
of the action most commonly is happy."

The Grecians, besides these satyric tragedies, had 30
another kind of poem, which they called *silli*, which
were more of kin to the Roman satire. Those *silli*
were indeed invective poems, but of a different species
from the Roman poems of Ennius, Pacuvius, Lucilius,
Horace, and the rest of their successors. They were 35

so called, says Casaubon in one place, from Silenus,
the foster-father of Bacchus ; but, in another place,
bethinking himself better, he derives their name ἀπὸ
τοῦ σιλλαίνειν, from their scoffing and petulancy. From
5 some fragments of the *silli*, written by Timon, we may
find that they were satyric poems, full of parodies ;
that is, of verses patched up from great poets, and
turned into another sense than their author intended
them. Such, amongst the Romans, is the famous *Cento*
10 of Ausonius ; where the words are Virgil's, but, by
applying them to another sense, they are made a relation of a wedding-night ; and the act of consummation
fulsomely described in the very words of the most
modest amongst all poets. Of the same manner are
15 our songs, which are turned into burlesque, and the
serious words of the author perverted into a ridiculous
meaning. Thus in Timon's *Silli* the words are generally those of Homer, and the tragic poets ; but he
applies them, satirically, to some customs and kinds
20 of philosophy, which he arraigns. But the Romans,
not using any of these parodies in their satires,—sometimes, indeed, repeating verses of other men, as Persius
cites some of Nero's, but not turning them into another
meaning,—the *silli* cannot be supposed to be the original
25 of Roman satire. To these *silli*, consisting of parodies,
we may properly add the satires which were written
against particular persons ; such as were the iambics
of Archilochus against Lycambes, which Horace undoubtedly imitated in some of his Odes and Epodes,
30 whose titles bear sufficient witness of it. I might also
name the invective of Ovid against Ibis, and many
others ; but these are the underwood of Satire, rather
than the timber-trees : they are not of general extension, as reaching only to some individual person. And
35 Horace seems to have purged himself from those

splenetic reflections in his Odes and Epodes, before
he undertook the noble work of Satires, which were
properly so called.

Thus, my Lord, I have at length disengaged myself
from those antiquities of Greece ; and have proved, 5
I hope, from the best critics, that the Roman Satire
was not borrowed from thence, but of their own manufacture. I am now almost gotten into my depth ; at
least, by the help of Dacier, I am swimming towards it.
Not that I will promise always to follow him, any more 10
than he follows Casaubon ; but to keep him in my eye,
as my best and truest guide ; and where I think he
may possibly mislead me, there to have recourse to my
own lights, as I expect that others should do by me.

Quintilian says, in plain words, *Satira quidem tota* 15
nostra est ; and Horace had said the same thing before
him, speaking of his predecessor in that sort of poetry,
et Græcis intacti carminis auctor. Nothing can be clearer
than the opinion of the poet, and the orator, both
the best critics of the two best ages of the Roman Em- 20
pire, that Satire was wholly of Latin growth, and not
transplanted to Rome from Athens. Yet, as I have
said, Scaliger, the father, according to his custom, that
is, insolently enough, contradicts them both ; and
gives no better reason, than the derivation of *satyrus* 25
from σαθυ, *salacitas ;* and so, from the lechery of
those Fauns, thinks he has sufficiently proved that
satire is derived from them : as if wantonness and
lubricity were essential to that sort of poem, which
ought to be avoided in it. His other allegation, which 30
I have already mentioned, is as pitiful ; that the Satyrs
carried platters and canisters full of fruit in their hands.
If they had entered empty-handed, had they been ever
the less Satyrs ? Or were the fruits and flowers, which
they offered, anything of kin to satire ? Or any argu- 35

ment that this poem was originally Grecian ? Casaubon
judged better, and his opinion is grounded on sure
authority, that Satire was derived from *satura*, a Roman
word, which signifies full and abundant, and full also
5 of variety, in which nothing is wanting to its due perfection.   It is thus, says Dacier, that we say *a full
colour*, when the wool has taken the whole tincture, and
drunk in as much of the dye as it can receive.   According to this derivation, from *satur* comes *satura ;* or
10 *satira*, according to the new spelling ; as *optumus* and
maxumus are now spelled *optimus* and *maximus*.   *Satura*,
as I have formerly noted, is an adjective, and relates
to the word *lanx*, which is understood ; and this *lanx*,
in English a charger, or large platter, was yearly filled
15 with all sorts of fruits, which were offered to the gods
at their festivals, as the *premices*, or first gatherings.
These offerings of several sorts thus mingled, it is true,
were not unknown to the Grecians, who called them
πανκαρπὸν θυσίαν, a sacrifice of all sorts of fruits ; and
20 πανσπερμίαν, when they offered all kinds of grain.   Virgil
has mentioned those sacrifices in his *Georgics* :—

> *Lancibus et pandis fumantia reddimus exta :*

and in another place, *lancesque et liba feremus :* that is,
we offer the smoking entrails in great platters, and *we will
25 offer the chargers and the cakes*.

The word *satura* has been afterwards applied to many
other sorts of mixtures ; as Festus calls it a kind of
olla, or hotchpotch, made of several sorts of meats.
Laws were also called *leges saturæ*, when they were
30 of several heads and titles, like our tacked bills of
Parliament.   And *per saturam legem ferre*, in the Roman
senate, was to carry a law without telling the senators,
or counting voices, when they were in haste.   Sallust
uses the word, *per saturam sententias exquirere*, when
35 the majority was visible on one side.   From hence it

may probably be conjectured, that the *Discourses,* or
Satires, of Ennius, Lucilius, and Horace, as we now
call them, took their name ; because they are full of
various matters, and are also written on various subjects, as Porphyrius says. But Dacier affirms that it 5
is not immediately from thence that these satires are
so called ; for that name had been used formerly for
other things, which bore a nearer resemblance to those
discourses of Horace. In explaining of which, continues Dacier, a method is to be pursued, of which 10
Casaubon himself has never thought, and which will
put all things into so clear a light, that no further room
will be left for the least dispute.

During the space of almost four hundred years, since
the building of their city, the Romans had never known 15
any entertainments of the stage. Chance and jollity
first found out those verses which they called *Saturnian*
and *Fescennine ;* or rather human nature, which is
inclined to poetry, first produced them, rude and barbarous, and unpolished, as all other operations of the 20
soul are in their beginnings, before they are cultivated
with art and study. However, in occasions of merri-
ment they were first practised ; and this rough-cast
unhewn poetry was instead of stage-plays for the space
of an hundred and twenty years together. They were 25
made *ex tempore,* and were, as the French call them,
impromptus ; for which the Tarsians of old were much
renowned ; and we see the daily examples of them in
the Italian farces of Harlequin and Scaramucha. Such
was the poetry of that savage people, before it was 30
turned into numbers, and the harmony of verse. Little
of the Saturnian verses is now remaining ; we only
know from authors that they were nearer prose than
poetry, without feet, or measure. They were ἐυρυθμοι,
but not ἔμμετροι ; perhaps they might be used in the 35

solemn part of their ceremonies ; and the Fescennine,
which were invented after them, in the afternoon's
debauchery, because they were scoffing and obscene.

The Fescennine and Saturnian were the same ; for
5 as they were called Saturnian from their ancientness,
when Saturn reigned in Italy, they were also called
Fescennine, from Fescennia, a town in the same
country, where they were first practised. The actors,
with a gross and rustic kind of raillery, reproached
10 each other with their failings ; and at the same time
were nothing sparing of it to their audience. Somewhat of this custom was afterwards retained in their
Saturnalia, or feasts of Saturn, celebrated in December ;
at least all kind of freedom in speech was then allowed
15 to slaves even against their masters ; and we are not
without some imitation of it in our Christmas gambols.
Soldiers also used those Fescennine verses, after
measure and numbers had been added to them, at
the triumph of their generals : of which we have an
20 example, in the triumph of Julius Cæsar over Gaul, in
these expressions :

> *Cæsar Gallias subegit, Nicomedes Cæsarem :*
> *Ecce Cæsar nunc triumphat, qui subegit Gallias :*
> *Nicomedes non triumphat, qui subegit Cæsarem.*

25 The vapours of wine made those first satirical poets
amongst the Romans ; which, says Dacier, we cannot
better represent, than by imagining a company of
clowns on a holiday, dancing lubberly, and upbraiding
one another, in *ex tempore* doggerel, with their defects
30 and vices, and the stories that were told of them in
bakehouses and barbers' shops.

When they began to be somewhat better bred, and
were entering, as I may say, into the first rudiments of
civil conversation, they left these hedge-notes for another
35 sort of poem, somewhat polished, which was also full

of pleasant raillery, but without any mixture of obscenity. This sort of poetry appeared under the name of satire, because of its variety ; and this satire was adorned with compositions of music, and with dances ; but lascivious postures were banished from it. In the Tuscan language, 5 says Livy, the word *hister* signifies a player ; and therefore those actors, which were first brought from Etruria to Rome, on occasion of a pestilence, when the Romans were admonished to avert the anger of the Gods by plays, in the year *ab urbe condita* CCCXC., those actors, 10 I say, were therefore called *histriones ;* and that name has since remained, not only to actors Roman born, but to all others of every nation. They played not the former *ex tempore* stuff of Fescennine verses, or clownish jests ; but what they acted was a kind of civil, cleanly 15 farce, with music and dances, and motions that were proper to the subject.

In this condition Livius Andronicus found the stage, when he attempted first, instead of farces, to supply it with a nobler entertainment of tragedies and comedies. 20 This man was a Grecian born, and being made a slave by Livius Salinator, and brought to Rome, had the education of his patron's children committed to him ; which trust he discharged so much to the satisfaction of his master, that he gave him his liberty. 25

Andronicus, thus become a freeman of Rome, added to his own name that of Livius his master ; and, as I observed, was the first author of a regular play in that commonwealth. Being already instructed, in his native country, in the manners and decencies of the 30 Athenian theatre, and conversant in the *Archæa Comœdia,* or Old Comedy of Aristophanes, and the rest of the Grecian poets, he took from that model his own designing of plays for the Roman stage ; the first of which was represented in the year 514 since the building of 35

Rome, as Tully, from the commentaries of Atticus, has
assured us : it was after the end of the first Punic war,
the year before Ennius was born.   Dacier has not
carried the matter altogether thus far ; he only says,
5 that one Livius Andronicus was the first stage-poet at
Rome ; but I will adventure on this hint, to advance
another proposition, which I hope the learned will
approve.   And though we have not anything of
Andronicus remaining to justify my conjecture, yet
10 it is exceeding probable, that, having read the works
of those Grecian wits, his countrymen, he imitated not
only the groundwork, but also the manner of their
writing ;   and how grave soever his tragedies might
be, yet, in his comedies, he expressed the way of
15 Aristophanes, Eupolis, and the rest, which was to
call some persons by their own names, and to expose
their defects to the laughter of the people : the examples
of which we have in the forementioned Aristophanes,
who turned the wise Socrates into ridicule, and is also
20 very free with the management of Cleon, Alcibiades, and
other ministers of the Athenian government.   Now, if
this be granted, we may easily suppose that the first
hint of satirical plays on the Roman stage was given
by the Greeks : not from their *Satyrica*, for that has
25 been reasonably exploded in the former part of this
discourse ; but from their Old Comedy, which was
imitated first by Livius Andronicus. And then Quintilian
and Horace must be cautiously interpreted, where they
affirm that Satire is wholly Roman, and a sort of verse,
30 which was not touched on by the Grecians.   The
reconcilement of my opinion to the standard of their
judgment is not, however, very difficult, since they spoke
of Satire, not as in its first elements, but as it was
formed into a separate work ; begun by Ennius, pursued
35 by Lucilius, and completed afterwards by Horace.   The

proof depends only on this *postulatum*, that the comedies of Andronicus, which were imitations of the Greek, were also imitations of their railleries, and reflections on particular persons. For, if this be granted me, which is a most probable supposition, 'tis easy to infer that 5 the first light which was given to the Roman theatrical satire was from the plays of Livius Andronicus ; which will be more manifestly discovered when I come to speak of Ennius. In the meantime I will return to Dacier.

The people, says he, ran in crowds to these new 10 entertainments of Andronicus, as to pieces which were more noble in their kind, and more perfect than their former satires, which for some time they neglected and abandoned. But not long after, they took them up again, and then they joined them to their comedies ; 15 playing them at the end of every drama, as the French continue at this day to act their farces, in the nature of a separate entertainment from their tragedies. But more particularly they were joined to the *Atellane* fables, says Casaubon ; which were plays invented by the Osci. 20 Those fables, says Valerius Maximus, out of Livy, were tempered with the Italian severity, and free from any note of infamy, or obsceneness ; and, as an old commentator of Juvenal affirms, the *Exodiarii*, which were singers and dancers, entered to entertain the people 25 with light songs, and mimical gestures, that they might not go away oppressed with melancholy, from those serious pieces of the theatre. So that the ancient Satire of the Romans was in extemporary reproaches ; the next was farce, which was brought from Tuscany ; 30 to that succeeded the plays of Andronicus, from the Old Comedy of the Grecians ; and out of all these sprung two several branches of new Roman Satire, like different scions from the same root, which I shall prove with as much brevity as the subject will allow. 35

A year after Andronicus had opened the Roman stage
with his new dramas, Ennius was born ; who, when he
was grown to man's estate, having seriously considered
the genius of the people, and how eagerly they followed
5 the first satires, thought it would be worth his pains to
refine upon the project, and to write satires, not to be
acted on the theatre, but read.   He preserved the
groundwork of their pleasantry, their venom, and their
raillery on particular persons, and general vices ; and
10 by this means, avoiding the danger of any ill success in
a public representation, he hoped to be as well received
in the cabinet, as Andronicus had been upon the stage.
The event was answerable to his expectation.   He
made discourses in several sorts of verse, varied often
15 in the same paper ; retaining still in the title their
original name of Satire.   Both in relation to the
subjects, and the variety of matters contained in them,
the satires of Horace are entirely like them ; only
Ennius, as I have said, confines not himself to one
20 sort of verse, as Horace does ; but taking example from
the Greeks, and even from Homer himself in his
Margites, which is a kind of Satire, as Scaliger
observes, gives himself the licence, when one sort of
numbers comes not easily, to run into another, as his
25 fancy dictates.   For he makes no difficulty to mingle
hexameter with iambic trimeters, or with trochaic tetra-
meters ; as appears by those fragments which are yet
remaining of him.   Horace has thought him worthy to
be copied ; inserting many things of his into his own
30 *Satires*, as Virgil has done into his *Æneids*.

Here we have Dacier making out that Ennius was the
first satirist in that way of writing, which was of his
invention ; that is, Satire abstracted from the stage, and
new-modelled into papers of verses on several subjects.
35 But he will have Ennius take the groundwork of Satire

from the first farces of the Romans, rather than from
the formed plays of Livius Andronicus, which were
copied from the Grecian comedies. It may possibly
be so ; but Dacier knows no more of it than I do. And
it seems to me the more probable opinion, that he rather 5
imitated the fine railleries of the Greeks, which he saw
in the pieces of Andronicus, than the coarseness of his
old countrymen, in their clownish extemporary way of
jeering.

But besides this, it is universally granted, that Ennius, 10
though an Italian, was excellently learned in the Greek
language. His verses were stuffed with fragments of it,
even to a fault ; and he himself believed, according to
the Pythagorean opinion, that the soul of Homer was
transfused into him ; which Persius observes, in his 15
Sixth Satire : *Postquam destertuit esse Mæonides.* But
this being only the private opinion of so inconsiderable
a man as I am, I leave it to the further disquisition of
the critics, if they think it worth their notice. Most
evident it is, that whether he imitated the Roman farce, 20
or the Greek comedies, he is to be acknowledged for
the first author of Roman Satire, as it is properly so
called, and distinguished from any sort of stage-play.

Of Pacuvius, who succeeded him, there is little to be
said, because there is so little remaining of him ; only 25
that he is taken to be the nephew of Ennius, his sister's
son ; that in probability he was instructed by his uncle,
in his way of satire, which we are told he has copied :
but what advances he made we know not.

Lucilius came into the world when Pacuvius flourished 30
most. He also made satires after the manner of Ennius,
but he gave them a more graceful turn, and endeavoured
to imitate more closely the *vetus comœdia* of the Greeks,
of the which the old original Roman Satire had no idea,
till the time of Livius Andronicus. And though Horace 35

seems to have made Lucilius the first author of satire in
verse amongst the Romans, in these words—

> . . . *Quid? cum est Lucilius ausus*
> *Primus in hunc operis componere carmina morem,—*

5 he is only thus to be understood ; that Lucilius had
given a more graceful turn to the satire of Ennius and
Pacuvius, not that he invented a new satire of his own :
and Quintilian seems to explain this passage of Horace
in these words : *Satira quidem tota nostra est ; in qua*
10 *primus insignem laudem adeptus est Lucilius.*

Thus, both Horace and Quintilian give a kind of
primacy of honour to Lucilius, amongst the Latin
satirists.   For, as the Roman language grew more
refined, so much more capable it was of receiving the
15 Grecian beauties, in his time.   Horace and Quintilian
could mean no more, than that Lucilius writ better than
Ennius and Pacuvius ; and on the same account we
prefer Horace to Lucilius.   Both of them imitated the
old Greek Comedy ; and so did Ennius and Pacuvius
20 before them.   The polishing of the Latin tongue, in
the succession of times, made the only difference ; and
Horace himself, in two of his satires, written purposely
on this subject, thinks the Romans of his age were too
partial in their commendations of Lucilius ; who writ
25 not only loosely, and muddily, with little art, and much
less care, but also in a time when the Latin tongue was
not yet sufficiently purged from the dregs of barbarism ;
and many significant and sounding words, which the
Romans wanted, were not admitted even in the times
30 of Lucretius and Cicero, of which both complain.

But to proceed :—Dacier justly taxes Casaubon, saying, that the Satires of Lucilius were wholly different in
specie from those of Ennius and Pacuvius.   Casaubon
was led into that mistake by Diomedes the grammarian,

who in effect says this : Satire amongst the Romans,
but not amongst the Greeks, was a biting invective
poem, made after the model of the ancient Comedy, for
the reprehension of vices ; such as were the poems of
Lucilius, of Horace, and of Persius. But in former 5
times the name of Satire was given to poems which
were composed of several sorts of verses, such as were
made by Ennius and Pacuvius ; more fully expressing
the etymology of the word satire, from *satura*, which
we have observed. Here 'tis manifest, that Diomedes 10
makes a specifical distinction betwixt the satires of
Ennius, and those of Lucilius. But this, as we say in
English, is only a distinction without a difference ; for
the reason of it is ridiculous, and absolutely false. This
was that which cozened honest Casaubon, who, relying 15
on Diomedes, had not sufficiently examined the origin
and nature of those two satires ; which were entirely
the same, both in the matter and the form : for all that
Lucilius performed beyond his predecessors, Ennius
and Pacuvius, was only the adding of more politeness, 20
and more salt, without any change in the substance of
the poem. And though Lucilius put not together in
the same satire several sorts of verses, as Ennius did,
yet he composed several satires, of several sorts of
verses, and mingled them with Greek verses : one poem 25
consisted only of hexameters, and another was entirely
of iambics ; a third of trochaics ; as is visible by the
fragments yet remaining of his works. In short, if the
satires of Lucilius are therefore said to be wholly
different from those of Ennius, because he added much 30
more of beauty and polishing to his own poems, than
are to be found in those before him, it will follow from
hence that the satires of Horace are wholly different
from those of Lucilius, because Horace has not less
surpassed Lucilius in the elegancy of his writing, than 35

Lucilius surpassed Ennius in the turn and ornament of his. This passage of Diomedes has also drawn Dousa, the son, into the same error of Casaubon, which I say, not to expose the little failings of those judicious men,
5 but only to make it appear, with how much diffidence and caution we are to read their works, when they treat a subject of so much obscurity, and so very ancient, as is this of Satire.

Having thus brought down the history of Satire from
10 its original to the times of Horace, and shown the several changes of it, I should here discover some of those graces which Horace added to it, but that I think it will be more proper to defer that undertaking, till I make thé comparison betwixt him and Juvenal. In
15 the meanwhile, following the order of time, it will be necessary to say somewhat of another kind of Satire, which also was descended from the ancients ; 'tis that which we call the Varronian Satire, (but which Varro himself calls the Menippean,) because Varro, the most
20 learned of the Romans, was the first author of it, who imitated, in his works, the manner of Menippus the Gardarenian, who professed the philosophy of the Cynics.

This sort of Satire was not only composed of several
25 sorts of verse, like those of Ennius, but was also mixed with prose ; and Greek was sprinkled amongst the Latin. Quintilian, after he had spoken of the satire of Lucilius, adds what follows : *There is another and former kind of satire, composed by Terentius Varro, the most learned of*
30 *the Romans ; in which he was not satisfied alone with mingling in it several sorts of verse.* The only difficulty of this passage is, that Quintilian tells us, that this satire of Varro was of a former kind. For how can we possibly imagine this to be, since Varro, who was
35 contemporary to Cicero, must consequently be after

Lucilius ? But Quintilian meant not, that the satire
of Varro was in order of time before Lucilius ; he
would only give us to understand, that the Varronian
Satire, with mixture of several sorts of verses, was more
after the manner of Ennius and Pacuvius, than that of 5
Lucilius, who was more severe, and more correct, and
gave himself less liberty in the mixture of his verses in
the same poem.

We have nothing remaining of those Varronian
satires, excepting some inconsiderable fragments, and 10
those for the most part much corrupted. The titles
of many of them are indeed preserved, and they are
generally double ; from whence, at least, we may
understand, how many various subjects were treated
by that author. Tully, in his *Academics*, introduces 15
Varro himself giving us some light concerning the
scope and design of these works. Wherein, after he
had shown his reasons why he did not *ex professo* write
of philosophy, he adds what follows : *Notwithstanding,*
says he, *that those pieces of mine, wherein I have imitated* 20
Menippus, though I have not translated him, are sprinkled
with a kind of mirth and gaiety, yet many things are there
inserted, which are drawn from the very entrails of philo-
sophy, and many things severely argued ; which I have
mingled with pleasantries on purpose, that they may more 25
easily go down with the common sort of unlearned readers.
The rest of the sentence is so lame, that we can only
make thus much out of it, that in the composition of
his satires he so tempered philology with philosophy,
that his work was a mixture of them both. And Tully 30
himself confirms us in this opinion, when a little after
he addresses himself to Varro in these words : *And*
you yourself have composed a most elegant and complete
poem ; you have begun philosophy in many places ; suffi-
cient to incite us, though too little to instruct us. Thus it 35

appears, that Varro was one of those writers whom they
called σπουδογέλοιοι, studious of laughter ; and that, as
learned as he was, his business was more to divert his
reader, than to teach him. And he entitled his own
5 satires *Menippean ;* not that Menippus had written any
satires (for his were either dialogues or epistles), but
that Varro imitated his style, his manner, and his face-
tiousness. All that we know further of Menippus and
his writings, which are wholly lost, is, that by some he
10 is esteemed, as, amongst the rest, by Varro ; by others
he is noted of cynical impudence, and obscenity : that
he was much given to those parodies, which I have
already mentioned ; that is, he often quoted the verses
of Homer and the tragic poets, and turned their serious
15 meaning into something that was ridiculous ; whereas
Varro's satires are by Tully called absolute, and most
elegant and various poems. Lucian, who was emulous
of this Menippus, seems to have imitated both his
manners and his style in many of his dialogues ; where
20 Menippus himself is often introduced as a speaker in
them, and as a perpetual buffoon ; particularly his
character is expressed in the beginning of that dialogue
which is called Νεκυομαντεία. But Varro, in imitating him,
avoids his impudence and filthiness, and only expresses
25 his witty pleasantry.

This we may believe for certain, that as his subjects
were various, so most of them were tales or stories of
his own invention. Which is also manifest from antiquity, by those authors who are acknowledged to have
30 written Varronian satires, in imitation of his ; of whom
the chief is Petronius Arbiter, whose satire, they say, is
now printed in Holland, wholly recovered, and made
complete : when 'tis made public, it will easily be seen
by any one sentence, whether it be supposititious, or
35 genuine. Many of Lucian's dialogues may also properly

be called Varronian satires, particularly his *True History ;* and consequently the *Golden Ass* of Apuleius, which is taken from him. Of the same stamp is the mock deification of Claudius, by Seneca : and the *Symposium* or *Cæsars* of Julian, the Emperor. Amongst 5 the moderns, we may reckon the *Encomium Moriæ* of Erasmus, Barclay's *Euphormio*, and a volume of German authors, which my ingenious friend, Mr. Charles Killigrew, once lent me. In the English, I remember none which are mixed with prose, as Varro's were ; but of 10 the same kind is *Mother Hubbard's Tale*, in Spenser ; and (if it be not too vain to mention anything of my own), the poems of *Absalom* and *MacFleckno*.

This is what I have to say in general of Satire : only, as Dacier has observed before me, we may take notice, 15 that the word *satire* is of a more general signification in Latin, than in French, or English. For amongst the Romans it was not only used for those discourses which decried vice, or exposed folly, but for others also, where virtue was recommended. But in our 20 modern languages we apply it only to invective poems, where the very name of Satire is formidable to those persons who would appear to the world what they are not in themselves ; for in English, to say satire, is to mean reflection, as we use that word in the worst sense ; 25 or as the French call it, more properly, *médisance*. In the criticism of spelling, it ought to be with *i*, and not with *y*, to distinguish its true derivation from *satura*, not from *satyrus*. And if this be so, then it is false spelled throughout this book ; for here it is written 30 *Satyr :* which having not considered at the first, I thought it not worth correcting afterwards. But the French are more nice, and never spell it any other way than *satire*.

I am now arrived at the most difficult part of my 35

undertaking, which is, to compare Horace with Juvenal
and Persius. It is observed by Rigaltius, in his preface
before Juvenal, written to Thuanus, that these three
poets have all their particular partisans, and favourers.
5 Every commentator, as he has taken pains with any of
them, thinks himself obliged to prefer his author to the
other two ; to find out their failings, and decry them,
that he may make room for his own darling. Such is
the partiality of mankind, to set up that interest which
10 they have once espoused, though it be to the prejudice
of truth, morality, and common justice ; and especially
in the productions of the brain. As authors generally
think themselves the best poets, because they cannot
go out of themselves to judge sincerely of their betters ;
15 so it is with critics, who, having first taken a liking to
one of these poets, proceed to comment on him, and to
illustrate him ; after which, they fall in love with their
own labours, to that degree of blind fondness, that at
length they defend and exalt their author, not so much
20 for his sake as for their own. 'Tis a folly of the same
nature with that of the Romans themselves, in the
games of the Circus. The spectators were divided in
their factions, betwixt the *Veneti* and the *Prasini ;* some
were for the charioteer in blue, and some for him in
25 green. The colours themselves were but a fancy ; but
when once a man had taken pains to set out those of
his party, and had been at the trouble of procuring
voices for them, the case was altered ; he was concerned
for his own labour, and that so earnestly, that disputes
30 and quarrels, animosities, commotions, and bloodshed,
often happened ; and in the declension of the Grecian
Empire the very sovereigns themselves engaged in it,
even when the barbarians were at their doors, and
stickled for the preference of colours, when the safety
35 of their people was in question. I am now myself on

the brink of the same precipice ; I have spent some
time on the translation of Juvenal and Persius ; and it
behoves me to be wary, lest, for that reason, I should
be partial to them, or take a prejudice against Horace.
Yet, on the other side, I would not be like some of our 5
judges, who would give the cause for a poor man, right
or wrong ; for, though that be an error on the better
hand, yet it is still a partiality : and a rich man, unheard,
cannot be concluded an oppressor. I remember a saying
of King Charles II on Sir Matthew Hale, (who was 10
doubtless an uncorrupt and upright man,) that his servants were sure to be cast on any trial which was heard
before him ; not that he thought the judge was possibly
to be bribed, but that his integrity might be too scrupu-
lous ; and that the causes of the crown were always 15
suspicious, when the privileges of subjects were concerned. It had been much fairer, if the modern critics,
who have embarked in the quarrels of their favourite
authors, had rather given to each his proper due ;
without taking from another's heap, to raise their own. 20
There is praise enough for each of them in particular,
without encroaching on his fellows, and detracting from
them, or enriching themselves with the spoils of others.
But to come to particulars. Heinsius and Dacier are
the most principal of those who raise Horace above 25
Juvenal and Persius. Scaliger the father, Rigaltius,
and many others, debase Horace, that they may set up
Juvenal ; and Casaubon, who is almost single, throws
dirt on Juvenal and Horace, that he may exalt Persius,
whom he understood particularly well, and better than 30
any of his former commentators ; even Stelluti, who
succeeded him. I will begin with him, who, in my
opinion, defends the weakest cause, which is that of
Persius ; and labouring, as Tacitus professes of his own
writing, to divest myself of partiality, or prejudice, con- 35

sider Persius, not as a poet whom I have wholly
translated, and who has cost me more labour and time
than Juvenal, but according to what I judge to be his
own merit ;· which I think not equal, in the main, to
5 that of Juvenal or Horace, and yet in some things to be
preferred to both of them.

First, then, for the verse ; neither Casaubon himself,
nor any for him, can defend either his numbers, or the
purity of his Latin. Casaubon gives this point for lost,
10 and pretends not to justify either the measures or the
words of Persius ; he is evidently beneath Horace and
Juvenal in both.

Then, as his verse is scabrous, and hobbling, and his
words not everywhere well chosen, the purity of Latin
15 being more corrupted than in the time of Juvenal, and
consequently of Horace, who writ when the language
was in the height of its perfection, so his diction is hard,
his figures are generally too bold and daring, and his
tropes, particularly his metaphors, insufferably strained.
20   In the third place, notwithstanding all the diligence
of Casaubon, Stelluti, and a Scotch gentleman, whom I
have heard extremely commended for his illustrations
of him, yet he is still obscure : whether he affected not
to be understood, but with difficulty ; or whether the
25 fear of his safety under Nero compelled him to this
darkness in some places ; or that it was occasioned by
his close way of thinking, and the brevity of his style,
and crowding of his figures ; or lastly, whether, after so
long a time, many of his words have been corrupted,
30 and many customs, and stories relating to them, lost to
us : whether some of these reasons, or all, concurred to
render him so cloudy, we may be bold to affirm, that
the best of commentators can but guess at his meaning,
in many passages ; and none can be certain that he has
35 divined rightly.

After all, he was a young man, like his friend and
contemporary Lucan ; both of them men of extraordinary parts, and great acquired knowledge, considering their youth : but neither of them had arrived
to that maturity of judgment which is necessary to the 5
accomplishing of a formed poet. And this consideration, as, on the one hand, it lays some imperfections to
their charge, so, on the other side, 'tis a candid excuse
for those failings which are incident to youth and
inexperience ; and we have more reason to wonder how 10
they, who died before the thirtieth year of their age,
could write so well, and think so strongly, than to
accuse them of those faults from which human nature,
and more especially in youth, can never possibly be
exempted. 15

To consider Persius yet more closely : he rather
insulted over vice and folly, than exposed them, like
Juvenal and Horace ; and as chaste and modest as he
is esteemed, it cannot be denied, but that in some
places he is broad and fulsome, as the latter verses of 20
the Fourth Satire, and of the Sixth, sufficiently witness.
And 'tis to be believed that he who commits the same
crime often, and without necessity, cannot but do it with
some kind of pleasure.

To come to a conclusion : he is manifestly below 25
Horace, because he borrows most of his greatest beauties from him ; and Casaubon is so far from denying
this, that he has written a treatise purposely concerning it, wherein he shows a multitude of his translations
from Horace, and his imitations of him, for the credit 30
of his author ; which he calls *Imitatio Horatiana*.

To these defects, which I casually observed while
I was translating this author, Scaliger has added others ;
he calls him, in plain terms, a silly writer, and a trifler,
full of ostentation of his learning, and, after all, un- 35

worthy to come into competition with Juvenal and
Horace.

After such terrible accusations, 'tis time to hear what
his patron Casaubon can allege in his defence. Instead
5 of answering, he excuses for the most part ; and, when
he cannot, accuses others ,of the same crimes. He
deals with Scaliger, as a modest scholar with a master.
He compliments him with so much reverence, that one
would swear he feared him as much at least as he
10 respected him. Scaliger will not allow Persius to have
any wit ; Casaubon interprets this in the mildest sense,
and confesses his author was not good at turning things
into a pleasant ridicule ; or, in other words, that he was
not a laughable writer. That he was *ineptus*, indeed,
15 but that was *non aptissimus ad jocandum* ; but that he
was ostentatious of his learning, that, by Scaliger's
good favour, he denies. Persius showed his learning,
but was no boaster of it ; he did *ostendere*, but not *osten-
tare* ; and so, he says, did Scaliger : where, methinks,
20 Casaubon turns it handsomely upon that supercilious
critic, and silently insinuates that he himself was sufficiently vainglorious, and a boaster of his own knowledge. All the writings of this venerable censor,
continues Casaubon, which are χρυσοῦ χρυσότερα, more
25 golden than gold itself, are everywhere smelling of
that thyme which, like a bee, he has gathered from
ancient authors ; but far be ostentation and vainglory
from a gentleman so well born, and so nobly educated
as Scaliger. But, says Scaliger, he is so obscure,
30 that he has got himself the name of Scotinus, a dark
writer. Now, says Casaubon, it is a wonder to me
that anything could be obscure to the divine wit of
Scaliger, from which nothing could be hidden. This
is indeed a strong compliment, but no defence ; and
35 Casaubon, who could not but be sensible of his author's

blind side, thinks it time to abandon a post that was untenable. He acknowledges that Persius is obscure in some places ; but so is Plato, so is Thucydides ; so are Pindar, Theocritus, and Aristophanes, amongst the Greek poets ; and even Horace and Juvenal, he might have added, amongst the Romans. The truth is, Persius is not sometimes, but generally, obscure ; and therefore Casaubon, at last, is forced to excuse him, by alleging that it was *se defendendo*, for fear of Nero ; and that he was commanded to write so cloudily by Cornutus, in virtue of holy obedience to his master. I cannot help my own opinion ; I think Cornutus needed not to have read many lectures to him on that subject. Persius was an apt scholar ; and when he was bidden to be obscure in some places, where his life and safety were in question, took the same counsel for all his books ; and never afterwards wrote ten lines together clearly. Casaubon, being upon this chapter, has not failed, we may be sure, of making a compliment to his own dear comment. If Persius, says he, be in himself obscure, yet my interpretation has made him intelligible. There is no question but he deserves that praise which he has given to himself ; but the nature of the thing, as Lucretius says, will not admit of a perfect explanation. Besides many examples, which I could urge, the very last verse of his last satire, upon which he particularly values himself in his preface, is not yet sufficiently explicated. 'Tis true, Holyday has endeavoured to justify his construction ; but Stelluti is against it ; and, for my part, I can have but a very dark notion of it. As for the chastity of his thoughts, Casaubon denies not but that one particular passage, in the Fourth Satire. *At si unctus cesses*, etc., is not only the most obscure, but the most obscene of all his works. I understood it ; but for that reason turned it over. In

defence of his boisterous metaphors, he quotes Longinus, who accounts them as instruments of the sublime ; fit to move and stir up the affections, particularly in narration. To which it may be replied, that where the
5 trope is far-fetched and hard it is fit for nothing but to puzzle the understanding ; and may be reckoned amongst those things of Demosthenes which Æschines called θαύματα, not ῥήματα, that is, prodigies, not words. It must be granted to Casaubon, that the knowledge of
10 many things is lost in our modern ages, which were of familiar notice to the ancients ; and that Satire is a poem of a difficult nature in itself, and is not written to vulgar readers : and through the relation which it has to comedy, the frequent change of persons makes the
15 sense perplexed, when we can but divine who it is that speaks ; whether Persius himself, or his friend and monitor ; or, in some places, a third person. But Casaubon comes back always to himself, and concludes, that if Persius had not been obscure there had been
20 no need of him for an interpreter. Yet when he had once enjoined himself so hard a task, he then considered the Greek proverb, that he must χελώνης φαγεῖν ἢ μὴ φαγεῖν, either eat the whole snail, or let it quite alone ; and so he went through with his laborious task, as I
25 have done with my difficult translation.

Thus far, my Lord, you see it has gone very hard with Persius : I think he cannot be allowed to stand in competition either with Juvenal or Horace. Yet for once I will venture to be so vain as to affirm, that none
30 of his hard metaphors, or forced expressions, are in my translation. But more of this in its proper place, where I shall say somewhat in particular of our general performance, in making these two authors English. In the meantime, I think myself obliged to give Persius his
35 undoubted due, and to acquaint the world, with Casau-

bon, in what he has equalled, and in what excelled, his
two competitors.

A man who has resolved to praise an author, with
any appearance of justice, must be sure to take him on
the strongest side, and where he is least liable to excep- 5
tions. He is therefore obliged to choose his mediums
accordingly. Casaubon, who saw that Persius could
not laugh with a becoming grace, that he was not made
for jesting, and that a merry conceit was not his talent,
turned his feather, like an Indian, to another light, that 10
he might give it the better gloss. Moral doctrine, says
he, and urbanity, or well-mannered wit, are the two
things which constitute the Roman satire ; but of the
two, that which is most essential to this poem, and
is, as it were, the very soul which animates it, is the 15
scourging of vice, and exhortation to virtue. Thus wit,
for a good reason, is already almost out of doors ; and
allowed only for an instrument, a kind of tool, or a
weapon, as he calls it, of which the satirist makes use
in the compassing of his design. The end and aim of 20
our three rivals is consequently the same. But by what
methods they have prosecuted their intention is further
to be considered. Satire is of the nature of moral
philosophy, as being instructive : he, therefore, who
instructs most usefully, will carry the palm from his 25
two antagonists. The philosophy in which Persius was
educated, and which he professes through his whole
book, is the Stoic ; the most noble, most generous,
most beneficial to human kind, amongst all the sects,
who have given us the rules of ethics, thereby to form 30
a severe virtue in the soul ; to raise in us an undaunted
courage against the assaults of fortune ; to esteem as
nothing the things that are without us, because they are
not in our power ; not to value riches, beauty, honours,
fame, or health, any further than as conveniences, and 35

so many helps to living as we ought, and doing good in
our generation.   In short, to be always happy, while
we possess our minds with a good conscience, are free
from the slavery of vices, and conform our actions and
5 conversations to the rules of right reason.   See here,
my Lord, an epitome of Epictetus ; the doctrine of
Zeno, and the education of our Persius.   And this he
expressed, not only in all his satires, but in the manner
of his life.   I will not lessen this commendation of the
10 Stoic philosophy by giving you an account of some
absurdities in their doctrine, and some perhaps impie-
ties, if we consider them by the standard of Christian
faith.   Persius has fallen into none of them ; and therefore is free from those imputations.   What he teaches
15 might be taught from pulpits, with more profit to the
audience than all the nice speculations of divinity, and
controversies concerning faith ; which are more for the
profit of the shepherd than for the edification of the
flock.   Passions, interest, ambition, and all their bloody
20 consequences of discord and of war, are banished from
this doctrine.   Here is nothing proposed but the quiet
and tranquillity of the mind ; virtue lodged at home,
and afterwards diffused in her general effects, to the
improvement and good of human kind.   And therefore
25 I wonder not that the present Bishop of Salisbury has
recommended this our author, and the Tenth Satire
of Juvenal, in his Pastoral Letter, to the serious perusal
and practice of the divines in his diocese, as the best
common-places for their sermons, as the store-houses
30 and magazines of moral virtues, from whence they may
draw out, as they have occasion, all manner of assistance for the accomplishment of a virtuous life, which
the Stoics have assigned for the great end and perfection of mankind.   Herein then it is, that Persius has
35 excelled both Juvenal and Horace.   He sticks to his

own philosophy ; he shifts not sides, like Horace, who
is sometimes an Epicurean, sometimes a Stoic, sometimes an Eclectic, as his present humour leads him ;
nor declaims like Juvenal against vices, more like an
orator than a philosopher. Persius is everywhere the 5
same ; true to the dogmas of his master. What he has
learnt, he teaches vehemently ; and what he teaches,
that he practises himself. There is a spirit of sincerity
in all he says ; you may easily discern that he is in
earnest, and is persuaded of that truth which he incul- 10
cates. In this I am of opinion that he excels Horace,
who is commonly in jest, and laughs while he instructs ;
and is equal to Juvenal, who was as honest and serious
as Persius, and more he could not be.

Hitherto I have followed Casaubon, and enlarged 15
upon him, because I am satisfied that he says no more
than truth ; the rest is almost all frivolous. For he
says that Horace, being the son of a tax-gatherer, or
a collector, as we call it, smells everywhere of the meanness of his birth and education : his conceits are vulgar, 20
like the subjects of his satires ; that he does *plebeium
sapere*, and writes not with that elevation which becomes
a satirist : that Persius, being nobly born, and of an
opulent family, had likewise the advantage of a better
master ; Cornutus being the most learned of his time, 25
a man of the most holy life, a chief of the Stoic sect
at Rome, and not only a great philosopher, but a poet
himself, and in probability a coadjutor of Persius : that,
as for Juvenal, he was long a declaimer, came late to
poetry, and has not been much conversant in philosophy. 30

'Tis granted that the father of Horace was *libertinus*,
that is, one degree removed from his grandfather, who
had been once a slave. But Horace, speaking of him,
gives him the best character of a father which I ever
read in history ; and I wish a witty friend of mine, now 35

living, had such another. He bred him in the best
school, and with the best company of young noblemen ;
and Horace, by his gratitude to his memory, gives
a certain testimony that his education was ingenuous.
5 After this, he formed himself abroad, by the conversation
of great men. Brutus found him at Athens, and was so
pleased with him, that he took him thence into the army,
and made him *tribunus militum*, a colonel in a legion,
which was the preferment of an old soldier. All this
10 was before his acquaintance with Mæcenas, and his introduction into the court of Augustus, and the familiarity
of that great emperor ; which, had he not been well-bred
before, had been enough to civilise his conversation,
and render him accomplished and knowing in all the
15 arts of complacency and good behaviour ; and, in short,
an agreeable companion for the retired hours and
privacies of a favourite, who was first minister. So that,
upon the whole matter, Persius may be acknowledged
to be equal with him in those respects, though better
20 born, and Juvenal inferior to both. If the advantage be
anywhere, 'tis on the side of Horace ; as much as the
court of Augustus Cæsar was superior to that of Nero.
As for the subjects which they treated, it will appear
hereafter that Horace writ not vulgarly on vulgar sub-
25 jects, nor always chose them. His style is constantly
accommodated to his subject, either high or low. If his
fault be too much lowness, that of Persius is the fault of
the hardness of his metaphors, and obscurity : and so
they are equal in the failings of their style ; where
30 Juvenal manifestly triumphs over both of them.

The comparison betwixt Horace and Juvenal is more
difficult ; because their forces were more equal. A dispute has always been, and ever will continue, betwixt
the favourers of the two poets. *Non nostrum est tantas*
35 *componere lites.* I shall only venture to give my own

opinion, and leave it for better judges to determine. If it be only argued in general, which of them was the better poet, the victory is already gained on the side of Horace. Virgil himself must yield to him in the delicacy of his turns, his choice of words, and perhaps 5 the purity of his Latin. He who says that Pindar is inimitable, is himself inimitable in his Odes. But the contention betwixt these two great masters is for the prize of Satire ; in which controversy all the Odes and Epodes of Horace are to stand excluded. I say this, 10 because Horace has written many of them satirically, against his private enemies ; yet these, if justly considered, are somewhat of the nature of the Greek *Silli*, which were invectives against particular sects and persons. But Horace had purged himself of this 15 choler before he entered on those discourses which are more properly called the Roman Satire. He has not now to do with a Lyce, a Canidia, a Cassius Severus, or a Menas ; but is to correct the vices and the follies of his time, and to give the rules of a happy and virtuous 20 life. In a word, that former sort of satire, which is known in England by the name of lampoon, is a dangerous sort of weapon, and for the most part unlawful. We have no moral right on the reputation of other men. 'Tis taking from them what we cannot restore to them. There 25 are only two reasons for which we may be permitted to write lampoons ; and I will not promise that they can always justify us. The first is revenge, when we have been affronted in the same nature, or have been any ways notoriously abused, and can make ourselves no 30 other reparation. And yet we know, that, in Christian charity, all offences are to be forgiven, as we expect the like pardon for those which we daily commit against Almighty God. And this consideration has often made me tremble when I was saying our Saviour's prayer ; 35

for the plain condition of the forgiveness which we beg
is the pardoning of others the offences which they have
done to us ; for which reason I have many times avoided
the commission of that fault, even when I have been
5 notoriously provoked. Let not this, my Lord, pass for
vanity in me ; for it is truth. More libels have been
written against me, than almost any man now living ;
and I had reason on my side, to have defended my own
innocence. I speak not of my poetry, which I have
10 wholly given up to the critics : let them use it as they
please : posterity, perhaps, may be more favourable to
me ; for interest and passion will lie buried in another
age, and partiality and prejudice be forgotten. I speak
of my mŏrals, which have been sufficiently aspersed :
15 that only sort of reputation ought to be dear to every
honest man, and is to me. But let the world witness
for me, that I have been often wanting to myself in that
particular ; I have seldom answered any scurrilous lampoon, when it was in my power to have exposed my
20 enemies : and, being naturally vindicative, have suffered
in silence, and possessed my soul in quiet.

Anything, though never so little, which a man speaks
of himself, in my opinion, is still too much ; and therefore I will waive this subject, and proceed to give the
25 second reason which may justify a poet when he writes
against a particular person ; and that is, when he is
become a public nuisance. All those, whom Horace in
his Satires, and Persius and Juvenal have mentioned in
theirs, with a brand of infamy, are wholly such. 'Tis an
30 action of virtue to make examples of vicious men. They
may and ought to be upbraided with their crimes and
follies ; both for their own amendment, if they are not
yet incorrigible, and for the terror of others, to hinder
them from falling into those enormities which they see
35 are so severely punished in the persons of others. The

first reason was only an excuse for revenge ; but this
second is absolutely of a poet's office to perform : but
how few lampooners are there now living, who are
capable of this duty ! When they come in my way, 'tis
impossible sometimes to avoid reading them. But, good 5
God ! how remote they are, in common justice, from the
choice of such persons as are the proper subject of
satire ! And how little wit they bring for the support
of their injustice ! The weaker sex is their most ordinary
theme ; and the best and fairest are sure to be the most 10
severely handled. Amongst men, those who are pros-
perously unjust are entitled to a panegyric ; but afflicted
virtue is insolently stabbed with all manner of reproaches. No decency is considered, no fulsomeness
omitted ; no venom is wanting, as far as dulness can 15
supply it. For there is a perpetual dearth of wit ; a barrenness of good sense and entertainment. The neglect
of the readers will soon put an end to this sort of scrib-
bling. There can be no pleasantry where there is no
wit ; no impression can be made where there is no truth 20
for the foundation. To conclude : they are like the fruits
of the earth in this unnatural season ; the corn which
held up its head is spoiled with rankness ; but the greater
part of the harvest is laid along, and little of good income
and wholesome nourishment is received into the barns. 25
This is almost a digression, I confess to your Lordship ;
but a just indignation forced it from me. Now I have
removed this rubbish, I will return to the comparison
of Juvenal and Horace.

I would willingly divide the palm betwixt them, upon 30
the two heads of profit and delight, which are the two
ends of poetry in general. It must be granted, by the
favourers of Juvenal, that Horace is the more copious
and profitable in his instructions of human life ; but, in
my particular opinion, which I set not up for a standard 35

to better judgments, Juvenal is the more delightful
author. I am profited by both, I am pleased with both ;
but I owe more to Horace for my instruction, and more
to Juvenal for my pleasure. This, as I said, is my
5 particular taste of these two authors : they who will
have either of them to excel the other in both qualities
can scarce give better reasons for their opinion than
I for mine. But all unbiassed readers will conclude,
that my moderation is not to be condemned : to such
10 impartial men I must appeal ; for they who have already
formed their judgment may justly stand suspected of
prejudice ; and though all who are my readers will set
up to be my judges, I enter my *caveat* against them, that
they ought not so much as to be of my jury ; or, if
15 they be admitted, 'tis but reason that they should
first hear what I have to urge in the defence of my
opinion.

   That Horace is somewhat the better instructor of the
two, is proved from hence, that his instructions are
20 more general, Juvenal's more limited. So that, granting that the counsels which they give are equally good
for moral use, Horace, who gives the most various
advice, and most applicable to all occasions which can
occur to us in the course of our lives,—as including in
25 his discourses, not only all the rules of morality, but
also of civil conversation,—is undoubtedly to be preferred to him who is more circumscribed in his
instructions, makes them to fewer people, and on fewer
occasions, than the other. I may be pardoned for
30 using an old saying, since 'tis true, and to the purpose :
Bonum quo communius, eo melius. Juvenal, excepting
only his First Satire, is in all the rest confined to the
exposing of some particular vice ; that he lashes, and
there he sticks. His sentences are truly shining and
35 instructive ; but they are sprinkled here and there.

Horace is teaching us in every line, and is perpetually
moral : he had found out the skill of Virgil, to hide
his sentences ; to give you the virtue of them, without
showing them in their full extent ; which is the ostentation of a poet, and not his art : and this Petronius charges 5
on the authors of his time, as a vice of writing which
was then growing on the age : *ne sententiæ extra corpus
orationis emineant :* he would have them weaved into
the body of the work, and not appear embossed upon
it, and striking directly on the reader's view.   Folly 10
was the proper quarry of Horace, and not vice ; and
as there are but few notoriously wicked men, in comparison with a shoal of fools and fops, so 'tis a harder
thing to make a man wise than to make him honest ;
for the will is only to be reclaimed in the one, but the 15
understanding is to be informed in the other.   There
are blind sides and follies, even in the professors of
moral philosophy ; and there is not any one sect of them
that Horace has not exposed : which, as it was not the
design of Juvenal, who was wholly employed in lashing 20
vices, some of them the most enormous that can be
imagined, so, perhaps, it was not so much his talent.

> *Omne vafer vitium ridenti Flaccus amico*
> *Tangit, et admissus circum præcordia ludit.*

This was the commendation which Persius gave him : 25
where, by *vitium*, he means those little vices which we
call follies, the defects of human understanding, or, at
most, the peccadillos of life, rather than the tragical
vices, to which men are hurried by their unruly passions
and exorbitant desires.   But in the word *omne*, which 30
is universal, he concludes with me, that the divine wit
of Horace left nothing untouched ; that he entered into
the inmost recesses of nature ; found out the imperfections even of the most wise and grave, as well as
of the common people ; discovering, even in the great 35

Trebatius, to whom he addresses the First Satire, his
hunting after business, and following the court, as well
as in the persecutor Crispinus, his impertinence and
importunity. 'Tis true, he exposes Crispinus openly,
5 as a common nuisance ; but he rallies the other, as
a friend, more finely. The exhortations of Persius
are confined to noblemen ; and the Stoic philosophy
is that alone which he recommends to them ; Juvenal
exhorts to particular virtues, as they are opposed to
10 those vices against which he declaims ; but Horace
laughs to shame all follies, and insinuates virtue rather
by familiar examples than by the severity of precepts.

This last consideration seems to incline the balance
on the side of Horace, and to give him the preference
15 to Juvenal, not only in profit, but in pleasure. But,
after all, I must confess, that the delight which Horace
gives me is but languishing. Be pleased still to understand, that I speak of my own taste only : he may ravish
other men ; but I am too stupid and insensible to be
20 tickled. Where he barely grins himself, and, as Scaliger
says, only shows his white teeth, he cannot provoke me
to any laughter. His urbanity, that is, his good manners,
are to be commended, but his wit is faint ; and his salt,
if I may dare to say so, almost insipid. Juvenal is of
25 a more vigorous and masculine wit ; he gives me as
much pleasure as I can bear ; he fully satisfies my
expectation ; he treats his subject home : his spleen is
raised, and he raises mine : I have the pleasure of concernment in all he says ; he drives his reader along
30 with him ; and when he is at the end of his way
I willingly stop with him. If he went another stage,
it would be too far ; it would make a journey of a progress, and turn delight into fatigue. When he gives
over, it is a sign the subject is exhausted, and the wit
35 of man can carry it no further. If a fault can be justly

found in him, 'tis that he is sometimes too luxuriant, too redundant; says more than he needs, like my friend the *Plain-Dealer*, but never more than pleases. Add to this, that his thoughts are as just as those of Hórace, and much more elevated. His expressions are sonorous and more noble; his verse more numerous, and his words are suitable to his thoughts, sublime and lofty. All these contribute to the pleasure of the reader; and the greater the soul of him who reads, his transports are the greater. Horace is always on the amble, Juvenal on the gallop; but his way is perpetually on carpet-ground. He goes with more impetuosity than Horace, but as securely; and the swiftness adds a more lively agitation to the spirits. The low style of Horace is according to his subject, that is, generally grovelling. I question not but he could have raised it; for the First Epistle of the Second Book, which he writes to Augustus, (a most instructive satire concerning poetry,) is of so much dignity in the words, and of so much elegancy in the numbers, that the author plainly shows the *sermo pedestris*, in his other Satires, was rather his choice than his necessity. He was a rival to Lucilius, his predecessor, and was resolved to sur-pass him in his own manner. Lucilius, as we see by his remaining fragments, minded neither his style, nor his numbers, nor his purity of words, nor his run of verse. Horace therefore copes with him in that humble way of satire, writes under his own force, and carries a dead-weight, that he may match his competitor in the race. This, I imagine, was the chief reason why he minded only the clearness of his satire, and the clean-ness of expression, without ascending to those heights to which his own vigour might have carried him. But, limiting his desires only to the conquest of Lucilius, he had his ends of his rival, who lived before him; but

made way for a new conquest over himself, by Juvenal,
his successor. He could not give an equal pleasure to
his reader, because he used not equal instruments. The
fault was in the tools, and not in the workman. But
5 versification and numbers are the greatest pleasures of
poetry : Virgil knew it, and practised both so happily,
that, for aught I know, his greatest excellency is in
his diction. In all other parts of poetry, he is faultless ; but in this he placed his chief perfection. And
10 give me leave, my Lord, since I have here an apt
occasion, to say that Virgil could have written sharper
satires than either Horace or Juvenal, if he would have
employed his talent that way. I will produce a verse
and half of his, in one of his Eclogues, to justify my
15 opinion ; and with commas after every word, to show
that he has given almost as many lashes as he has
written syllables. 'Tis against a bad poet, whose ill
verses he describes :—

> . . . *non tu, in triviis, indocte, solebas*
20 *Stridenti, miserum, stipula disperdere carmen?*

But to return to my purpose : when there is anything
deficient in numbers and sound, the reader is uneasy
and unsatisfied ; he wants something of his complement,
desires somewhat which he finds not : and this being
25 the manifest defect of Horace, 'tis no wonder that,
finding it supplied in Juvenal, we are more delighted
with him. And, besides this, the sauce of Juvenal is
more poignant, to create in us an appetite of reading
him. The meat of Horace is more nourishing ; but the
30 cookery of Juvenal more exquisite : so that, granting
Horace to be the more general philosopher, we cannot
deny that Juvenal was the greater poet, I mean in
satire. His thoughts are sharper ; his indignation
against vice is more vehement ; his spirit has more of
35 the commonwealth genius ; he treats tyranny, and all

the vices attending it, as they deserve, with the utmost
rigour : and consequently, a noble soul is better pleased
with a zealous vindicator of Roman liberty, than with
a temporising poet, a well-mannered court-slave, and
a man who is often afraid of laughing in the right 5
place ; who is ever decent, because he is naturally
servile. After all, Horace had the disadvantage of the
times in which he lived ; they were better for the man,
but worse for the satirist. 'Tis generally said, that
those enormous vices which were practised under the 10
reign of Domitian were unknown in the time of
Augustus Cæsar ; that therefore Juvenal had a larger
field than Horace. Little follies were out of doors
when oppression was to be scourged instead of avarice :
it was no longer time to turn into ridicule the false 15
opinions of philosophers when the Roman liberty was
to be asserted. There was more need of a Brutus in
Domitian's days, to redeem or mend, than of a Horace,
if he had then been living, to laugh at a fly-catcher.
This reflection at the same time excuses Horace, but 20
exalts Juvenal. I have ended, before I was aware, the
comparison of Horace and Juvenal, upon the topics of
instruction and delight ; and, indeed, I may safely here
conclude that common-place ; for, if we make Horace
our minister of state in Satire, and Juvenal of our private 25
pleasures, I think the latter has no ill bargain of it.
Let profit have the pre-eminence of honour, in the end
of poetry. Pleasure, though but the second in degree,
is the first in favour. And who would not choose to be
loved better, rather than to be more esteemed ? But 30
I am entered already upon another topic, which concerns the particular merits of these two satirists.
However, I will pursue my business where I left it,
and carry it farther than that common observation of
the several ages in which these authors flourished. 35

When Horace writ his *Satires*, the monarchy of his
Cæsar was in its newness, and the government but just
made easy to the conquered people. They could not
possibly have forgotten the usurpation of that prince
5 upon their freedom, nor the violent methods which he
had used, in the compassing that vast design : they yet
remembered his proscriptions, and the slaughter of so
many noble Romans, their defenders : amongst the
rest, that horrible action of his, when he forced Livia
10 from the arms of her husband, who was constrained to
see her married, as Dion relates the story, and, big
with child as she was, conveyed to the bed of his insult-
ing rival. The same Dion Cassius gives us another
instance of the crime before mentioned ; that Cornelius
15 Sisenna being reproached, in full senate, with the
licentious conduct of his wife, returned this answer,
that he had married her by the counsel of Augustus ;
intimating, says my author, that Augustus had obliged
him to that marriage, that he might, under that covert,
20 have the more free access to her. His adulteries were
still before their eyes : but they must be patient where
they had not power. In other things that emperor was
moderate enough : propriety was generally secured ;
and the people entertained with public shows and
25 donatives, to make them more easily digest their lost
liberty. But Augustus, who was conscious to himself
of so many crimes which he had committed, thought, in
the first place, to provide for his own reputation, by
making an edict against lampoons and satires, and the
30 authors of those defamatory writings which my author
Tacitus, from the law-term, calls *famosos libellos*.

In the first book of his *Annals*, he gives the following
account of it, in these words : *Primus Augustus cogni-
tionem de famosis libellis, specie legis ejus, tractavit ;*
35 *commotus Cassii Severi libidine, qua viros fœminasque*

illustres procacibus scriptis diffamaverat. Thus in English : ' Augustus was the first who under the colour of
that law took cognisance of lampoons ; being provoked to
it by the petulancy of Cassius Severus, who had defamed
many illustrious persons of both sexes in his writings.' 5
The law to which Tacitus refers was *Lex læsæ Majes-
tatis* ; commonly called, for the sake of brevity, *Majestas ;*
or, as we say, high treason. He means not, that this
law had not been enacted formerly : for it had been
made by the Decemviri, and was inscribed amongst the 10
rest in the Twelve Tables ; to prevent the aspersion of
the Roman majesty, either of the people themselves, or
their religion, or their magistrates : and the infringe-
ment of it was capital ; that is, the offender was whipt to
death, with the *fasces*, which were borne before their 15
chief officers of Rome. But Augustus was the first
who restored that intermitted law. By the words,
under colour of that law, he insinuates that Augustus
caused it to be executed on pretence of those libels,
which were written by Cassius Severus, against the 20
nobility ; but, in truth, to save himself from such defamatory verses. Suetonius likewise makes mention of it
thus : *Sparsos de se in curia famosos libellos, nec expavit,
et magna cura redarguit. Ac ne requisitis quidem auc-
toribus, id modo censuit, cognoscendum posthac de iis qui* 25
*libellos aut carmina ad infamiam cujuspiam sub alieno
nomine edant.* ' Augustus was not afraid of libels,' says
that author ; ' yet he took all care imaginable to have
them answered ; and then decreed, that for the time to
come the authors of them should be punished.' But 30
Aurelius makes it yet more clear, according to my
sense, that this emperor for his own sake durst not
permit them : *Fecit id Augustus in speciem, ut quasi
gratificaretur populo Romano, et primoribus urbis ; sed
revera ut sibi consuleret : nam habuit in animo, compri-* 35

mere nimiam quorundam procacitatem in loquendo, a qua
nec ipse exemptus fuit. Nam suo nomine compescere erat
invidiosum, sub alieno facile et utile. Ergo specie legis
tractavit, quasi populi Romani majestas infamaretur.
5 This, I think, is a sufficient comment on that passage of
Tacitus. I will add only by the way, that the whole
family of the Cæsars, and all their relations, were
included in the law ; because the majesty of the Romans, in the time of the empire, was wholly in that
10 house ; *omnia Cæsar erat :* they were all accounted
sacred who belonged to him. As for Cassius Severus,
he was contemporary with Horace ; and was the same
poet against whom he writes in his Epodes, under this
title, *In Cassium Severum maledicum poetam ;* perhaps
15 intending to kill two crows, according to our proverb,
with one stone, and revenge both himself and his
emperor together.

From hence I may reasonably conclude, that Augustus, who was not altogether so good as he was wise,
20 had some by-respect in the enacting of this law ; for to
do anything for nothing was not his maxim. Horace,
as he was a courtier, complied with the interest of his
master ; and, avoiding the lashing of greater crimes,
confined himself to the ridiculing of petty vices and com-
25 mon follies ; excepting only some reserved cases, in his
Odes and Epodes, of his own particular quarrels, which
either with permission of the magistrate, or without it,
every man will revenge, though I say not that he should ;
for *prior læsit* is a good excuse in the civil law, if Chris-
30 tianity had not taught us to forgive. However, he was
not the proper man to arraign great vices, at least if the
stories which we hear of him are true, that he practised some, which I will not here mention, out of honour
to him. It was not for a Clodius to accuse adulterers,
35 especially when Augustus was of that number ; so that

though his age was not exempted from the worst of
villanies, there was no freedom left to reprehend them
by reason of the edict ; and our poet was not fit to
represent them in an odious character, because himself
was dipt in the same actions.   Upon this account, with- 5
out further insisting on the different tempers of Juvenal
and Horace, I conclude, that the subjects which Horace
chose for satire are of a lower nature than those of
which Juvenal has written.

Thus I have treated, in a new method, the comparison 10
betwixt Horace, Juvenal, and Persius ; somewhat of
their particular manner belonging to all of them is yet
remaining to be considered.   Persius was grave, and
particularly opposed his gravity to lewdness, which was
the predominant vice in Nero's court, at the time when 15
he published his Satires, which was before that emperor fell into the excess of cruelty.   Horace was
a mild admonisher, a court-satirist, fit for the gentle
times of Augustus, and more fit, for the reasons which
I have already given.   Juvenal was as proper for his 20
times, as they for theirs ; his was an age that deserved
a more severe chastisement ; vices were more gross
and open, more flagitious, more encouraged by the
example of a tyrant, and more protected by his authority.   Therefore, wheresoever Juvenal mentions Nero, 25
he means Domitian, whom he dares not attack in his
own person, but scourges him by proxy.   Heinsius
urges in praise of Horace, that, according to the ancient
art and law of satire, it should be nearer to comedy
than tragedy ; not declaiming against vice, but only 30
laughing at it.   Neither Persius nor Juvenal were
ignorant of this, for they had both studied Horace.
And the thing itself is plainly true.   But as they had
read Horace, they had likewise read Lucilius, of whom
Persius says *secuit urbem ; . . . et genuinum fregit in* 35

illis ; meaning Mutius and Lupus ; and Juvenal also
mentions him in these words : *Ense velut stricto, quoties
Lucilius ardens infremuit,* &c. So that they thought the
imitation of Lucilius was more proper to their purpose
5 than that of Horace. ' They changed satire ', says
Holyday, ' but they changed it for the better ; for the
business being to reform great vices, chastisement goes
further than admonition ; whereas a perpetual grin, like
that of Horace, does rather anger than amend a man.'
10   Thus far that learned critic, Barten Holyday, whose
interpretation and illustrations of Juvenal are as excellent, as the verse of his translation and his English are
lame and pitiful. For 'tis not enough to give us the
meaning of a poet, which I acknowledge him to have
15 performed most faithfully, but he must also imitate his
genius and his numbers, as far as the English will
come up to the elegance of the original. In few words,
'tis only for a poet to translate a poem. Holyday and
Stapylton had not enough considered this, when they
20 attempted Juvenal : but I forbear reflections ; only
I beg leave to take notice of this sentence, where
Holyday says, ' a perpetual grin, like that of Horace,
rather angers than amends a man.' I cannot give him
up the manner of Horace in low satire so easily. Let
25 the chastisement of Juvenal be never so necessary
for his new kind of satire ; let him declaim as wittily
and sharply as he pleases ; yet still the nicest and
most delicate touches of satire consist in fine raillery.
This, my Lord, is your particular talent, to which even
30 Juvenal could not arrive. 'Tis not reading, 'tis not
imitation of an author, which can produce this fineness ;
it must be inborn ; it must proceed from a genius, and
particular way of thinking, which is not to be taught ;
and therefore not to be imitated by him who has it not
35 from nature. How easy is it to call rogue and villain,

and that wittily ! But how hard to make a man appear
a fool, a blockhead, or a knave, without using any of
those opprobrious terms ! To spare the grossness of
the names, and to do the thing yet more severely, is to
draw a full face, and to make the nose and cheeks 5
stand out, and yet not to employ any depth of shadow-
ing. This is the mystery of that noble trade, which yet
no master can teach to his apprentice ; he may give the
rules, but the scholar is never the nearer in his practice. Neither is it true, that this fineness of raillery 10
is offensive. A witty man is tickled while he is hurt in
this manner, and a fool feels it not. The occasion of
an offence may possibly be given, but he cannot take it.
If it be granted, that in effect this way does more mischief ; that a man is secretly wounded, and though he 15
be not sensible himself, yet the malicious world will
find it out for him ; yet there is still a vast difference
betwixt the slovenly butchering of a man, and the fineness of a stroke that separates the head from the body,
and leaves it standing in its place. A man may be capa- 20
ble, as Jack Ketch's wife said of his servant, of a plain
piece of work, a bare hanging ; but to make a male-
factor die sweetly was only belonging to her husband.
I wish I could apply it to myself, if the reader would be
kind enough to think it belongs to me. The character 25
of Zimri in my *Absalom* is, in my opinion, worth the
whole poem : it is not bloody, but it is ridiculous
enough ; and he, for whom it was intended, was too
witty to resent it as an injury. If I had railed, I might
have suffered for it justly ; but I managed my own work 30
more happily, perhaps more dexterously. I avoided
the mention of great crimes, and applied myself to the
representing of blindsides, and little extravagancies ;
to which, the wittier a man is, he is generally the more
obnoxious. It succeeded as I wished ; the jest went 35

round, and he was laught at in his turn who began the frolic.

And thus, my Lord, you see I have preferred the manner of Horace, and of your Lordship, in this kind 5 of satire, to that of Juvenal, and, I think, reasonably. Holyday ought not to have arraigned so great an author, for that which was his excellency and his merit : or if he did, on such a palpable mistake, he might expect that some one might possibly arise, either in his 10 own time, or after him, to rectify his error, and restore to Horace that commendation of which he has so unjustly robbed him. And let the *Manes* of Juvenal forgive me if I say, that this way of Horace was the best for amending manners, as it is the most difficult. 15 His was an *ense rescindendum ;* but that of Horace was a pleasant cure, with all the limbs preserved entire ; and, as our mountebanks tell us in their bills, without keeping the patient within-doors for a day. What they promise only, Horace has effectually performed : yet I 20 contradict not the proposition which I formerly advanced. Juvenal's times required a more painful kind of operation ; but if he had lived in the age of Horace, I must needs affirm, that he had it not about him. He took the method which was prescribed him by his own 25 genius, which was sharp and eager ; he could not rally, but he could declaim ; and as his provocations were great, he has revenged them tragically. This notwithstanding, I am to say another word, which, as true as it is, will yet displease the partial admirers of our 30 Horace. I have hinted it before, but it is time for me now to speak more plainly.

This manner of Horace is indeed the best ; but Horace has not executed it altogether so happily, at least not often. The manner of Juvenal is confessed to 35 be inferior to the former, but Juvenal has excelled him

in his performance. Juvenal has railed more wittily
than Horace has rallied. Horace means to make his
readers laugh, but he is not sure of his experiment.
Juvenal always intends to move your indignation, and
he always brings about his purpose. Horace, for aught 5
I know, might have tickled the people of his age; but
amongst the moderns he is not so successful. They
who say he entertains so pleasantly may perhaps value
themselves on the quickness of their own understandings, that they can see a jest further off than other men. 10
They may find occasion of laughter in the wit-battle of
the two buffoons, Sarmentus and Cicerrus; and hold
their sides for fear of bursting, when Rupilius and
Persius are scolding. For my own part, I can only
like the characters of all four, which are judiciously 15
given; but for my heart I cannot so much as smile at
their insipid raillery. I see not why Persius should call
upon Brutus to revenge him on his adversary; and
that because he had killed Julius Cæsar, for endeavouring to be a king, therefore he should be desired to 20
murder Rupilius, only because his name was Mr. King.
A miserable clench, in my opinion, for Horace to
record: I have heard honest Mr. Swan make many
a better, and yet have had the grace to hold my
countenance. But it may be puns were then in fashion, 25
as they were wit in the sermons of the last age, and in
the court of King Charles the Second. I am sorry to
say it, for the sake of Horace; but certain it is, he has
no fine palate who can feed so heartily on garbage.

But I have already wearied myself, and doubt not 30
but I have tired your Lordship's patience, with this long,
rambling, and, I fear, trivial discourse. Upon the one
half of the merits, that is, pleasure, I cannot but conclude
that Juvenal was the better satirist. They, who will
descend into his particular praises, may find them at 35

large in the Dissertation of the learned Rigaltius to
Thuanus. As for Persius, I have given the reasons
why I think him inferior to both of them ; yet I have
one thing to add on that subject.

5   Barten Holyday, who translated both Juvenal and
Persius, has made this distinction betwixt them, which
is no less true than witty ; that in Persius the difficulty
is to find a meaning, in Juvenal to choose a meaning :
so crabbed is Persius, and so copious is Juvenal ; so
10 much the understanding is employed in one, and so
much the judgment in the other ; so difficult it is to find
any sense in the former, and the best sense of the latter.

If, on the other side, any one suppose I have commended Horace below his merit, when I have allowed
15 him but the second place, I desire him to consider, if
Juvenal, a man of excellent natural endowments, besides
the advantages of diligence and study, and coming after
him, and building upon his foundations, might not
probably, with all these helps, surpass him ; and whether
20 it be any dishonour to Horace to be thus surpassed,
since no art or science is at once begun and perfected,
but that it must pass first through many hands, and
even through several ages. If Lucilius could add to
Ennius, and Horace to Lucilius, why, without any
25 diminution to the fame of Horace, might not Juvenal
give the last perfection to that work ? Or rather, what
disreputation is it to Horace, that Juvenal excels in the
tragical satire, as Horace does in the comical ? I have
read over attentively both Heinsius and Dacier, in
30 their commendations of Horace ; but I can find no
more in either of them, for the preference of him to
Juvenal, than the instructive part ; the part of wisdom,
and not that of pleasure ; which, therefore, is here
allowed him, notwithstanding what Scaliger and Rigal-
35 tius have pleaded to the contrary for Juvenal. And to

show I am impartial, I will here translate what Dacier
has said on that subject.

'I cannot give a more just idea of the two books of
Satires made by Horace, than by comparing them to
the statues of the Sileni, to which Alcibiades compares 5
Socrates in the *Symposium*. They were figures, which
had nothing of agreeable, nothing of beauty, on their
outside ; but when any one took the pains to open them,
and search into them, he there found the figures of all
the deities. So, in the shape that Horace presents 10
himself to us in his *Satires*, we see nothing, at the first
view, which deserves our attention. It seems that he is
rather an amusement for children, than for the serious
consideration of men. But, when we take away his
crust, and that which hides him from our sight, when 15
we discover him to the bottom, then we find all the
divinities in a full assembly ; that is to say, all the
virtues which ought to be the continual exercise of
those, who seriously endeavour to correct their vices.'

'Tis easy to observe, that Dacier, in this noble 20
similitude, has confined the praise of his author wholly
to the instructive part ; the commendation turns on
this, and so does that which follows.

'In these two books of Satire, 'tis the business of
Horace to instruct us how to combat our vices, to 25
regulate our passions, to follow nature, to give bounds
to our desires, to distinguish betwixt truth and falsehood, and betwixt our conceptions of things, and things
themselves ; to come back from our prejudicate opinions,
to understand exactly the principles and motives of all 30
our actions ; and to avoid the ridicule into which all
men necessarily fall, who are intoxicated with those
notions which they have received from their masters,
and which they obstinately retain, without examining
whether or no they be founded on right reason. 35

'In a word, he labours to render us happy in relation to ourselves ; agreeable and faithful to our friends ; and discreet, serviceable, and well-bred, in relation to those with whom we are obliged to live, and to converse.
5 To make his figures intelligible, to conduct his readers through the labyrinth of some perplexed sentence, or obscure parenthesis, is no great matter ; and as Epictetus says, there is nothing of beauty in all this, or what is worthy of a prudent man.   The principal business,
10 and which is of most importance to us, is to show the use, the reason, and the proof of his precepts.

'They who endeavour not to correct themselves according to so exact a model, are just like the patients who have open before them a book of admirable receipts
15 for their diseases, and please themselves with reading it, without comprehending the nature of the remedies, or how to apply them to their cure.'

Let Horace go off with these encomiums, which he has so well deserved.
20   To conclude the contention betwixt our three poets, I will use the words of Virgil, in his fifth *Æneid*, where Æneas proposes the rewards of the foot-race to the three first who should reach the goal :—

. . . tres præmia primi
25   *Accipient, flavaque caput nectentur oliva.*

Let these three ancients be preferred to all the moderns, as first arriving at the goal ; let them all be crowned, as victors, with the wreath that properly belongs to satire ; but, after that, with this distinction amongst themselves—

30   *Primus equum phaleris insignem victor habeto :—*

let Juvenal ride first in triumph ;

Alter Amazoniam pharetram, plenamque sagittis
Threiciis, lato quam circumplectitur auro
Balteus, et tereti subnectit fibula gemma :—

let Horace, who is the second, and but just the second,
carry off the quivers and the arrows, as the badges of
his satire, and the golden belt, and the diamond button ;

Tertius Argolico hoc clypeo contentus abito :—

and let Persius, the last of the first three worthies, be 5
contented with this Grecian shield, and with victory,
not only over all the Grecians, who were ignorant of
the Roman satire, but over all the moderns in succeeding ages, excepting Boileau and your Lordship.

And thus I have given the history of Satire, and 10
derived it as far as from Ennius to your Lordship ; that
is, from its first rudiments of barbarity to its last
polishing and perfection ; which is, with Virgil, in his
address to Augustus—

> . . . *nomen fama tot ferre per annos,*   15
> *Tithoni prima quot abest ab origine Cæsar.*

I said only from Ennius ; but I may safely carry it
higher, as far as Livius Andronicus ; who, as I have
said formerly, taught the first play at Rome, in the year
ab urbe condita DXIV. I have since desired my learned 20
friend, Mr. Maidwell, to compute the difference of
times betwixt Aristophanes and Livius Andronicus ;
and he assures me, from the best chronologers, that
Plutus, the last of Aristophanes his plays, was represented at Athens in the year of the 97th Olympiad ; 25
which agrees with the year *urbis conditæ* CCCLXIV. So
that the difference of years betwixt Aristophanes and
Andronicus is 150 ; from whence I have probably
deduced, that Livius Andronicus, who was a Grecian,
had read the plays of the Old Comedy, which were 30
satirical, and also of the New ; for Menander was fifty
years before him, which must needs be a great light to
him in his own plays, that were of the satirical nature.
That the Romans had farces before this, 'tis true ; but

then they had no communication with Greece ; so that
Andronicus was the first who wrote after the manner of
the Old Comedy in his plays : he was imitated by
Ennius, about thirty years afterwards. Though the
5 former writ fables, the latter, speaking properly, began
the Roman satire ; according to that description, which
Juvenal gives of it in his first :

> *Quicquid agunt homines, votum, timor, ira, voluptas,*
> *Gaudia, discursus, nostri est farrago libelli.*

10 This is that in which I have made bold to differ from
Casaubon, Rigaltius, Dacier, and indeed from all the
modern critics, that not Ennius, but Andronicus was
the first who, by the *Archæa Comædia* of the Greeks,
added many beauties to the first rude and barbarous
15 Roman satire : which sort of poem, though we had not
derived from Rome, yet nature teaches it mankind in
all ages, and in every country.

'Tis but necessary, that after so much has been
said of Satire some definition of it should be given.
20 Heinsius, in his dissertations on Horace, makes it for
me, in these words : ' Satire is a kind of poetry, without a series of action, invented for the purging of our
minds ; in which human vices, ignorance, and errors,
and all things besides, which are produced from them
25 in every man, are severely reprehended ; partly dra-
matically, partly simply, and sometimes in both kinds
of speaking ; but, for the most part, figuratively, and
occultly ; consisting in a low familiar way, chiefly in
a sharp and pungent manner of speech ; but partly,
30 also, in a facetious and civil way of jesting ; by which
either hatred, or laughter, or indignation, is moved.'—
Where I cannot but observe, that this obscure and perplexed definition, or rather description, of satire, is
wholly accommodated to the Horatian way ; and ex-

cluding the works of Juvenal and Persius, as foreign
from that kind of poem. The clause in the beginning
of it *without a series of action* distinguishes satire properly from stage-plays, which are all of one action, and
one continued series of action. The end or scope of 5
satire is to purge the passions ; so far it is common to
the satires of Juvenal and Persius. The rest which
follows is also generally belonging to all three ; till he
comes upon us, with the excluding clause *consisting in
a low familiar way of speech*, which is the proper character 10
of Horace ; and from which the other two, for their
honour be it spoken, are far distant. But how come
lowness of style, and the familiarity of words, to be so
much the propriety of satire, that without them a poet
can be no more a satirist, than without risibility he can 15
be a man ? Is the fault of Horace to be made the
virtue and standing rule of this poem ? Is the *grande
sophos* of Persius, and the sublimity of Juvenal, to be
circumscribed with the meanness of words and vulgarity
of expression ? If Horace refused the pains of num- 20
bers, and the loftiness of figures, are they bound to
follow so ill a precedent ? Let him walk afoot, with
his pad in his hand, for his own pleasure ; but let not
them be accounted no poets, who choose to mount, and
show their horsemanship. Holyday is not afraid to 25
say, that there was never such a fall, as from his Odes
to his Satires, and that he, injuriously to himself, un-
tuned his harp. The majestic way of Persius and
Juvenal was new when they began it, but 'tis old to us ;
and what poems have not, with time, received an altera- 30
tion in their fashion ? ' Which alteration,' says Holyday, ' is to aftertimes as good a warrant as the first.'
Has not Virgil changed the manners of Homer's heroes
in his *Æneis* ? Certainly he has, and for the better :
for Virgil's age was more civilised, and better bred ; 35

and he writ according to the politeness of Rome, under
the reign of Augustus Cæsar, not to the rudeness of
Agamemnon's age, or the times of Homer. Why
should we offer to confine free spirits to one form,
5 when we cannot so much as confine our bodies to one
fashion of apparel ? Would not Donne's *Satires*, which
abound with so much wit, appear more charming, if he
had taken care of his words, and of his numbers ? But
he followed Horace so very close, that of necessity he
10 must fall with him ; and I may safely say it of this
present age, that if we are not so great wits as Donne,
yet certainly we are better poets.

But I have said enough, and it may be too much, on
this subject. Will your Lordship be pleased to prolong
15 my audience, only so far, till I tell you my own trivial
thoughts, how a modern satire should be made ? I will
not deviate in the least from the precepts and examples
of the Ancients, who were always our best masters.
I will only illustrate them, and discover some of the
20 hidden beauties in their designs, that we thereby may
form our own in imitation of them. Will you please
but to observe, that Persius, the least in dignity of all
the three, has notwithstanding been the first who has
discovered to us this important secret, in the design-
25 ing of a perfect satire ; that it ought only to treat of one
subject ; to be confined to one particular theme ; or at
least, to one principally. If other vices occur in the
management of the chief, they should only be transiently lashed, and not be insisted on, so as to make
30 the design double. As in a play of the English fashion,
which we call a tragi-comedy, there is to be but one
main design ; and though there be an underplot, or
second walk of comical characters and adventures, yet
they are subservient to the chief fable, carried along
35 under it, and helping to it ; so that the drama may not

seem a monster with two heads. Thus, the Copernican system of the planets makes the moon to be moved by the motion of the earth, and carried about her orb, as a dependent of hers. Mascardi, in his discourse of the *Doppia Favola*, or double tale in plays, gives an instance 5 of it in the famous pastoral of Guarini, called *Il Pastor Fido ;* where Corisca and the Satyr are the under parts ; yet we may observe, that Corisca is brought into the body of the plot, and made subservient to it. 'Tis certain, that the divine wit of Horace was not ignorant 10 of this rule,—that a play, though it consists of many parts, must yet be one in the action, and must drive on the accomplishment of one design ; for he gives this very precept, *sit quodvis simplex duntaxat et unum ;* yet he seems not much to mind it in his *Satires*, many 15 of them consisting of more arguments than one ; and the second without dependence on the first. Casaubon has observed this before me, in his preference of Persius to Horace ; and will have his own beloved author to be the first who found out and introduced this 20 method of confining himself to one subject. I know it may be urged in defence of Horace, that this unity is not necessary ; because the very word *satura* signifies a dish plentifully stored with all variety of fruit and grains. Yet Juvenal, who calls his poems a *farrago*, 25 which is a word of the same signification with *satura*, has chosen to follow the same method of Persius, and not of Horace ; and Boileau, whose example alone is a sufficient authority, has wholly confined himself, in all his *Satires*, to this unity of design. That variety, 30 which is not to be found in any one satire, is, at least, in many, written on several occasions. And if variety be of absolute necessity in every one of them, according to the etymology of the word, yet it may arise naturally from one subject, as it is diversely treated, in the several 35

subordinate branches of it, all relating to the chief. It
may be illustrated accordingly with variety of examples
in the subdivisions of it, and with as many precepts as
there are members of it ; which, altogether, may com-
5 plete that *olla*, or hotchpotch, which is properly a
satire.

Under this unity of theme, or subject, is comprehended another rule for perfecting the design of true
satire. The poet is bound, and that *ex officio*, to give
10 his reader some one precept of moral virtue, and to
caution him against some one particular vice or folly.
Other virtues, subordinate to the first, may be recommended under that chief head ; and other vices or
follies may be scourged, besides that which he prin-
15 cipally intends. But he is chiefly to inculcate one
virtue, and insist on that. Thus Juvenal, in every
satire excepting the first, ties himself to one principal
instructive point, or to the shunning of moral evil.
Even in the Sixth, which seems only an arraignment
20 of the whole sex of womankind, there is a latent admonition to avoid ill women, by showing how very few,
who are virtuous and good, are to be found amongst
them. But this, though the wittiest of all his satires,
has yet the least of truth or instruction in it. He
25 has run himself into his old declamatory way, and
almost forgotten that he was now setting up for
a moral poet.

Persius is never wanting to us in some profitable
doctrine, and in exposing the opposite vices to it. His
30 kind of philosophy is one, which is the Stoic ; and
every satire is a comment on one particular dogma of
that sect, unless we will except the first, which is against
bad writers ; and yet even there he forgets not the precepts of the Porch. In general, all virtues are every-
35 where to be praised and recommended to practice ; and

all vices to be reprehended, and made either odious or
ridiculous ; or else there is a fundamental error in the
whole design.

I have already declared who are the only persons
that are the adequate object of private satire, and who 5
they are that may properly be exposed by name for
public examples of vices and follies ; and therefore
I will trouble your Lordship no further with them.   Of
the best and finest manner of Satire, I have said enough
in the comparison betwixt Juvenal and Horace : 'tis 10
that sharp, well-mannered way of laughing a folly out
of countenance, of which your Lordship is the best
master in this age.   I will proceed to the versification,
which is most proper for it, and add somewhat to
what I have said already on that subject.   The sort of 15
verse which is called *burlesque*, consisting of eight syllables, or four feet, is that which our excellent Hudibras has chosen.   I ought to have mentioned him
before, when I spoke of Donne ; but by a slip of an old
man's memory he was forgotten.   The worth of his 20
poem is too well known to need my commendation, and
he is above my censure.   His satire is of the Varronian kind, though unmixed with prose.   The choice of
his numbers is suitable enough to his design, as he has
managed it ; but in any other hand, the shortness of his 25
verse, and the quick returns of rhyme, had debased
the dignity of style.   And besides, the double rhyme,
(a necessary companion of burlesque writing,) is not so
proper for manly satire ; for it turns earnest too much
to jest, and gives us a boyish kind of pleasure.   It 30
tickles awkwardly with a kind of pain, to the best sort
of readers : we are pleased ungratefully, and, if I may
say so, against our liking.   We thank him not for
giving us that unseasonable delight, when we know he
could have given us a better, and more solid.   He 35

might have left that task to others, who, not being able to put in thought, can only make us grin with the excrescence of a word of two or three syllables in the close. 'Tis, indeed, below so great a master to make
5 use of such a little instrument. But his good sense is perpetually shining through all he writes ; it affords us not the time of finding faults. We pass through the levity of his rhyme, and are immediately carried into some admirable useful thought. After all, he has
10 chosen this kind of verse, and has written the best in it : and had he taken another, he would always have excelled : as we say of a court favourite, that whatsoever his office be, he still makes it uppermost, and most beneficial to himself.

15   The quickness of your imagination, my Lord, has already prevented me ; and you know beforehand, that I would prefer the verse of ten syllables, which we call the English heroic, to that of eight. This is truly my opinion. For this sort of number is more roomy ; the
20 thought can turn itself with greater ease in a larger compass. When the rhyme comes too thick upon us, it straitens the expression ; we are thinking of the close, when we should be employed in adorning the thought. It makes a poet giddy with turning in a space too
25 narrow for his imagination ; he loses many beauties, without gaining one advantage. For a burlesque rhyme I have already concluded to be none ; or, if it were, 'tis more easily purchased in ten syllables than in eight. In both occasions 'tis as in a tennis-court, when
30 the strokes of greater force are given, when we strike out and play at length. Tassoni and Boileau have left us the best examples of this way, in the *Secchia Rapita*, and the *Lutrin ;* and next them Merlin Coccaius in his *Baldus*. I will speak only of the two former, because
35 the last is written in Latin verse. The *Secchia Rapita*

is an Italian poem, a satire of the Varronian kind. 'Tis
written in the stanza of eight, which is their measure
for heroic verse. The words are stately, the numbers
smooth, the turn both of thoughts and words is happy.
The first six lines of the stanza seem majestical and 5
severe ; but the two last turn them all into a pleasant
ridicule. Boileau, if I am not much deceived, has
modelled from hence his famous *Lutrin*. He had read
the burlesque poetry of Scarron, with some kind of
indignation, as witty as it was, and found nothing in 10
France that was worthy of his imitation ; but he copied
the Italian so well, that his own may pass for an
original. He writes it in the French heroic verse, and
calls it an heroic poem ; his subject is trivial, but his
verse is noble. I doubt not but he had Virgil in his 15
eye, for we find many admirable imitations of him, and
some parodies ; as particularly this passage in the
fourth of the *Æneids*—

> *Nec tibi diva parens, generis nec Dardanus auctor,*
> *Perfide ; sed duris genuit te cautibus horrens* 20
> *Caucasus ; Hyrcanæque admorunt ubera tigres :*

which he thus translates, keeping to the words, but
altering the sense—

> *Non, ton Père à Paris, ne fut point boulanger :*
> *Et tu n'es point du sang de Gervais, l'horloger ;*
> *Ta mère ne fut point la maitresse d'un coche :* 25
> *Caucase dans ses flancs te forma d'une roche :*
> *Une tigresse affreuse, en quelque antre écarté,*
> *Te fit, avec son lait, sucer sa cruauté.*

And, as Virgil in his fourth Georgic, of the Bees, per- 30
petually raises the lowness of his subject, by the loftiness
of his words, and ennobles it by comparisons drawn
from empires, and from monarchs—

> *Admiranda tibi levium spectacula rerum,*
> *Magnanimosque duces, totiusque ordine gentis* 35
> *Mores et studia, et populos, et prœlia dicam.*

And again—

> *Sed genus immortale manet ; multosque per annos*
> *Stat fortuna domus, et avi numerantur avorum ;—*

we see Boileau pursuing him in the same flights, and
5 scarcely yielding to his master. This, I think, my
Lord, to be the most beautiful, and most noble kind of
satire. Here is the majesty of the heroic, finely mixed
with the venom of the other ; and raising the delight
which otherwise would be flat and vulgar, by the
10 sublimity of the expression. I could say somewhat
more of the delicacy of this and some other of his satires ;
but it might turn to his prejudice, if 'twere carried back
to France.

I have given your Lordship but this bare hint, in what
15 verse and in what manner this sort of satire may be best
managed. Had I time, I could enlarge on the beautiful
turns of words and thoughts, which are as requisite in
this, as in heroic poetry itself, of which the satire is
undoubtedly a species. With these beautiful turns,
20 I confess myself to have been unacquainted, till about
twenty years ago, in a conversation which I had with
that noble wit of Scotland, Sir George Mackenzie, he
asked me why I did not imitate in my verses the turns
of Mr. Waller and Sir John Denham, of which he
25 repeated many to me. I had often read with pleasure,
and with some profit, those two fathers of our English
poetry, but had not seriously enough considered those
beauties which gave the last perfection to their works.
Some sprinklings of this kind I had also formerly in my
30 plays ; but they were casual, and not designed. But
this hint, thus seasonably given me, first made me
sensible of my own wants, and brought me afterwards
to seek for the supply of them in other English authors.
I looked over the darling of my youth, the famous
35 Cowley ; there I found, instead of them, the points of

wit, and quirks of epigram, even in the *Davideis*, an
heroic poem, which is of an opposite nature to those
puerilities ; but no elegant turns either on the word or
on the thought. Then I consulted a greater genius,
(without offence to the *Manes* of that noble author,) 5
I mean Milton. But as he endeavours everywhere to
express Homer, whose age had not arrived to that
fineness, I found in him a true sublimity, lofty thoughts,
which were clothed with admirable Grecisms, and
ancient words, which he had been digging from the 10
mines of Chaucer and Spenser, and which, with all
their rusticity, had somewhat of venerable in them ;
but I found not there neither that for which I looked.
At last I had recourse to his master, Spenser, the author
of that immortal poem called the *Fairy Queen ;* and 15
there I met with that which I had been looking for so
long in vain. Spenser had studied Virgil to as much
advantage as Milton had done Homer ; and amongst
the rest of his excellencies had copied that. Looking
farther into the Italian, I found Tasso had done the 20
same ; nay more, that all the sonnets in that language
are on the turn of the first thought ; which Mr. Walsh,
in his late ingenious preface to his poems, has observed.
In short, Virgil and Ovid are the two principal fountains
of them in Latin poetry. And the French at this day 25
are so fond of them, that they judge them to be the first
beauties: *délicat et bien tourné*, are the highest commendations which they bestow on somewhat which they think
a masterpiece.

An example of the turn on words, amongst a 30
thousand others, is that in the last book of Ovid's
Metamorphoses—

> *Heu ! quantum scelus est, in viscera, viscera condi !*
> *Congestoque avidum pinguescere corpore corpus ;*
> *Alteriusque animantem animantis vivere leto.* 35

An example on the turn both of thoughts and words is to be found in Catullus, in the complaint of Ariadne, when she was left by Theseus—

5
> *Tum jam nulla viro juranti fœmina credat ;*
> *Nulla viri speret sermones esse fideles ;*
> *Qui, dum aliquid cupiens animus prægestit apisci,*
> *Nil metuunt jurare, nihil promittere parcunt :*
> *Sed simul ac cupidæ mentis satiata libido est,*
> *Dicta nihil metuere, nihil perjuria curant.*

10 An extraordinary turn upon the words is that in Ovid's *Epistolæ Heroidum*, of Sappho to Phaon—

> *Si, nisi quæ forma poterit te digna videri,*
> *Nulla futura tua est, nulla futura tua est.*

Lastly, a turn, which I cannot say is absolutely on
15 words, for the thought turns with them, is in the fourth *Georgic* of Virgil, where Orpheus is to receive his wife from Hell, on express condition not to look on her till she was come on earth—

> *Cum subita incautum dementia cepit amantem ;*
20 > *Ignoscenda quidem, scirent si ignoscere Manes.*

I will not burthen your Lordship with more of them ; for I write to a master who understands them better than myself. But I may safely conclude them to be great beauties. I might descend also to the mechanic
25 beauties of heroic verse ; but we have yet no English *prosodia*, not so much as a tolerable dictionary, or a grammar ; so that our language is in a manner barbarous ; and what government will encourage any one, or more, who are capable of refining it, I know
30 not : but nothing under a public expense can go through with it. And I rather fear a declination of the language, than hope an advancement of it in the present age.

I am still speaking to you, my Lord, though, in all
35 probability, you are already out of hearing.   Nothing,

which my meanness can produce, is worthy of this
long attention.   But I am come to the last petition of
Abraham ; if there be ten righteous lines, in this vast
Preface, spare it for their sake ; and also spare the next
city, because it is but a little one.   5
I would excuse the performance of this translation,
if it were all my own ; but the better, though not the
greater part, being the work of some gentlemen, who
have succeeded very happily in their undertaking, let
their excellencies atone for my imperfections, and those 10
of my sons.   I have perused some of the satires, which
are done by other hands ; and they seem to me as
perfect in their kind, as anything I have seen in English
verse.   The common way which we have taken is not
a literal translation, but a kind of paraphrase ; or some- 15
what, which is yet more loose, betwixt a paraphrase and
imitation.   It was not possible for us, or any men, to
have made it pleasant any other way.   If rendering
the exact sense of those authors, almost line for line,
had been our business, Barten Holyday had done it 20
already to our hands : and by the help of his learned
notes and illustrations not only of Juvenal and Persius,
but what yet is more obscure, his own verses, might be
understood.
But he wrote for fame, and wrote to scholars : we 25
write only for the pleasure and entertainment of those
gentlemen and ladies, who, though they are not scholars,
are not ignorant : persons of understanding and good
sense, who, not having been conversant in the original,
or at least not having made Latin verse so much their 30
business as to be critics in it, would be glad to find if
the wit of our two great authors be answerable to their
fame and reputation in the world.   We have, therefore,
endeavoured to give the public all the satisfaction we are
able in this kind.   35

And if we are not altogether so faithful to our author, as our predecessors Holyday and Stapylton, yet we may challenge to ourselves this praise, that we shall be far more pleasing to our readers. We have followed 5 our authors at greater distance, though not step by step, as they have done : for oftentimes they have gone so close, that they have trod on the heels of Juvenal and Persius, and hurt them by their too near approach. A noble author would not be pursued too close by a 10 translator. We lose his spirit, when we think to take his body. The grosser part remains with us, but the soul is flown away in some noble expression, or some delicate turn of words, or thought. Thus Holyday, who made this way his choice, seized the meaning of Juvenal ; 15 but the poetry has always escaped him.

They who will not grant me, that pleasure is one of the ends of poetry, but that it is only a means of compassing the only end, which is instruction, must yet allow, that, without the means of pleasure, the instruc- 20 tion is but a bare and dry philosophy : a crude preparation of morals, which we may have from Aristotle and Epictetus, with more profit than from any poet. Neither Holyday nor Stapylton have imitated Juvenal in the poetical part of him, his diction and his elocution. Nor 25 had they been poets, as neither of them were, yet, in the way they took, it was impossible for them to have succeeded in the poetic part.

The English verse, which we call heroic, consists of no more than ten syllables ; the Latin hexameter some- 30 times rises to seventeen ; as, for example, this verse in Virgil—

Pulverulenta putrem sonitu quatit ungula campum.

Here is the difference of no less than seven syllables in a line, betwixt the English and the Latin. Now the 35 medium of these is about fourteen syllables ; because

the dactyl is a more frequent foot in hexameters than
the spondee. But Holyday, without considering that
he wrote with the disadvantage of four syllables less in
every verse, endeavours to make one of his lines to
comprehend the sense of one of Juvenal's. According 5
to the falsity of the proposition was the success. He
was forced to crowd his verse with ill-sounding monosyllables, of which our barbarous language affords him
a wild plenty ; and by that means he arrived at his
pedantic end, which was to make a literal translation. 10
His verses have nothing of verse in them, but only the
worst part of it, the rhyme ; and that, into the bargain,
is far from good. But, which is more intolerable, by
cramming his ill-chosen, and worse-sounding monosyllables so close together, the very sense which he 15
endeavours to explain is become more obscure than
that of his author ; so that Holyday himself cannot be
understood, without as large a commentary as that which
he makes on his two authors. For my own part, I can
make a shift to find the meaning of Juvenal without his 20
notes : but his translation is more difficult than his author.
And I find beauties in the Latin to recompense my
pains ; but, in Holyday and Stapylton, my ears, in the
first place, are mortally offended ; and then their sense
is so perplexed, that I return to the original, as the more 25
pleasing task, as well as the more easy.

This must be said for our translation, that, if we give
not the whole sense of Juvenal, yet we give the most
considerable part of it : we give it, in general, so clearly,
that few notes are sufficient to make us intelligible. We 30
make our author at least appear in a poetic dress.
We have actually made him more sounding, and
more elegant, than he was before in English ; and have
endeavoured to make him speak that kind of English,
which he would have spoken had he lived in England, 35

and had written to this age. If sometimes any of us (and 'tis but seldom) make him express the customs and manners of our native country rather than of Rome, 'tis either when there was some kind of analogy
5 betwixt their customs and ours, or when, to make him more easy to vulgar understandings, we give him those manners which are familiar to us. But I defend not this innovation, 'tis enough if I can excuse it. For to speak sincerely, the manners of nations and ages are
10 not to be confounded ; we should either make them English, or leave them Roman. If this can neither be defended nor excused, let it be pardoned at least, because it is acknowledged ; and so much the more easily, as being a fault which is never committed without
15 some pleasure to the reader.

Thus, my Lord, having troubled you with a tedious visit, the best manners will be shown in the least ceremony. I will slip away while your back is turned, and while you are otherwise employed ; with great con-
20 fusion for having entertained you so long with this discourse, and for having no other recompense to make you, than the worthy labours of my fellow-undertakers in this work, and the thankful acknowledgments, prayers, and perpetual good wishes, of,

MY LORD,

Your Lordship's

Most obliged, most humble,

and most obedient Servant,

JOHN DRYDEN.

Aug. 18, 1692.

A PARALLEL

OF POETRY AND PAINTING

PREFIXED TO THE VERSION OF DU FRESNOY

DE ARTE GRAPHICA

[1695]

IT may be reasonably expected that I should say
something on my own behalf, in respect to my present
undertaking. First, then, the reader may be pleased to
know, that it was not of my own choice that I undertook
this work. Many of our most skilful painters, and 5
other artists, were pleased to recommend this author to
me, as one who perfectly understood the rules of painting ; who gave the best and most concise instructions
for performance, and the surest to inform the judgment
of all who loved this noble art : that they who before 10
were rather fond of it, than knowingly admired it, might
defend their inclination by their reason ; that they
might understand those excellencies which they blindly
valued, so as not to be farther imposed on by bad
pieces, and to know when nature was well imitated by 15
the most able masters. 'Tis true, indeed, and they
acknowledge it, that beside the rules which are given
in this treatise, or which can be given in any other,
that to make a perfect judgment of good pictures, and
to value them more or less, when compared with one 20
another, there is farther required a long conversation
with the best pieces, which are not very frequent either
in France or England ; yet some we have, not only

from the hands of Holbein, Rubens, and Vandyck (one
of them admirable for history-painting, and the other
two for portraits), but of many Flemish masters, and
those not inconsiderable, though for design not equal
5 to the Italians. And of these latter also, we are not
unfurnished with some pieces of Raphael, Titian,
Correggio, Michael Angelo, and others.

But to return to my own undertaking of this translation, I freely own that I thought myself uncapable of
10 performing it, either to their satisfaction, or my own
credit. Not but that I understood the original Latin,
and the French author, perhaps as well as most Eng-
lishmen ; but I was not sufficiently versed in the terms
of art ; and therefore thought that many of those per-
15 sons who put this honourable task on me were more
able to perform it themselves, as undoubtedly they
were. But they assuring me of their assistance in
correcting my faults where I spoke improperly, I was
encouraged to attempt it, that I might not be wanting
20 in what I could, to satisfy the desires of so many gentlemen who were willing to give the world this useful
work. They have effectually performed their promise
to me, and I have been as careful, on my side, to take
their advice in all things ; so that the reader may
25 assure himself of a tolerable translation. Not elegant,
for I proposed not that to myself, but familiar, clear,
and instructive. In any of which parts if I have failed,
the fault lies wholly at my door. In this one particular
only, I must beg the reader's pardon. The prose trans-
30 lation of this poem is not free from poetical expressions,
and I dare not promise that some of them are not
fustian, or at least highly metaphorical ; but this being
a fault in the first digestion (that is, the original Latin),
was not to be remedied in the second, *viz.* the trans-
35 lation. And I may confidently say, that whoever had

attempted it must have fallen into the same inconvenience, or a much greater, that of a false version.

When I undertook this work, I was already engaged in the translation of Virgil, from whom I have borrowed only two months ; and am now returning to that which I ought to understand better. In the meantime I beg the reader's pardon, for entertaining him so long with myself : 'tis an usual part of ill manners in all authors, and almost in all mankind, to trouble others with their business ; and I was so sensible of it beforehand, that I had not now committed it, unless some concernments of the reader's had been interwoven with my own. But I know not, while I am atoning for one error, if I am not falling into another ; for I have been importuned to say something farther of this art ; and to make some observations on it, in relation to the likeness and agreement which it has with poetry, its sister. But before I proceed, it will not be amiss if I copy from Bellori (a most ingenious author yet living) some part of his Idea of a Painter, which cannot be unpleasing, at least to such who are conversant in the philosophy of Plato. And, to avoid tediousness, I will not translate the whole discourse, but take and leave as I find occasion.

' God Almighty, in the fabric of the Universe, first contemplated himself, and reflected on his own excellencies ; from which he drew and constituted those first forms which are called ideas. So that every species which was afterwards expressed was produced from that first idea, forming that wonderful contexture of all created beings. But the celestial bodies above the moon being incorruptible, and not subject to change, remained for ever fair, and in perpetual order ; on the contrary, all things which are sublunary are subject to change, to deformity, and to decay. And though

Nature always intends a consummate beauty in her productions, yet through the inequality of the matter the forms are altered ; and in particular, human beauty suffers alteration for the worse, as we see to our morti-
5 fication, in the deformities and disproportions which are in us. For which reason, the artful painter and the sculptor, imitating the Divine Maker, form to themselves, as well as they are able, a model of the superior beauties ; and reflecting on them, endeavour to correct
10 and amend the common nature, and to represent it as it was at first created, without fault, either in colour, or in lineament.

' This idea, which we may call the goddess of painting and of sculpture, descends upon the marble and the
15 cloth, and becomes the original of those arts ; and being measured by the compass of the intellect, is itself the measure of the performing hand ; and being animated by the imagination, infuses life into the image. The idea of the painter and the sculptor is undoubtedly that per-
20 fect and excellent example of the mind, by imitation of which imagined form all things are represented which fall under human sight : such is the definition which is made by Cicero in his book of the *Orator* to Brutus :—
" As therefore in forms and figures there is somewhat
25 which is excellent and perfect, to which imagined species all things are referred by imitation, which are the objects of sight, in like manner we behold the species of eloquence in our minds, the *effigies* or actual image of which we seek in the organs of our hearing."
30 This is likewise confirmed by Proclus in the dialogue of Plato, called *Timæus*. If, says he, you take a man as he is made by nature, and compare him with another, who is the effect of art, the work of nature will always appear the less beautiful, because art is more
35 accurate than nature. But Zeuxis, who, from the

choice which he made of five virgins, drew that wonderful picture of Helena, which Cicero, in his *Orator*
before-mentioned, sets before us as the most perfect
example of beauty, at the same time admonishes a
painter to contemplate the ideas of the most natural 5
forms, and to make a judicious choice of several bodies,
all of them the most elegant which he can find ; by
which we may plainly understand, that he thought it
impossible to find in any one body all those perfections
which he sought for the accomplishment of a Helena, 10
because nature in any individual person makes nothing
that is perfect in all its parts. For this reason Maximus Tyrius also says, that the image which is taken
by a painter from several bodies produces a beauty
which it is impossible to find in any single natural body, 15
approaching to the perfection of the fairest statues.
Thus nature on this account is so much inferior to art,
that those artists who propose to themselves only the
imitation and likeness of such or such a particular
person, without election of those ideas before-men- 20
tioned, have often been reproached for that omission.
Demetrius was taxed for being too natural ; Dionysius
was also blamed for drawing men like us, and was
commonly called ἀνθρωπογράφος, that is, a painter of
men. In our times, Michael Angelo da Caravaggio 25
was esteemed too natural. He drew persons as they
were ; and Bamboccio, and most of the Dutch painters,
have drawn the worst likeness. Lysippus of old
upbraided the common sort of sculptors, for making
men such as they were found in nature ; and boasted 30
of himself, that he made them as they ought to be :
which is a precept of Aristotle, given as well to poets
as to painters. Phidias raised an admiration, even to
astonishment, in those who beheld his statues, with the
forms which he gave to his gods and heroes, by imitat- 35

ing the idea, rather than nature. And Cicero, speaking of him, affirms, that figuring Jupiter and Pallas, he did not contemplate any object from whence he took the likeness, but considered in his own mind a great and 5 admirable form of beauty ; and according to that image in his soul he directed the operation of his hand. Seneca also seems to wonder, that Phidias, having never beheld either Jove or Pallas, yet could conceive their divine images in his mind. Apollonius Tyanæus 10 says the same in other words,—that the fancy more instructs the painter, than the imitation ; for the last makes only the things which it sees, but the first makes also the things which it never sees.

‘ Leon Battista Alberti tells us, that we ought not so 15 much to love the likeness as the beauty, and to choose from the fairest bodies severally the fairest parts. Leonardo da Vinci instructs the painter to form this idea to himself ; and Raphael, the greatest of all modern masters, writes thus to Castiglione, concerning his 20 *Galatea :* " To paint a fair one, it is necessary for me to see many fair ones ; but because there is so great a scarcity of lovely women, I am constrained to make use of one certain idea, which I have formed to myself in my own fancy." Guido Reni sending to Rome his 25 *St. Michael*, which he had painted for the church of the Capuchins, at the same time wrote to Monsignor Massano, who was *Maestro di Casa* (or Steward of the House) to Pope Urban the Eighth, in this manner : " I wish I had the wings of an angel, to have ascended 30 into Paradise, and there to have beheld the forms of those beautiful spirits, from which I might have copied my archangel. But not being able to mount so high, it was in vain for me to search his resemblance here below ; so that I was forced to make an introspection 35 into my own mind, and into that idea of beauty which

I have formed in my own imagination. I have likewise created there the contrary idea of deformity and ugliness ; but I leave the consideration of it, till I paint the Devil : and in the meantime shun the very thought of it as much as possibly I can, and am even endeavouring 5 to blot it wholly out of my remembrance."

' There was not any lady in all antiquity, who was mistress of so much beauty as was to be found in the *Venus* of Gnidus, made by Praxiteles, or the *Minerva* of Athens, by Phidias ; which was therefore called the 10 *beautiful form.* Neither is there any man of the present age equal in the strength, proportion, and knitting of his limbs, to the *Hercules* of Farnese, made by Glycon ; or any woman, who can justly be compared with the Medicean *Venus* of Cleomenes. And upon this account, 15 the noblest poets and the best orators, when they desired to celebrate any extraordinary beauty, are forced to have recourse to statues and pictures, and to draw their persons and faces into comparison. Ovid, endeavouring to express the beauty of Cyllarus, the fairest 20 of the Centaurs, celebrates him as next in perfection to the most admirable statues :

> *Gratus in ore vigor, cervix, humerique, manusque,*
> *Pectoraque artificum laudatis proxima signis.*

> A pleasing vigour his fair face expressed ; 25
> His neck, his hands, his shoulders, and his breast,
> Did next, in gracefulness and beauty, stand
> To breathing figures of the sculptor's hand.

In another place he sets Apelles above Venus :

> *Si Venerem Cous nunquam pinxisset Apelles,* 30
> *Mersa sub æquoreis illa lateret aquis.*

Thus varied :

> One birth to seas the Cyprian goddess owed,
> A second birth the painter's art bestowed :
> Less by the seas than by his power was given ; 35
> They made her live, but he advanced to heaven.

' The idea of this beauty is indeed various, according
to the several forms which the painter or sculptor would
describe ; as one in strength, another in magnanimity :
and sometimes it consists in cheerfulness, and some-
5 times in delicacy ; and is always diversified by the sex
and age.

' The beauty of Jove is one, and that of Juno another ;
Hercules and Cupid are perfect beauties, though of
different kinds ; for beauty is only that which makes
10 all things as they are in their proper and perfect nature,
which the best painters always choose by contemplating
the forms of each. We ought farther to consider, that
a picture being the representation of a human action,
the painter ought to retain in his mind the examples of
15 all affections and passions, as a poet preserves the idea
of an angry man, of one who is fearful, sad, or merry,
and so of all the rest. For 'tis impossible to express that
with the hand, which never entered into the imagination.
In this manner, as I have rudely and briefly shewn
20 you, painters and sculptors, choosing the most elegant
natural beauties, perfectionate the idea, and advance
their art even above nature itself in her individual
productions ; which is the utmost mastery of human
performance.

25   ' From hence arises that astonishment, and almost
adoration, which is paid by the knowing to those divine
remainders of antiquity. From hence Phidias, Lysippus,
and other noble sculptors, are still held in veneration ;
and Apelles, Zeuxis, Protogenes, and other admirable
30 painters, though their works are perished, are and will
be eternally admired ; who all of them drew after the
ideas of perfection, which are the miracles of nature,
the providence of the understanding, the exemplars of
the mind, the light of the fancy ; the sun, which, from
35 its rising, inspired the statue of Memnon, and the fire,

which warmed into life the image of Prometheus. 'Tis
this, which causes the Graces and the Loves to take
up their habitations in the hardest marble, and to
subsist in the emptiness of light and shadows. But
since the idea of eloquence is as far inferior to that of 5
painting, as the force of words is to the sight, I must
here break off abruptly, and having conducted the
reader, as it were, to a secret walk, there leave him
in the midst of silence, to contemplate those ideas
which I have only sketched, and which every man must 10
finish for himself.'

In these pompous expressions, or such as these, the
Italian has given you his Idea of a Painter ; and though
I cannot much commend the style, I must needs say,
there is somewhat in the matter. Plato himself is 15
accustomed to write loftily, imitating, as the critics tell
us, the manner of Homer ; but surely that inimitable
poet had not so much of smoke in his writing, though
not less of fire. But in short, this is the present genius
of Italy. What Philostratus tells us in the proem of 20
his *Figures*, is somewhat plainer ; and therefore I will
translate it almost word for word :—' He who will
rightly govern the art of painting, ought of necessity
first to understand human nature. He ought likewise
to be endued with a genius to express the signs of their 25
passions, whom he represents ; and to make the dumb,
as it were, to speak. He must yet further understand
what is contained in the constitution of the cheeks, in
the temperament of the eyes, in the naturalness (if
I may so call it) of the eyebrows ; and in short, 30
whatsoever belongs to the mind and thought. He
who thoroughly possesses all these things will obtain
the whole ; and the hand will exquisitely represent the
action of every particular person, if it happen that he
be either mad or angry, melancholic or cheerful, a 35

sprightly youth or a languishing lover ; in one word,
he will be able to paint whatsoever is proportionable
to any one.   And even in all this there is a sweet
error, without causing any shame.   For the eyes and
5 minds of the beholders being fastened on objects which
have no real being, as if they were truly existent, and
being induced by them to believe them so, what pleasure
is it not capable of giving ?   The Ancients, and other
wise men, have written many things concerning the
10 symmetry which is in the art of painting,—constituting,
as it were, some certain laws for the proportion of
every member ;   not thinking it possible for a painter
to undertake the expression of those motions which
are in the mind, without a concurrent harmony in the
15 natural measure.   For that which is out of its own
kind and measure is not received from Nature, whose
motion is always right.   On a serious consideration
of this matter, it will be found that the art of painting
has a wonderful affinity with that of poetry ;   and that
20 there is betwixt them a certain common imagination.
For as the poets introduce the gods and heroes, and
all those things which are either majestical, honest, or
delightful, in like manner the painters, by the virtue
of their outlines, colours, lights, and shadows, represent
25 the same things and persons in their pictures.'

Thus, as convoy-ships either accompany or should
accompany their merchants, till they may prosecute the
rest of their voyage without danger ;   so Philostratus
has brought me thus far on my way, and I can now
30 sail on without him.   He has begun to speak of the
great relation betwixt painting and poetry, and thither
the greatest part of this discourse, by my promise, was
directed.   I have not engaged myself to any perfect
method, neither am I loaded with a full cargo.   'Tis
35 sufficient if I bring a sample of some goods in this

voyage. It will be easy for others to add more, when the commerce is settled ; for a treatise twice as large as this of painting could not contain all that might be said on the parallel of these two sister arts. I will take my rise from Bellori, before I proceed to the author 5 of this book.

The business of his preface is to prove that a learned painter should form to himself an idea of perfect nature. This image he is to set before his mind in all his undertakings, and to draw from thence, as from a store- 10 house, the beauties which are to enter into his work ; thereby correcting Nature from what actually she is in individuals, to what she ought to be, and what she was created. Now, as this idea of perfection is of little use in portraits, or the resemblances of particular persons, 15 so neither is it in the characters of Comedy and Tragedy, which are never to be made perfect, but always to be drawn with some specks of frailty and deficience ; such as they have been described to us in history, if they were real characters, or such as the poet began to 20 shew them at their first appearance, if they were only fictitious or imaginary. The perfection of such stage-characters consists chiefly in their likeness to the deficient faulty nature, which is their original ; only, as it is observed more at large hereafter, in such cases 25 there will always be found a better likeness and a worse, and the better is constantly to be chosen ; I mean in tragedy, which represents the figures of the highest form amongst mankind. Thus in portraits, the painter will not take that side of the face which has some 30 notorious blemish in it ; but either draw it in profile (as Apelles did Antigonus, who had lost one of his eyes), or else shadow the more imperfect side. For an ingenious flattery is to be allowed to the professors of both arts, so long as the likeness is not destroyed. 'Tis 35

true, that all manner of imperfections must not be taken
away from the characters ; and the reason is, that there
may be left some grounds of pity for their misfortunes.
We can never be grieved for their miseries who are
5 thoroughly wicked, and have thereby justly called their
calamities on themselves.   Such men are the natural
objects of our hatred, not of our commiseration.   If,
on the other side, their characters were wholly perfect
(such as, for example, the character of a saint or martyr
10 in a play), his or her misfortunes would produce impious thoughts in the beholders ; they would accuse
the heavens of injustice, and think of leaving a religion
where piety was so ill requited.   I say, the greater
part would be tempted so to do, I say not that they
15 ought ; and the consequence is too dangerous for the
practice.   In this I have accused myself for my own
St. Catharine ; but let truth prevail.   Sophocles has
taken the just medium in his *Œdipus.*   He is somewhat
arrogant at his first entrance, and is too inquisitive
20 through the whole tragedy ; yet these imperfections
being balanced by great virtues, they hinder not our
compassion for his miseries ; neither yet can they
destroy that horror which the nature of his crimes
has excited in us.   Such in painting are the warts and
25 moles, which, adding a likeness to the face, are not
therefore to be omitted ; but these produce no loathing
in us ; but how far to proceed, and where to stop, is
left to the judgment of the poet and the painter.   In
Comedy there is somewhat more of the worse likeness
30 to be taken, because that is often to produce laughter,
which is occasioned by the sight of some deformity ;
but for this I refer the reader to Aristotle.   'Tis a sharp
manner of instruction for the vulgar, who are never
well amended till they are more than sufficiently
35 exposed.

That I may return to the beginning of this remark concerning perfect ideas, I have only this to say,—that the parallel is often true in Epic Poetry. The heroes of the poets are to be drawn according to this rule. There is scarce a frailty to be left in the best of them, any more than is to be found in a divine nature ; and if Æneas sometimes weeps, it is not in bemoaning his own miseries, but those which his people undergo. If this be an imperfection, the Son of God, when he was incarnate, shed tears of compassion over Jerusalem ; and Lentulus describes him often weeping, but never laughing ; so that Virgil is justified even from the Holy Scriptures. I have but one word more, which for once I will anticipate from the author of this book. Though it must be an idea of perfection, from which both the epic poet and the history painter draws, yet all perfections are not suitable to all subjects ; but every one must be designed according to that perfect beauty which is proper to him. An Apollo must be distinguished from a Jupiter, a Pallas from a Venus ; and so, in poetry, an Æneas from any other hero ; for piety is his chief perfection. Homer's Achilles is a kind of exception to this rule ; but then he is not a perfect hero, nor so intended by the poet. All his gods had somewhat of human imperfection, for which he has been taxed by Plato, as an imitator of what was bad ; but Virgil observed his fault, and mended it. Yet, Achilles was perfect in the strength of his body, and the vigour of his mind. Had he been less passionate, or less revengeful, the poet well foresaw that Hector had been killed, and Troy taken, at the first assault ; which had destroyed the beautiful contrivance of his *Iliads*, and the moral of preventing discord amongst confederate princes, which was his principal intention. For the moral (as Bossu observes) is the first business

of the poet, as being the groundwork of his instruction.
This being formed, he contrives such a design, or fable,
as may be most suitable to the moral ; after this he
begins to think of the persons whom he is to employ
5 in carrying on his design ; and gives them the manners
which are most proper to their several characters. The
thoughts and words are the last parts, which give
beauty and colouring to the piece.

When I say that the manners of the hero ought to
10 be good in perfection, I contradict not the Marquis
of Normanby's opinion, in that admirable verse, where,
speaking of a perfect character, he calls it *A faultless
monster, which the world ne'er knew.* For that excellent
critic intended only to speak of dramatic characters,
15 and not of epic.

Thus at least I have shewn, that in the most perfect
poem, which is that of Virgil, a perfect idea was required and followed ; and consequently that all succeeding poets ought rather to imitate him, than even Homer.
20 I will now proceed as I promised, to the author of this
book.

He tells you almost in the first lines of it, that ' the
chief end of Painting is, to please the eyes ; and 'tis one
great end of Poetry to please the mind.' Thus far the
25 parallel of the arts holds true ; with this difference, that
the principal end of Painting is to please, and the chief
design of Poetry is to instruct. In this the latter seems
to have the advantage of the former ; but if we consider
the artists themselves on both sides, certainly their aims
30 are the very same ; they would both make sure of
pleasing, and that in preference to instruction. Next,
the means of this pleasure is by deceit ; one imposes
on the sight, and the other on the understanding.
Fiction is of the essence of Poetry, as well as of paint-
35 ing ; there is a resemblance in one, of human bodies,

things, and actions, which are not real; and in the
other, of a true story by a fiction; and as all stories
are not proper subjects for an epic poem or a tragedy,
so neither are they for a noble picture. The subjects
both of the one and of the other ought to have nothing 5
of immoral, low, or filthy in them; but this being
treated at large in the book itself, I wave it, to avoid
repetition. Only I must add, that though Catullus,
Ovid, and others, were of another opinion,—that the
subject of poets, and even their thoughts and expres- 10
sions, might be loose, provided their lives were chaste
and holy, yet there are no such licences permitted in
that art, any more than, in painting, to design and
colour obscene nudities. *Vita proba est*, is no excuse;
for it will scarcely be admitted, that either a poet or 15
a painter can be chaste, who give us the contrary
examples in their writings and their pictures. We see
nothing of this kind in Virgil; that which comes the
nearest to it is the adventure of the cave, where Dido
and Æneas were driven by the storm; yet even there 20
the poet pretends a marriage before the consummation,
and Juno herself was present at it. Neither is there
any expression in that story, which a Roman matron
might not read without a blush. Besides, the poet
passes it over as hastily as he can, as if he were afraid 25
of staying in the cave with the two lovers, and of being
a witness to their actions. Now I suppose that a
painter would not be much commended, who should
pick out this cavern from the whole *Æneids*, when
there is not another in the work. He had better leave 30
them in their obscurity, than let in a flash of lightning
to clear the natural darkness of the place, by which
he must discover himself, as much as them. The altar-
pieces and holy decorations of Painting shew *that* art
may be applied to better uses, as well as Poetry; and 35

amongst many other instances, the Farnesian gallery, painted by Annibàle Caracci, is a sufficient witness yet remaining ; the whole work being morally instructive, and particularly the *Herculis Bivium*, which is a perfect
5 triumph of virtue over vice ; as it is wonderfully well described by the ingenious Bellori.

Hitherto I have only told the reader, what ought not to be the subject of a picture or of a poem. What it ought to be on either side, our author tells us : it must
10 in general be great and noble ; and in this the parallel is exactly true. The subject of a poet, either in Tragedy or in an Epic Poem, is a great action of some illustrious hero. It is the same in painting ; not every action, nor every person, is considerable enough to enter into the
15 cloth. It must be the anger of an Achilles, the piety of an Æneas, the sacrifice of an Iphigenia, for heroines as well as heroes are comprehended in the rule ; but the parallel is more complete in tragedy, than in an epic poem. For as a tragedy may be made out of
20 many particular episodes of Homer or of Virgil, so may a noble picture be designed out of this or that particular story in either author. History is also fruitful of designs both for the painter and the tragic poet : Curtius throwing himself into a gulph, and the two
25 Decii sacrificing themselves for the safety of their country, are subjects for tragedy and picture. Such is Scipio restoring the Spanish bride, whom he either loved, or may be supposed to love ; by which he gained the hearts of a great nation to interess themselves for
30 Rome against Carthage. These are all but particular pieces in Livy's History ; and yet are full complete subjects for the pen and pencil. Now the reason of this is evident. Tragedy and Picture are more narrowly circumscribed by the mechanic rules of time and place,
35 than the Epic Poem. The time of this last is left

indefinite. 'Tis true, Homer took up only the space of eight-and-forty days for his *Iliads*; but whether Virgil's action was comprehended in a year, or somewhat more, is not determined by Bossu. Homer made the place of his action Troy, and the Grecian camp besieging it. Virgil introduces his Æneas sometimes in Sicily, sometimes in Carthage, and other times at Cumæ, before he brings him to Laurentum; and even after that, he wanders again to the kingdom of Evander, and some parts of Tuscany, before he returns to finish the war by the death of Turnus. But Tragedy, according to the practice of the ancients, was always confined within the compass of twenty-four hours, and seldom takes up so much time. As for the place of it, it was always one, and that not in a larger sense (as for example, a whole city, or two or three several houses in it), but the market, or some other public place, common to the chorus and all the actors; which established law of theirs I have not an opportunity to examine in this place, because I cannot do it without digression from my subject; though it seems too strict at the first appearance, because it excludes all secret intrigues, which are the beauties of the modern stage; for nothing can be carried on with privacy, when the chorus is supposed to be always present. But to proceed; I must say this to the advantage of Painting, even above Tragedy, that what this last represents in the space of many hours, the former shews us in one moment. The action, the passion, and the manners of so many persons as are contained in a picture are to be discerned at once, in the twinkling of an eye; at least they would be so, if the sight could travel over so many different objects all at once, or the mind could digest them all at the same instant, or point of time. Thus, in the famous picture of Poussin, which repre-

sents the *Institution of the Blessed Sacrament*, you see
our Saviour and his twelve disciples, all concurring in
the same action, after different manners, and in different
postures ; only the manners of Judas are distinguished
5 from the rest. Here is but one indivisible point of
time observed ; but one action performed by so many
persons, in one room, and at the same table ; yet the
eye cannot comprehend at once the whole object, nor
the mind follow it so fast ; 'tis considered at leisure,
10 and seen by intervals. Such are the subjects of noble
pictures ; and such are only to be undertaken by noble
hands.

There are other parts of Nature, which are meaner,
and yet are the subjects both of painters and of poets.
15 For, to proceed in the parallel ; as Comedy is a representation of human life in inferior persons, and low
subjects, and by that means creeps into the nature of
poetry, and is a kind of juniper, a shrub belonging to
the species of cedar, so is the painting of clowns, the
20 representation of a Dutch kermis, the brutal sport of
snick-or-snee, and a thousand other things of this mean
invention ; a kind of picture which belongs to nature,
but of the lowest form. Such is a Lazar in comparison
to a Venus : both are drawn in human figures ; they
25 have faces alike, though not like faces. There is yet
a lower sort of poetry and painting, which is out of
nature ; for a farce is that in poetry, which *grotesque*
is in a picture. The persons and action of a farce are
all unnatural, and the manners false, that is, inconsisting
30 with the characters of mankind. Grotesque painting
is the just resemblance of this ; and Horace begins his
Art of Poetry by describing such a figure, with a man's
head, a horse's neck, the wings of a bird, and a fish's
tail ; parts of different species jumbled together, accord-
35 ing to the mad imagination of the dauber ; and the end

of all this, as he tells you afterward, to cause laughter :
a very monster in a Bartholomew Fair, for the mob
to gape at for their two-pence. Laughter is indeed the
propriety of a man, but just enough to distinguish him
from his elder brother with four legs. 'Tis a kind of 5
bastard-pleasure too, taken in at the eyes of the vulgar
gazers, and at the ears of the beastly audience. Church-
painters use it to divert the honest countryman at
public prayers, and keep his eyes open at a heavy
sermon ; and farce-scribblers make use of the same 10
noble invention, to entertain citizens, country-gentle-
men, and Covent Garden fops. If they are merry, all
goes well on the poet's side. The better sort go thither
too, but in despair of sense and the just images of
Nature, which are the adequate pleasures of the mind. 15
But the author can give the stage no better than what
was given him by Nature ; and the actors must represent such things as they are capable to perform, and
by which both they and the scribbler may get their
living. After all, 'tis a good thing to laugh at any rate ; 20
and if a straw can tickle a man, it is an instrument
of happiness. Beasts can weep when they suffer, but
they cannot laugh. And as Sir William D'Avenant
observes in his Preface to *Gondibert*, ' 'Tis the wisdom
of a government to permit plays ' (he might have added 25
—farces), ' as 'tis the prudence of a carter to put bells
upon his horses, to make them carry their burthens
cheerfully.'

I have already shewn, that one main end of Poetry
and Painting is to please, and have said something of 30
the kinds of both, and of their subjects, in which they
bear a great resemblance to each other. I must now
consider them, as they are great and noble arts ; and as
they are arts, they must have rules, which may direct
them to their common end. 35

To all arts and sciences, but more particularly to these, may be applied what Hippocrates says of physic, as I find him cited by an eminent French critic : ' Medicine has long subsisted in the world. The prin-
5 ciples of it are certain, and it has a certain way ; by both which there has been found, in the course of many ages, an infinite number of things, the experience of which has confirmed its usefulness and goodness. All that is wanting to the perfection of this art will
10 undoubtedly be found, if able men, and such as are instructed in the ancient rules, will make a farther inquiry into it ; and endeavour to arrive at that which is hitherto unknown, by that which is already known. But all who, having rejected the ancient rules, and taken
15 the opposite ways, yet boast themselves to be masters of this art, do but deceive others, and are themselves deceived ; for that is absolutely impossible.'

This is notoriously true in these two arts ; for the way to please being to imitate Nature, both the poets
20 and the painters in ancient times, and in the best ages, have studied her ; and from the practice of both these arts the rules have been drawn by which we are instructed how to please, and to compass that end which they obtained, by following their example. For Nature
25 is still the same in all ages, and can never be contrary to herself. Thus, from the practice of Æschylus, Sophocles, and Euripides, Aristotle drew his rules for tragedy ; and Philostratus for painting. Thus, amongst the moderns, the Italian and French critics,
30 by studying the precepts of Aristotle and Horace, and having the example of the Grecian poets before their eyes, have given us the rules of modern tragedy ; and thus the critics of the same countries in the art of painting have given the precepts of perfecting that art.
35. 'Tis true that Poetry has one advantage over Painting

in these last ages, that we have still the remaining
examples both of the Greek and Latin poets ; whereas
the painters have nothing left them from Apelles,
Protogenes, Parrhasius, Zeuxis, and the rest, but only
the testimonies which are given of their incomparable 5
works. But instead of this, they have some of their
best statues, bass-relievos, columns, obelisks, &c. which
were saved out of the common ruin, and are still preserved in Italy ; and by well distinguishing what is
proper to Sculpture, and what to Painting, and what is 10
common to them both, they have judiciously repaired
that loss. And the great genius of Raphael, and others,
having succeeded to the times of barbarism and ignorance, the knowledge of Painting is now arrived to
a supreme perfection, though the performance of it is 15
much declined in the present age. The greatest age
for Poetry amongst the Romans was certainly that of
Augustus Cæsar : and yet we are told that painting
was then at its lowest ebb ; and perhaps sculpture
was also declining at the same time. In the reign of 20
Domitian, and some who succeeded him, Poetry was
but meanly cultivated,but Painting eminently flourished.
I am not here to give the history of the two arts ; how
they were both in a manner extinguished by the irrup-
tion of the barbarous nations, and both restored about 25
the times of Leo the Tenth, Charles the Fifth, and
Francis the First ; though I might observe, that neither
Ariosto, nor any of his contemporary poets, ever arrived
at the excellency of Raphael, Titian, and the rest, in
painting. But in revenge, at this time, or lately, in 30
many countries, Poetry is better practised than her
sister-art. To what height the magnificence and encouragement of the present King of France may carry
Painting and Sculpture, is uncertain ; but by what he has
done before the war in which he is engaged, we may 35

expect what he will do after the happy conclusion of
a peace, which is the prayer and wish of all those who
have not an interest to prolong the miseries of Europe.
For 'tis most certain, as our author, amongst others, has
5 observed, that reward is the spur of virtue, as well in all
good arts, as in all laudable attempts ; and emulation,
which is the other spur, will never be wanting, either
amongst poets or painters, when particular rewards and
prizes are proposed to the best deservers.

10   But to return from this digression, though it was
almost necessary : all the rules of Painting are methodi-
cally, concisely, and yet clearly delivered in this present
treatise, which I have translated. Bossu has not given
more exact rules for the Epic Poem, nor Dacier for
15 Tragedy, in his late excellent translation of Aristotle,
and his notes upon him, than our Fresnoy has made
for Painting ; with the parallel of which I must resume
my discourse, following my author's text, though with
more brevity than I intended, because Virgil calls me.

20   *The principal and most important part of painting* is,
to know what *is most beautiful in nature, and most proper
for that art*. That which is the most beautiful is the
most noble subject : so in Poetry, Tragedy is more
beautiful than Comedy ; because, as I said, the persons
25 are greater whom the poet instructs, and consequently
the instructions of more benefit to mankind : the action
is likewise greater and more noble, and thence is derived
the greater and more noble pleasure.

To imitate Nature well in whatsoever subject, is the
30 perfection of both arts ; and that picture, and that poem,
which comes nearest to the resemblance of Nature, is
the best. But it follows not, that what pleases most
in either kind is therefore good, but what ought to
please. Our depraved appetites, and ignorance of the
35 arts, mislead our judgments, and cause us often to take

that for true imitation of Nature which has no resemblance of Nature in it. To inform our judgments, and to reform our tastes, rules were invented, that by them we might discern when Nature was imitated, and how nearly. I have been forced to recapitulate these things, 5 because mankind is not more liable to deceit, than it is willing to continue in a pleasing error, strengthened by a long habitude. The imitation of Nature is therefore justly constituted as the general, and indeed the only, rule of pleasing, both in Poetry and Painting. Aristotle 10 tells us, that imitation pleases, because it affords matter for a reasoner to inquire into the truth or falsehood of imitation, by comparing its likeness, or unlikeness, with the original ; but by this rule every speculation in nature, whose truth falls under the inquiry of a philo- 15 sopher, must produce the same delight ; which is not true. I should rather assign another reason. Truth is the object of our understanding, as good is of our will ; and the understanding can no more be delighted with a lie, than the will can choose an apparent evil. As truth 20 is the end of all our speculations, so the discovery of it is the pleasure of them ; and since a true knowledge of Nature gives us pleasure, a lively imitation of it, either in Poetry or Painting, must of necessity produce a much greater : for both these arts, as I said before, are not 25 only true imitations of Nature, but of the best Nature, of that which is wrought up to a nobler pitch. They present us with images more perfect than the life in any individual ; and we have the pleasure to see all the scattered beauties of Nature united by a happy 30 chemistry, without its deformities or faults. They are imitations of the passions, which always move, and therefore consequently please ; for without motion there can be no delight, which cannot be considered but as an active passion. When we view these elevated ideas of 35 nature, the result of that view is admiration, which is always the cause of pleasure.

This foregoing remark, which gives the reason why imitation pleases, was sent me by Mr. Walter Moyle, 5 a most ingenious young gentleman, conversant in all the studies of humanity much above his years. He had also furnished me, according to my request, with all the particular passages in Aristotle and Horace which are used by them to explain the art of Poetry 10 by that of Painting; which, if ever I have time to retouch this Essay, shall be inserted in their places.

Having thus shewn that imitation pleases, and why it pleases in both these arts, it follows, that some rules of imitation are necessary to obtain the end; for without 15 rules there can be no art, any more than there can be a house without a door to conduct you into it.

The principal parts of Painting and Poetry next follow. Invention is the first part, and absolutely necessary to them both; yet no rule ever was or ever 20 can be given, how to compass it. A happy genius is the gift of nature: it depends on the influence of the stars, say the astrologers; on the organs of the body, say the naturalists; it is the particular gift of Heaven, say the divines, both Christians and heathens. How to improve 25 it, many books can teach us; how to obtain it, none; that nothing can be done without it, all agree:

Tu nihil invita dices faciesve Minerva.

Without invention, a painter is but a copier, and a poet but a plagiary of others. Both are allowed sometimes 30 to copy, and translate; but, as our author tells you, that is not the best part of their reputation. *Imitators are but a servile kind of cattle*, says the poet; or at best, the keepers of cattle for other men: they have nothing which is properly their own: that is a sufficient mortification for me, while I am translating Virgil. But to copy the best author is a kind of praise, if I perform it as I ought ; as a copy after Raphael is more to be commended than an original of any indifferent painter.

Under this head of *Invention* is placed the disposition 5 of the work ; to put all things in a beautiful order and harmony, that the whole may be of a piece. The compositions of the painter should be conformable to the text of ancient authors, to the customs, and the times. And this is exactly the same in Poetry ; Homer and 10 Virgil are to be our guides in the Epic ; Sophocles and Euripides in Tragedy : in all things we are to imitate the customs and the times of those persons and things which we represent : not to make new rules of the drama, as Lopez de Vega has attempted unsuc- 15 cessfully to do, but to be content to follow our masters, who understood Nature better than we. But if the story which we treat be modern, we are to vary the customs, according to the time and the country where the scene of action lies ; for this is still to imitate Nature, which 20 is always the same, though in a different dress.

As in the composition of a picture the painter is to take care that nothing enter into it which is not proper or convenient to the subject, so likewise is the poet to reject all incidents which are foreign to his poem, 25 and are naturally no parts of it ; they are wens, and other excrescences, which belong not to the body, but deform it. No person, no incident, in the piece, or in the play, but must be of use to carry on the main design. All things else are like six fingers to the hand, when 30 Nature, which is superfluous in nothing, can do her work with five. A painter must reject all trifling ornaments ; so must a poet refuse all tedious and unnecessary descriptions. A robe which is too heavy is less an ornament than a burthen. 35

In poetry Horace calls these things *versus inopes rerum, nugæque canoræ ;* these are also the *lucus et ara Dianæ,* which he mentions in the same *Art of Poetry.* But since there must be ornaments both in painting and
5 poetry, if they are not necessary, they must at least be decent ; that is, in their due place, and but moderately used. The painter is not to take so much pains about the drapery, as about the face, where the principal resemblance lies ; neither is the poet, who is working
10 up a passion, to make similes, which will certainly make it languish. My Montezuma dies with a fine one in his mouth ; but it is ambitious, and out of season. When there are more figures in a picture than are necessary, or at least ornamental, our author calls them *figures to*
15 *be let ;* because the picture has no use of them. So I have seen in some modern plays above twenty actors, when the action has not required half the number. In the principal figures of a picture, the painter is to employ the sinews of his art ; for in them consists the principal
20 beauty of his work. Our author saves me the comparison with Tragedy ; for he says, that herein he is to imitate the tragic poet, who employs his utmost force in those places wherein consists the height and beauty of the action.

Du Fresnoy, whom I follow, makes *design*, or *drawing*,
25 the second part of painting ; but the rules which he gives concerning the posture of the figures are almost wholly proper to that art, and admit not any comparison, that I know, with poetry. The posture of a poetic figure is, as I conceive, the description of his heroes in the
30 performance of such or such an action ; as of Achilles, just in the act of killing Hector, or of Æneas, who has Turnus under him. Both the poet and the painter vary the posture, according to the action or passion which they represent, of the same person ; but all must be great
35 and graceful in them. The same Æneas must be drawn

a suppliant to Dido, with respect in his gestures, and humility in his eyes ; but when he is forced, in his own defence, to kill Lausus, the poet shows him compassionate, and tempering the severity of his looks with a reluctance to the action which he is going to perform. 5 He has pity on his beauty and his youth, and is loth to destroy such a masterpiece of nature. He considers Lausus, rescuing his father at the hazard of his own life, as an image of himself, when he took Anchises on his shoulders, and bore him safe through the rage of the 10 fire, and the opposition of his enemies ; and therefore, in the posture of a retiring man, who avoids the combat, he stretches out his arm in sign of peace, with his right foot drawn a little back, and his breast bending inward, more like an orator than a soldier ; and seems to dis- 15 suade the young man from pulling on his destiny, by attempting more than he was able to perform. Take the passage as I have thus translated it :

> Shouts of applause ran ringing through the field,
> To see the son the vanquish'd father shield :   20
> All, fir'd with noble emulation, strive,
> And with a storm of darts to distance drive
> The *Trojan* chief ; who, held at bay, from far
> On his *Vulcanian* orb sustain'd the war.
> *Æneas*, thus o'erwhelm'd on every side,   25
> Their first assault undaunted did abide,
> And thus to *Lausus*, loud with friendly threatening cry'd :—
> Why wilt thou rush to certain death, and rage,
> In rash attempts, beyond thy tender age,
> Betray'd by pious love ?   30

And afterwards :

> He griev'd, he wept ; the sight an image brought
> Of his own filial love ; a sadly pleasing thought.

But besides the outlines of the posture, the design of the picture comprehends, in the next place, the forms 35 of faces, which are to be different ; and so in a poem or

a play must the several characters of the persons be distinguished from each other. I knew a poet, whom out of respect I will not name, who, being too witty himself, could draw nothing but wits in a comedy of his ;
5 even his fools were infected with the disease of their author. They overflowed with smart reparties, and were only distinguished from the intended wits by being called coxcombs, though they deserved not so scandalous a name. Another, who had a great genius for
10 Tragedy, following the fury of his natural temper, made every man, and woman too, in his plays, stark raging mad ; there was not a sober person to be had for love or money. All was tempestuous and blustering ; heaven and earth were coming together at every word ; a mere
15 hurricane from the beginning to the end, and every actor seemed to be hastening on the day of judgment.

Let every member be made for its own head, says our author ; not a withered hand to a young face. So, in the persons of a play, whatsoever is said or done by any
20 of them must be consistent with the manners which the poet has given them distinctly ; and even the habits must be proper to the degrees and humours of the persons, as well as in a picture. He who entered in the first act a young man, like Pericles, Prince of Tyre, must not
25 be in danger, in the fifth act, of committing incest with his daughter ; nor an usurer, without great probability, and causes of repentance, be turned into a cutting Morecraft.

I am not satisfied, that the comparison betwixt the
30 two arts in the last paragraph is altogether so just as it might have been ; but I am sure of this which follows :

The principal figure of the subject must appear in the midst of the picture, under the principal light, to distinguish
35 *it from the rest, which are only its attendants.* Thus, in

a tragedy, or an epic poem, the hero of the piece must be advanced foremost to the view of the reader, or spectator : he must outshine the rest of all the characters ; he must appear the prince of them, like the sun in the Copernican system, encompassed with the less noble 5 planets : because the hero is the centre of the main action ; all the lines from the circumference tend to him alone : he is the chief object of pity in the drama, and of admiration in the epic poem.

As in a picture, besides the principal figures which 10 compose it, and are placed in the midst of it, there are less groups or knots of figures disposed at proper distances, which are parts of the piece, and seem to carry on the same design in a more inferior manner ; so, in epic poetry there are episodes, and a chorus in 15 tragedy, which are members of the action, as growing out of it, not inserted into it. Such in the ninth book of the *Æneids* is the episode of Nisus and Euryalus. The adventure belongs to them alone ; they alone are the objects of compassion and admiration ; but their 20 business which they carry on is the general concernment of the Trojan camp, then beleaguered by Turnus and the Latins, as the Christians were lately by the Turks. They were to advertise the chief hero of the distresses of his subjects occasioned by his absence, to 25 crave his succour, and solicit him to hasten his return.

The Grecian Tragedy was at first nothing but a chorus of singers ; afterwards one actor was introduced, which was the poet himself, who entertained the people with a discourse in verse, betwixt the pauses of the singing. 30 This succeeding with the people, more actors were added, to make the variety the greater ; and, in process of time, the chorus only sung betwixt the acts, and the Coryphæus, or chief of them, spoke for the rest, as an actor concerned in the business of the play. 35

Thus Tragedy was perfected by degrees ; and being arrived at that perfection, the painters might probably take the hint from thence of adding groups to their pictures. But as a good picture may be without a
5 group, so a good tragedy may subsist without a chorus, notwithstanding any reasons which have been given by Dacier to the contrary.

Monsieur Racine has, indeed, used it in his *Esther* ; but not that he found any necessity of it, as the French
10 critic would insinuate. The chorus at St. Cyr was only to give the young ladies an occasion of entertaining the king with vocal music, and of commending their own voices. The play itself was never intended for the public stage, nor, without disparagement to the learned
15 author, could possibly have succeeded there ; and much less the translation of it here. Mr. Wycherley, when we read it together, was of my opinion in this, or rather I of his ; for it becomes me so to speak of so excellent a poet, and so great a judge. But since I am in this
20 place, as Virgil says, *spatiis exclusus iniquis*, that is, shortened in my time, I will give no other reason, than that it is impracticable on our stage. A new theatre, much more ample and much deeper, must be made for that purpose, besides the cost of sometimes forty or
25 fifty habits, which is an expence too large to be supplied by a company of actors. 'Tis true, I should not be sorry to see a chorus on a theatre more than as large and as deep again as ours, built and adorned at a king's charges ; and on that condition, and another, which is,
30 that my hands were not bound behind me, as now they are, I should not despair of making such a tragedy as might be both instructive and delightful, according to the manner of the Grecians.

To make a sketch, or a more perfect model of
35 a picture, is, in the language of poets, to draw up the

scenary of a play ; and the reason is the same for both ; to guide the undertaking, and to preserve the remembrance of such things, whose natures are difficult to retain.

To avoid absurdities and incongruities, is the same law established for both arts. The painter is not to paint a cloud at the bottom of a picture, but in the uppermost parts ; nor the poet to place what is proper to the end or middle, in the beginning of a poem. I might enlarge on this ; but there are few poets or painters who can be supposed to sin so grossly against the laws of nature and of art. I remember only one play, and for once I will call it by its name, *The Slighted Maid*, where there is nothing in the first act but what might have been said or done in the fifth ; nor anything in the midst, which might not have been placed as well in the beginning, or the end. To express the passions which are seated in the heart, by outward signs, is one great precept of the painters, and very difficult to perform. In poetry, the same passions and motions of the mind are to be expressed ; and in this consists the principal difficulty, as well as the excellency of that art. This, says my author, is the gift of Jupiter ; and, to speak in the same heathen language, we call it the gift of our Apollo—not to be obtained by pains or study, if we are not born to it ; for the motions which are studied are never so natural as those which break out in the height of a real passion. Mr. Otway possessed this part as thoroughly as any of the Ancients or Moderns. I will not defend everything in his *Venice Preserved ;* but I must bear this testimony to his memory, that the passions are truly touched in it, though perhaps there is somewhat to be desired, both in the grounds of them, and in the height and elegance of expression ; but nature is there, which is the greatest beauty.

In the passions, says our author, *we must have a very great regard to the quality of the persons who are actually possessed with them.* The joy of a monarch for the news of a victory must not be expressed like the
5 ecstacy of a Harlequin on the receipt of a letter from his mistress : this is so much the same in both the arts, that it is no longer a comparison. What he says of face-painting, or the portrait of any one particular person, concerning the likeness, is also as applicable to
10 poetry. In the character of an hero, as well as in an inferior figure, there is a better or worse likeness to be taken : the better is a panegyric, if it be not false, and the worse is a libel. Sophocles, says Aristotle, always drew men as they ought to be, that is, better than they
15 were ; another, whose name I have forgotten, drew them worse than naturally they were : Euripides altered nothing in the character, but made them such as they were represented by history, epic poetry, or tradition. Of the three, the draught of Sophocles is most com-
20 mended by Aristotle. I have followed it in that part of *Œdipus* which I writ, though perhaps I have made him too good a man. But my characters of Antony and Cleopatra, though they are favourable to them, have nothing of outrageous panegyric. Their passions were
25 their own, and such as were given them by history ; only the deformities of them were cast into shadows, that they might be objects of compassion : whereas if I had chosen a noon-day light for them, somewhat must have been discovered which would rather have moved
30 our hatred than our pity.

The Gothic manner, and the barbarous ornaments, which are to be avoided in a picture, are just the same with those in an ill-ordered play. For example, our English tragi-comedy must be confessed to be wholly
35 Gothic, notwithstanding the success which it has found

upon our theatre, and in the *Pastor Fido* of Guarini ;
even though Corisca and the Satyr contribute somewhat
to the main action.   Neither can I defend my *Spanish
Friar*, as fond as otherwise I am of it, from this imputation : for though the comical parts are diverting, and 5
the serious moving, yet they are of an unnatural mingle :
for mirth and gravity destroy each other, and are no
more to be allowed for decent than a gay widow laughing in a mourning habit.

I had almost forgotten one considerable resemblance. 10
Du Fresnoy tells us, *That the figures of the groups must
not be all on a side, that is, with their face and bodies all
turned the same way ; but must contrast each other by their
several positions.*   Thus in a play, some characters must
be raised, to oppose others, and to set them off the 15
better ; according to the old maxim, *contraria juxta se
posita magis elucescunt.*   Thus, in *The Scornful Lady*,
the usurer is set to confront the prodigal : thus, in my
Tyrannic Love, the atheist Maximin is opposed to the
character of St. Catherine.   20

I am now come, though with the omission of many
likenesses, to the Third Part of Painting, which is called
the Cromatic, or Colouring.   Expression, and all that
belongs to words, is that in a poem which colouring
is in a picture.   The colours well chosen in their proper 25
places, together with the lights and shadows which
belong to them, lighten the design, and make it pleasing
to the eye.   The words, the expressions, the tropes and
figures, the versification, and all the other elegancies
of sound, as cadences, turns of words upon the thought, 30
and many other things, which are all parts of expression,
perform exactly the same office both in dramatic and
epic poetry.   Our author calls Colouring, *lena sororis ;*
in plain English, the bawd of her sister, the design or
drawing : she clothes, she dresses her up, she paints 35

her, she makes her appear more lovely than naturally she is ; she procures for the design, and makes lovers for her : for the design of itself is only so many naked lines.   Thus in poetry, the expression is that which
5 charms the reader, and beautifies the design, which is only the outlines of the fable.   'Tis true, the design must of itself be good ; if it be vicious, or, in one word, unpleasing, the cost of colouring is thrown away upon it : 'tis an ugly woman in a rich habit set out with
10 jewels ; nothing can become her ; but granting the design to be moderately good, it is like an excellent complexion with indifferent features : the white and red well mingled on the face make what was before but passable appear beautiful. *Operum colores* is the very
15 word which Horace uses to signify words and elegant expressions, of which he himself was so great a master in his Odes.   Amongst the ancients, Zeuxis was most famous for his colouring ; amongst the moderns, Titian and Correggio.   Of the two ancient epic poets, who
20 have so far excelled all the moderns, the invention and design were the particular talents of Homer. Virgil must yield to him in both ; for the design of the Latin was borrowed from the Grecian : but the *dictio Virgiliana*, the expression of Virgil, his colour-
25 ing, was incomparably the better ; and in that I have always endeavoured to copy him.   Most of the pedants, I know, maintain the contrary, and will have Homer excel even in this part.   But of all people, as they are the most ill-mannered, so they are the worst judges.
30 Even of words, which are their province, they seldom know more than the grammatical construction, unless they are born with a poetical genius, which is a rare portion amongst them.   Yet some I know may stand excepted ; and such I honour.   Virgil is so exact in
35 every word, that none can be changed but for a worse ;

nor any one removed from its place, but the harmony will be altered. He pretends sometimes to trip ; but it is only to make you think him in danger of a fall, when he is most secure : like a skilful dancer on the ropes (if you will pardon the meanness of the simili- 5 tude), who slips willingly, and makes a seeming stumble, that you may think him in great hazard of breaking his neck, while at the same time he is only giving you a proof of his dexterity. My late Lord Roscommon was often pleased with this reflection, and with the examples 10 of it in this admirable author.

I have not leisure to run through the whole comparison of lights and shadows with tropes and figures ; yet I cannot but take notice of metaphors, which like them have power to lessen or greaten anything. Strong and 15 glowing colours are the just resemblances of bold metaphors : but both must be judiciously applied ; for there is a difference betwixt daring and fool-hardiness. Lucan and Statius often ventured them too far ; our Virgil never. But the great defect of the *Pharsalia* 20 and the *Thebais* was in the design : if that had been more perfect, we might have forgiven many of their bold strokes in the colouring, or at least excused them : yet some of them are such as Demosthenes or Cicero could not have defended. Virgil, if he could have seen 25 the first verses of the *Sylvæ*, would have thought Statius mad, in his fustian description of the statue on the brazen horse. But that poet was always in a foam at his setting out, even before the motion of the race had warmed him. The soberness of Virgil, whom 30 he read, it seems, to little purpose, might have shewn him the difference betwixt

> *Arma virumque cano . . .*

and

> *Magnanimum Æacidem, formidatamque tonanti* 35
> *Progeniem.*

But Virgil knew how to rise by degrees in his expressions : Statius was in his towering heights at the first stretch of his pinions. The description of his running horse, just starting in the Funeral Games for Arche-
5 morus, though the verses are wonderfully fine, are the true image of their author :

> Stare adeo nescit, pereunt vestigia mille
> Ante fugam; absentemque ferit gravis ungula campum;

which would cost me an hour, if I had the leisure to
10 translate them, there is so much of beauty in the original.

Virgil, as he better knew his colours, so he knew better how and where to place them. In as much haste as I am, I cannot forbear giving one example.
15 It is said of him, that he read the Second, Fourth, and Sixth Books of his *Æneids* to Augustus Cæsar. In the Sixth (which we are sure he read, because we know Octavia was present, who rewarded him so bountifully for the twenty verses which were made in honour of
20 her deceased son, Marcellus), in this Sixth Book, I say, the poet, speaking of Misenus, the trumpeter, says :

> . . . quo non præstantior alter
> Ære ciere viros, . . .

and broke off in the hemistic, or midst of the verse ;
25 but in the very reading, seized as it were with a divine fury, he made up the latter part of the hemistic with these following words :

> . . . Martemque accendere cantu.

How warm, nay, how glowing a colouring is this ! In
30 the beginning of his verse, the word *æs*, or brass, was taken for a trumpet, because the instrument was made of that metal, which of itself was fine ; but in the latter end, which was made *ex tempore*, you see three metaphors, *Martemque,—accendere,—cantu*. Good Heavens !

how the plain sense is raised by the beauty of the words !
But this was happiness, the former might be only judgment : this was the *curiosa felicitas*, which Petronius
attributes to Horace ; it is the pencil thrown luckily
full upon the horse's mouth, to express the foam which 5
the painter with all his skill could not perform without
it.   These hits of words a true poet often finds, as
I may say, without seeking ; but he knows their value
when he finds them, and is infinitely pleased.   A bad
poet may sometimes light on them, but he discerns not 10
a diamond from a Bristol-stone ; and would have been
of the cock's mind in Æsop ; a grain of barley would
have pleased him better than the jewel.

The lights and shadows which belong to colouring
put me in mind of that verse in Horace :   15

Hoc amat obscurum, vult hoc sub luce videri.

Some parts of a poem require to be amply written, and
with all the force and elegance of words ; others must
be cast into shadows, that is, passed over in silence, or
but faintly touched.   This belongs wholly to the judg- 20
ment of the poet and the painter.   The most beautiful
parts of the picture, and the poem, must be the most
finished, the colours and words most chosen ; many
things in both, which are not deserving of this care,
must be shifted off ; content with vulgar expressions, 25
and those very short, and left, as in a shadow, to the
imagination of the reader.

We have the proverb, *manum de tabula*, from the
painters ; which signifies, to know when to give over,
and to lay by the pencil.   Both Homer and Virgil 30
practised this precept wonderfully well, but Virgil the
better of the two.   Homer knew, that when Hector
was slain Troy was as good as already taken ; therefore he concludes his action there : for what follows in

the funerals of Patroclus, and the redemption of Hector's body, is not, properly speaking, a part of the main action. But Virgil concludes with the death of Turnus ; for after that difficulty was removed Æneas might
5 marry, and establish the Trojans, when he pleased. This rule I had before my eyes in the conclusion of the *Spanish Friar*, when the discovery was made that the king was living, which was the knot of the play untied ; the rest is shut up in the compass of some few lines,
10 because nothing then hindered the happiness of Torrismond and Leonora. The faults of that drama are in the kind of it, which is tragi-comedy. But it was given to the people : and I never writ anything for myself but *Antony and Cleopatra*.
15   This remark, I must acknowledge, is not so proper for the colouring, as the design ; but it will hold for both. As the words, &c., are evidently shown to be the clothing of the thought, in the same sense as colours are the clothing of the design, so the painter and the
20 poet ought to judge exactly, when the colouring and expressions are perfect, and then to think their work is truly finished. Apelles said of Protogenes,—that he knew not when to give over. A work may be overwrought, as well as under-wrought ; too much labour
25 often takes away the spirit by adding to the polishing, so that there remains nothing but a dull correctness, a piece without any considerable faults, but with few beauties ; for when the spirits are drawn off, there is nothing but a *caput mortuum*. Statius never thought
30 an expression could be bold enough ; and if a bolder could be found, he rejected the first. Virgil had judgment enough to know daring was necessary ; but he knew the difference betwixt a glowing colour and a glaring : as when he compared the shocking of the
35 fleets at Actium to the jostling of islands rent from their

foundations, and meeting in the ocean. He knew the comparison was forced beyond nature, and raised too high ; he therefore softens the metaphor with a *credas* : you would almost believe that mountains or islands rushed against each other : 5

> . . . *credas innare revulsas*
> *Cycladas, aut montes concurrere montibus altos.*

But here I must break off without finishing the discourse. *Cynthius aurem vellit, et admonuit,* &c. The things which are behind are of too nice a consideration 10 for an essay, begun and ended in twelve mornings ; and perhaps the judges of painting and poetry, when I tell them how short a time it cost me, may make me the same answer which my late Lord Rochester made to one, who, to commend a tragedy, said it was written in 15 three weeks : ' How the devil could he be so long about it ? ' For that poem was infamously bad ; and I doubt this Parallel is little better ; and then the shortness of the time is so far from being a commendation, that it is scarcely an excuse. But if I have really drawn a por- 20 trait to the knees, or an half-length, with a tolerable likeness, then I may plead, with some justice, for myself, that the rest is left to the imagination. Let some better artist provide himself of a deeper canvas, and, taking these hints which I have given, set the figure 25 on its legs, and finish it in the invention, design, and colouring.

DEDICATION OF THE ÆNEIS

[1697]

TO THE MOST HONOURABLE

JOHN,

LORD MARQUESS OF NORMANBY, EARL OF

MULGRAVE, ETC., AND KNIGHT OF

THE MOST NOBLE ORDER OF

THE GARTER

A HEROIC POEM, truly such, is undoubtedly the greatest work which the soul of man is capable to perform. The design of it is to form the mind to heroic virtue by example ; 'tis conveyed in verse, that it may 5 delight, while it instructs. The action of it is always one, entire, and great. The least and most trivial episodes, or under-actions, which are interwoven in it, are parts either necessary or convenient to carry on the main design ; either so necessary, that, without them, 10 the poem must be imperfect, or so convenient, that no others can be imagined more suitable to the place in which they are. There is nothing to be left void in a firm building ; even the cavities ought not to be filled with rubbish which is of a perishable kind, destructive

to the strength, but with brick or stone, though of less
pieces, yet of the same nature, and fitted to the cran-
nies. Even the least portions of them must be of the
epic kind : all things must be grave, majestical, and
sublime ; nothing of a foreign nature, like the trifling 5
novels, which Ariosto [1], and others, have inserted in
their poems ; by which the reader is misled into another
sort of pleasure, opposite to that which is designed in
an epic poem. One raises the soul, and hardens it to
virtue ; the other softens it again, and unbends it into 10
vice. One conduces to the poet's aim, the completing
of his work, which he is driving on, labouring and
hastening in every line ; the other slackens his pace,
diverts him from his way, and locks him up like a knight-
errant in an enchanted castle, when he should be pur- 15
suing his first adventure. Statius, as Bossu has well
observed was ambitious of trying his strength with
his master Virgil, as Virgil had before tried his with
Homer. The Grecian gave the two Romans an example,
in the games which were celebrated at the funerals of 20
Patroclus. Virgil imitated the invention of Homer, but
changed the sports. But both the Greek and Latin poet
took their occasions from the subject ; though, to confess the truth, they were both ornamental, or, at best,
convenient parts of it, rather than of necessity arising 25
from it. Statius, who, through his whole poem, is
noted for want of conduct and judgment, instead of
staying, as he might have done, for the death of Capaneus, Hippomedon, Tydeus, or some other of his seven
champions (who are heroes all alike), or more properly 30
for the tragical end of the two brothers, whose exequies
the next successor had leisure to perform when the
siege was raised, and in the interval betwixt the poet's

---

[1] 'The early editions, by an absurd and continued blunder, read
Aristotle.' (Scott.)

first action and his second—went out of his way, as it
were on prepense malice, to commit a fault. For he took
his opportunity to kill a royal infant by the means of
a serpent (that author of all evil), to make way for those
5 funeral honours which he intended for him. Now, if
this innocent had been of any relation to his *Thebais* ;
if he had either furthered or hindered the taking of the
town ; the poet might have found some sorry excuse at
least for detaining the reader from the promised siege.
10 I can think of nothing to plead for him but what
I verily believe he thought himself, which was, that
as the funerals of Anchises were solemnised in Sicily,
so those of Archemorus should be celebrated in Candy.
For the last was an island, and a better than the first,
15 because Jove was born there. On these terms, this
Capaneus of a poet engaged his two immortal predecessors ; and his success was answerable to his
enterprise.

If this œconomy must be observed in the minutest
20 parts of an epic poem, which, to a common reader,
seems to be detached from the body, and almost independent of it ; what soul, though sent into the world
with great advantages of Nature, cultivated with the
liberal arts and sciences, conversant with histories of
25 the dead, and enriched with observations on the living,
can be sufficient to inform the whole body of so great
a work ? I touch here but transiently, without any
strict method, on some few of those many rules of
imitating nature which Aristotle drew from Homer's
30 *Iliads* and *Odysseys*, and which he fitted to the drama ;
furnishing himself also with observations from the
practice of the theatre, when it flourished under
Æschylus, Euripides, and Sophocles. For the original
of the stage was from the Epic Poem. Narration,
35 doubtless, preceded acting, and gave laws to it : what

at first was told artfully, was, in process of time, represented gracefully to the sight and hearing. Those
episodes of Homer, which were proper for the stage,
the poets amplified each into an action ; out of his limbs
they formed their bodies ; what he had contracted, they 5
enlarged ; out of one Hercules were made infinity of
pigmies, yet all endued with human souls ; for from
him, their great creator, they have each of them the
divinæ particulam auræ. They flowed from him at
first, and are at last resolved into him. Nor were 10
they only animated by him, but their measure and
symmetry was owing to him. His one, entire, and
great action was copied by them according to the proportions of the drama. If he finished his orb within
the year, it sufficed to teach them, that their action 15
being less, and being also less diversified with incidents,
their orb, of consequence, must be circumscribed in
a less compass, which they reduced within the limits
either of a natural or an artificial day ; so that, as he
taught them to amplify what he had shortened, by the 20
same rule, applied the contrary way, he taught them
to shorten what he had amplified. Tragedy is the
miniature of human life ; an epic poem is the draught
at length. Here, my Lord, I must contract also ; for,
before I was aware, I was almost running into a long 25
digression, to prove that there is no such absolute
necessity that the time of a stage action should so
strictly be confined to twenty-four hours as never to
exceed them, for which Aristotle contends, and the
Grecian stage has practised. Some longer space, on 30
some occasions, I think, may be allowed, especially for
the English theatre, which requires more variety of
incidents than the French. Corneille himself, after
long practice, was inclined to think that the time allotted
by the Ancients was too short to raise and finish a great 35

action : and better a mechanic rule were stretched or
broken, than a great beauty were omitted. To raise,
and afterwards to calm the passions—to purge the soul
from pride, by the examples of human miseries, which
5 befall the greatest—in few words, to expel arrogance,
and introduce compassion, are the great effects of
tragedy. Great, I must confess, if they were altogether
as true as they are pompous. But are habits to be
introduced at three hours' warning ? are radical diseases
10 so suddenly removed. A mountebank may promise
such a cure, but a skilful physician will not undertake
it. An epic poem is not in so much haste : it works
leisurely ; the changes which it makes are slow ; but
the cure is likely to be more perfect. The effects of
15 tragedy, as I said, are too violent to be lasting. If it
be answered that, for this reason, tragedies are often
to be seen, and the dose to be repeated, this is tacitly
to confess that there is more virtue in one heroic poem
than in many tragedies. A man is humbled one day,
20 and his pride returns the next. Chymical medicines
are observed to relieve oftener than to cure : for 'tis
the nature of spirits to make swift impressions, but not
deep. Galenical decoctions, to which I may properly
compare an epic poem, have more of body in them ;
25 they work by their substance and their weight. It is
one reason of Aristotle's to prove that Tragedy is the
more noble, because it turns in a shorter compass ;
the whole action being circumscribed within the space
of four-and-twenty hours. He might prove as well that
30 a mushroom is to be preferred before a peach, because
it shoots up in the compass of a night. A chariot may
be driven round the pillar in less space than a large
machine, because the bulk is not so great. Is the
Moon a more noble planet than Saturn, because she
35 makes her revolution in less than thirty days, and he

in little less than thirty years ? Both their orbs are in proportion to their several magnitudes ; and consequently the quickness or slowness of their motion, and the time of their circumvolutions, is no argument of the greater or less perfection. And, besides, what virtue is 5 there in a tragedy which is not contained in an epic poem, where pride is humbled, virtue rewarded, and vice punished ; and those more amply treated than the narrowness of the drama can admit ? The shining quality of an epic hero, his magnanimity, his constancy, 10 his patience, his piety, or whatever characteristical virtue his poet gives him, raises first our admiration ; we are naturally prone to imitate what we admire ; and frequent acts produce a habit. If the hero's chief quality be vicious, as, for example, the choler and obstinate 15 desire of vengeance in Achilles, yet the moral is instructive : and, besides, we are informed in the very proposition of the *Iliads*, that this anger was pernicious ; that it brought a thousand ills on the Grecian camp. The courage of Achilles is proposed to imitation, 20 not his pride and disobedience to his general, nor his brutal cruelty to his dead enemy, nor the selling of his body to his father. We abhor these actions while we read them ; and what we abhor we never imitate. The poet only shows them, like rocks or quicksands, to be 25 shunned.

By this example, the critics have concluded that it is not necessary the manners of the hero should be virtuous. They are poetically good, if they are of a piece : though where a character of perfect virtue is set before us, it is 30 more lovely ; for there the whole hero is to be imitated. This is the Æneas of our author ; this is that idea of perfection in an epic poem which painters and statuaries have only in their minds, and which no hands are able to express. These are the beauties of a god in a human 35

body. When the picture of Achilles is drawn in tragedy,
he is taken with those warts, and moles, and hard features by those who represent him on the stage, or he
is no more Achilles ; for his creator, Homer, has so
5 described him. Yet even thus he appears a perfect
hero, though an imperfect character of virtue. Horace
paints him after Homer, and delivers him to be copied
on the stage with all those imperfections. Therefore
they are either not faults in a heroic poem, or faults
10 common to the drama. After all, on the whole merits
of the cause, it must be acknowledged that the Epic
Poem is more for the manners, and Tragedy for the
passions. The passions, as I have said, are violent ;
and acute distempers require medicines of a strong and
15 speedy operation. Ill habits of the mind are like chro-
nical diseases, to be corrected by degrees, and cured
by alteratives ; wherein, though purges are sometimes
necessary, yet diet, good air, and moderate exercise
have the greatest part. The matter being thus stated,
20 it will appear that both sorts of poetry are of use for
their proper ends. The stage is more active ; the Epic
Poem works at greater leisure, yet is active too, when
need requires ; for dialogue is imitated by the drama
from the more active parts of it. One puts off a fit,
25 like the quinquina, and relieves us only for a time ; the
other roots out the distemper, and gives a healthful
habit. The sun enlightens and cheers us, dispels fogs,
and warms the ground with his daily beams ; but the
corn is sowed, increases, is ripened, and is reaped for
30 use in process of time, and in its proper season. I proceed, from the greatness of the action, to the dignity of
the actors ; I mean to the persons employed in both
poems. There likewise Tragedy will be seen to borrow
from the Epopee ; and that which borrows is always of
35 less dignity, because it has not of its own. A subject,

it is true, may lend to his sovereign ; but the act of
borrowing makes the king inferior, because he wants,
and the subject supplies. And suppose the persons
of the drama wholly fabulous, or of the poet's invention,
yet Heroic Poetry gave him the examples of that inven- 5
tion, because it was first, and Homer the common father
of the stage. I know not of any one advantage which
Tragedy can boast above Heroic Poetry, but that it is
represented to the view, as well as read, and instructs
in the closet, as well as on the theatre. This is an 10
uncontended excellence, and a chief branch of its prerogative ; yet I may be allowed to say, without partiality,
that herein the actors share the poet's praise. Your
Lordship knows some modern tragedies which are
beautiful on the stage, and yet I am confident you would 15
not read them. Tryphon the stationer complains they
are seldom asked for in his shop. The poet who
flourished in the scene is damned in the *ruelle ;* nay
more, he is not esteemed a good poet by those, who
see and hear his extravagances with delight. They 20
are a sort of stately fustian, and lofty childishness.
Nothing but Nature can give a sincere pleasure ; where
that is not imitated, 'tis grotesque painting ; the fine
woman ends in a fish's tail.

I might also add that many things, which not only 25
please, but are real beauties in the reading, would
appear absurd upon the stage ; and those not only the
speciosa miracula, as Horace calls them, of transforma-
tions, of Scylla, Antiphates, and the Læstrygons, which
cannot be represented even in operas ; but the prowess 30
of Achilles or Æneas would appear ridiculous in our
dwarf heroes of the theatre. We can believe they
routed armies, in Homer or in Virgil ; but *ne Hercules
contra duos* in the drama. I forbear to instance in many
things, which the stage cannot, or ought not to repre- 35

sent ; for I have said already more than I intended on
this subject, and should fear it might be turned against
me, that I plead for the pre-eminence of Epic Poetry
because I have taken some pains in translating Virgil,
5 if this were the first time that I had delivered my
opinion in this dispute. But I have more than once
already maintained the rights of my two masters against
their rivals of the scene, even while I wrote tragedies
myself, and had no thoughts of this present under-
10 taking. I submit my opinion to your judgment, who
are better qualified than any man I know, to decide
this controversy. You come, my Lord, instructed in
the cause, and needed not that I should open it. Your
Essay of Poetry, which was published without a name,
15 and of which I was not honoured with the confidence,
I read over and over with much delight, and as
much instruction, and, without flattering you, or making
myself more moral than I am, not without some envy.
I was loath to be informed how an epic poem should
20 be written, or how a tragedy should be contrived and
managed, in better verse, and with more judgment, than
I could teach others. A native of Parnassus, and bred
up in the studies of its fundamental laws, may receive
new lights from his contemporaries ; but it is a grudging
25 kind of praise which he gives his benefactors. He is
more obliged than he is willing to acknowledge ; there
is a tincture of malice in his commendations. For
where I own I am taught, I confess my want of knowledge. A judge upon the bench may, out of good
30 nature, or at least interest, encourage the pleadings of
a puny counsellor ; but he does not willingly commend
his brother serjeant at the bar, especially when he
controuls his law, and exposes that ignorance which
is made sacred by his place. I gave the unknown
35 author his due commendation, I must confess ; but

who can answer for me and for the rest of the poets
who heard me read the poem, whether we should not
have been better pleased to have seen our own names
at the bottom of the title-page ?   Perhaps we commended it the more, that we might seem to be above 5
the censure.   We are naturally displeased with an
unknown critic, as the ladies are with a lampooner,
because we are bitten in the dark, and know not where
to fasten our revenge.   But great excellencies will work
their way through all sorts of opposition.   I applauded 10
rather out of decency than affection ;   and was ambitious, as some yet can witness, to be acquainted with
a man with whom I had the honour to converse, and
that almost daily, for so many years together.   Heaven
knows, if I have heartily forgiven you this deceit.   You 15
extorted a praise, which I should willingly have given,
had I known you.   Nothing had been more easy than
to commend a patron of a long standing.   The world
would join with me, if the encomiums were just ;   and,
if unjust, would excuse a grateful flatterer.   But to 20
come anonymous upon me, and force me to commend
you against my interest, was not altogether so fair, give
me leave to say, as it was politic.   For, by concealing
your quality, you might clearly understand how your
work succeeded, and that the general approbation was 25
given to your merit, not your titles.   Thus, like Apelles,
you stood unseen behind your own Venus, and received
the praises of the passing multitude ;   the work was
commended, not the author ;   and I doubt not, this was
one of the most pleasing adventures of your life.   30
    I have detained your Lordship longer than I in-
tended in this dispute of preference betwixt the Epic
Poem and the Drama, and yet have not formally
answered any of the arguments which are brought by
Aristotle on the other side, and set in the fairest light 35

by Dacier.   But I suppose, without looking on the
book, I may have touched on some of the objections ;
for, in this address to your Lordship, I design not a
Treatise of Heroic Poetry, but write in a loose episto-
5 lary way, somewhat tending to that subject, after the
example of Horace, in his *First Epistle* of the Second
Book *to Augustus Cæsar*, and in that to the Piso's,
which we call his *Art of Poetry* ; in both of which he
observes no method that I can trace, whatever Scaliger
10 the father, or Heinsius, may have seen, or rather think
they had seen.   I have taken up, laid down, and resumed
as often as I pleased, the same subject ; and this loose
proceeding I shall use through all this prefatory Dedication.   Yet all this while I have been sailing with
15 some side-wind or other toward the point I proposed
in the beginning, the greatness and excellency of a
Heroic Poem, with some of the difficulties which attend
that work.   The comparison, therefore, which I made
betwixt the Epopee and the Tragedy was not altogether
20 a digression ; for 'tis concluded on all hands that they
are both the master-pieces of human wit.

In the meantime, I may be bold to draw this corollary
from what has been already said, that the file of heroic
poets is very short ; all are not such who have assumed
25 that lofty title in ancient or modern ages, or have been
so esteemed by their partial and ignorant admirers.

There have been but one great *Ilias* and one *Æneis*
in so many ages.   The next, but the next with a long
interval betwixt, was the *Jerusalem* : I mean not so
30 much in distance of time, as in excellency.   After these
three are entered, some Lord Chamberlain should be
appointed, some critic of authority should be set before
the door, to keep out a crowd of little poets, who press
for admission, and are not of quality.   Mævius would
35 be deafening your Lordship's ears with his

Fortunam Priami cantabo, et nobile bellum ;

mere fustian, as Horace would tell you from behind,
without pressing forward, and more smoke than fire.
Pulci, Boiardo, and Ariosto, would cry out, ' make room
for the Italian poets, the descendants of Virgil in a right 5
line : ' Father Le Moine, with his *Saint Louis*, and
Scudery with his *Alaric*, for a godly king and a Gothic
conqueror ; and Chapelain would take it ill that his
Maid should be refused a place with Helen and
Lavinia. Spenser has a better plea for his *Fairy* 10
Queen, had his action been finished, or had been one.
And Milton, if the Devil had not been his hero, instead
of Adam ; if the giant had not foiled the knight, and
driven him out of his stronghold, to wander through the
world with his lady errant ; and if there had not been 15
more machining persons than human in his poem.
After these, the rest of our English poets shall not
be mentioned. I have that honour for them which
I ought to have ; but, if they are worthies, they are
not to be ranked amongst the three whom I have 20
named, and who are established in their reputation.

Before I quitted the comparison betwixt Epic Poetry
and Tragedy, I should have acquainted my judge with
one advantage of the former over the latter, which I now
casually remember out of the preface of Segrais before 25
his translation of the *Æneis*, or out of Bossu, no matter
which : *the style of the Heroic Poem is, and ought to be,*
more lofty than that of the drama. The critic is certainly
in the right, for the reason already urged ; the work of
Tragedy is on the passions, and in dialogue ; both 30
of them abhor strong metaphors, in which the Epopee
delights. A poet cannot speak too plainly on the stage :
for *volat irrevocabile verbum ;* the sense is lost, if it be
not taken flying. But what we read alone, we have
leisure to digest ; there an author may beautify his 35

sense by the boldness of his expression, which if we understand not fully at the first, we may dwell upon it till we find the secret force and excellence. That which cures the manners by alterative physic, as I said before, 5 must proceed by insensible degrees ; but that which purges the passions must do its business all at once, or wholly fail of its effect, at least in the present operation, and without repeated doses. We must beat the iron while it is hot, but we may polish it at leisure. Thus, 10 my Lord, you pay the fine of my forgetfulness ; and yet the merits of both causes are where they were, and undecided, till you declare whether it be more for the benefit of mankind to have their manners in general corrected, or their pride and hard-heartedness removed.

15 I must now come closer to my present business, and not think of making more invasive wars abroad, when, like Hannibal, I am called back to the defence of my own country. Virgil is attacked by many enemies ; he has a whole confederacy against him ; and I must 20 endeavour to defend him as well as I am able. But their principal objections being against his moral, the duration or length of time taken up in the action of the poem, and what they have to urge against the manners of his hero, I shall omit the rest as mere 25 cavils of grammarians ; at the worst, but casual slips of a great man's pen, or inconsiderable faults of an admirable poem, which the author had not leisure to review before his death. Macrobius has answered what the ancients could urge against him ; and some 30 things I have lately read in Tanneguy le Fèvre, Valois, and another whom I name not, which are scarce worth answering. They begin with the moral of his poem, which I have elsewhere confessed, and still must own, not to be so noble as that of Homer. But let both be 35 fairly stated ; and, without contradicting my first opinion,

I can show that Virgil's was as useful to the Romans of his age, as Homer's was to the Grecians of his, in what time soever he may be supposed to have lived and flourished.   Homer's moral was to urge the necessity of union, and of a good understanding betwixt con- 5 federate states and princes engaged in a war with a mighty monarch ; as also of discipline in an army, and obedience in the several chiefs to the supreme commander of the joint forces.   To inculcate this, he sets forth the ruinous effects of discord in the camp of 10 those allies, occasioned by the quarrel betwixt the general and one of the next in office under him. Agamemnon gives the provocation, and Achilles resents the injury.   Both parties are faulty in the quarrel ; and accordingly they are both punished : the aggressor is 15 forced to sue for peace to his inferior on dishonourable conditions : the deserter refuses the satisfaction offered, and his obstinacy costs him his best friend.   This works the natural effect of choler, and turns his rage against him by whom he was last affronted, and most sensibly. 20 The greater anger expels the less ; but his character is still preserved.   In the meantime, the Grecian army receives loss on loss, and is half destroyed by a pestilence into the bargain :—

Quidquid delirant reges, plectuntur Achivi.   25

As the poet, in the first part of the example, had shown the bad effects of discord, so, after the reconcilement, he gives the good effects of unity ; for Hector is slain, and then Troy must fall.   By this it is probable that Homer lived when the Persian Monarchy was 30 grown formidable to the Grecians, and that the joint endeavours of his countrymen were little enough to preserve their common freedom from an encroaching enemy.   Such was his moral, which all critics have

allowed to be more noble than that of Virgil, though
not adapted to the times in which the Roman poet
lived. Had Virgil flourished in the age of Ennius,
and addressed to Scipio, he had probably taken the
5 same moral, or some other not unlike it : for then
the Romans were in as much danger from the
Carthaginian commonwealth as the Grecians were
from the Persian monarchy. But we are to consider
him as writing his poem in a time when the old form
10 of government was subverted, and a new one just
established by Octavius Cæsar, in effect by force of
arms, but seemingly by the consent of the Roman
people. The Commonwealth had received a deadly
wound in the former civil wars betwixt Marius and
15 Sylla. The commons, while the first prevailed, had
almost shaken off the yoke of the nobility ; and Marius
and Cinna, like the captains of the mob, under the
specious pretence of the public good, and of doing
justice on the oppressors of their liberty, revenged
20 themselves, without form of law, on their private
enemies. Sylla, in his turn, proscribed the heads of
the adverse party : he too had nothing but liberty and
reformation in his mouth ; (for the cause of religion is
but a modern motive to rebellion, invented by the
25 Christian priesthood, refining on the heathen ;) Sylla,
to be sure, meant no more good to the Roman people
than Marius before him, whatever he declared ; but
sacrificed the lives, and took the estates, of all his
enemies, to gratify those who brought him into power.
30 Such was the reformation of the government by both
parties. The Senate and the Commons were the two
bases on which it stood ; and the two champions of
either faction, each, destroyed the foundations of the
other side ; so the fabric, of consequence, must fall
35 betwixt them, and tyranny must be built upon their

ruins. This comes of altering fundamental laws and constitutions ; like him, who, being in good health, lodged himself in a physician's house, and was over-persuaded by his landlord to take physic (of which he died), for the benefit of his doctor. *Stavo ben* (was written on his monument), *ma, per star meglio, sto quì.*

After the death of those two usurpers, the Commonwealth seemed to recover, and held up its head for a little time. But it was all the while in a deep consumption, which is a flattering disease. Pompey, Crassus, and Cæsar had found the sweets of arbitrary power ; and, each being a check to the other's growth, struck up a false friendship amongst themselves, and divided the government betwixt them, which none of them was able to assume alone. These were the public-spirited men of their age ; that is, patriots for their own interest. The Commonwealth looked with a florid countenance in their management, spread in bulk, and all the while was wasting in the vitals. Not to trouble your Lordship with the repetition of what you know : after the death of Crassus, Pompey found himself out-witted by Cæsar, broke with him, overpowered him in the Senate, and caused many unjust decrees to pass against him. Cæsar, thus injured, and unable to resist the faction of the nobles which was now uppermost (for he was a Marian), had recourse to arms ; and his cause was just against Pompey, but not against his country, whose constitution ought to have been sacred to him, and never to have been violated on the account of any private wrong. But he prevailed ; and Heaven declaring for him, he became a providential monarch, under the title of perpetual dictator. He being murdered by his own son, whom I neither dare commend, nor can justly blame (though Dante, in his *Inferno*, has put him and Cassius, and Judas Iscariot betwixt them, into the

great Devil's mouth), the Commonwealth popped up its
head for the third time, under Brutus and Cassius, and
then sunk for ever.

Thus the Roman people were grossly gulled twice or
5 thrice over, and as often enslaved in one century, and
under the same pretence of reformation. At last the
two battles of Philippi gave the decisive stroke against
liberty ; and, not long after, the Commonwealth was
turned into a Monarchy by the conduct and good fortune
10 of Augustus. 'Tis true, that the despotic power could
not have fallen into better hands than those of the
first and second Cæsar. Your Lordship well knows
what obligations Virgil had to the latter of them : he
saw, beside, that the Commonwealth was lost without
15 resource ; the heads of it destroyed ; the Senate new
moulded, grown degenerate, and either bought off, or
thrusting their own necks into the yoke, out of fear of
being forced. Yet I may safely affirm for our great
author (as men of good sense are generally honest), that
20 he was still of republic principles in his heart.

Secretosque pios, his dantem jura Catonem.

I think I need use no other argument to justify my
opinion, than that of this one line, taken from the
Eighth Book of the *Æneis*. If he had not well studied
25 his patron's temper, it might have ruined him with
another prince. But Augustus was not discontented,
at least that we can find, that Cato was placed, by his
own poet, in Elysium, and there giving laws to the
holy souls who deserved to be separated from the
30 vulgar sort of good spirits ; for his conscience could
not but whisper to the arbitrary Monarch that the
Kings of Rome were at first elective, and governed not
without a Senate ; that Romulus was no hereditary
prince ; and though, after his death, he received divine

honours for the good he did on earth, yet he was but
a god of their own making ; that the last Tarquin was
expelled justly for overt acts of tyranny, and mal-
administration ; for such are the conditions of an
elective kingdom : and I meddle not with others, being, 5
for my own opinion, of Montaigne's principles, that
an honest man ought to be contented with that form
of government, and with those fundamental constitutions of it, which he received from his ancestors, and
under which himself was born ; though at the same 10
time he confessed freely, that, if he could have chosen
his place of birth, it should have been at Venice ;
which, for many reasons, I dislike, and am better
pleased to have been born an Englishman.

But, to return from my long rambling : I say, that 15
Virgil having maturely weighed the condition of the
times in which he lived ; that an entire liberty was
not to be retrieved ; that the present settlement had
the prospect of a long continuance in the same family,
or those adopted into it ; that he held his paternal 20
estate from the bounty of the conqueror, by whom he
was likewise enriched, esteemed and cherished ; that
this conqueror, though of a bad kind, was the very
best of it ; that the arts of peace flourished under him ;
that all men might be happy, if they would be quiet ; 25
that, now he was in possession of the whole, yet he
shared a great part of his authority with the Senate ;
that he would be chosen into the ancient offices of
the Commonwealth, and ruled by the power which
he derived from them ; and prorogued his government 30
from time to time, still, as it were, threatening to dis-
miss himself from public cares, which he exercised
more for the common good than for any delight he
took in greatness ; these things, I say, being considered
by the poet, he concluded it to be the interest of his 35

country to be so governed ; to infuse an awful respect
into the people towards such a prince ; by that respect
to confirm their obedience to him, and by that obedience
to make them happy. This was the moral of his divine
5 poem ; honest in the poet ; honourable to the Emperor,
whom he derives from a divine extraction ; and reflecting part of that honour on the Roman people, whom
he derives also from the Trojans ; and not only profitable, but necessary, to the present age, and likely to
10 be such to their posterity. That it was the received
opinion, that the Romans were descended from the
Trojans, and Julius Cæsar from Iulus the son of Æneas,
was enough for Virgil ; though perhaps he thought not
so himself, or that Æneas ever was in Italy ; which
15 Bochartus manifestly proves. And Homer, where he
says that Jupiter hated the house of Priam, and was
resolved to transfer the kingdom to the family of Æneas,
yet mentions nothing of his leading a colony into a
foreign country, and settling there. But that the
20 Romans valued themselves on their Trojan ancestry is
so undoubted a truth that I need not prove it. Even
the seals which we have remaining of Julius Cæsar,
which we know to be antique, have the star of Venus
over them (though they were all graven after his death),
25 as a note that he was deified. I doubt not but it was
one reason why Augustus should be so passionately
concerned for the preservation of the *Æneis*, which its
author had condemned to be burnt, as an imperfect
poem, by his last will and testament, because it did
30 him a real service, as well as an honour ; that a work
should not be lost where his divine original was celebrated in verse which had the character of immortality
stamped upon it.

Neither were the great Roman families, which
35 flourished in his time, less obliged by him than the

Emperor. Your Lordship knows with what address
he makes mention of them, as captains of ships, or
leaders in the war ; and even some of Italian extraction
are not forgotten. These are the single stars which
are sprinkled through the *Æneis* : but there are whole 5
constellations of them in the Fifth Book. And I could
not but take notice, when I translated it, of some
favourite families to which he gives the victory and
awards the prizes, in the person of his hero, at the
funeral games which were celebrated in honour of 10
Anchises. I insist not on their names ; but am pleased
to find the Memmii amongst them, derived from Mnes-
theus, because Lucretius dedicates to one of that family,
a branch of which destroyed Corinth. I likewise either
found or formed an image to myself of the contrary 15
kind ; that those who lost the prizes were such as had
disobliged the poet, or were in disgrace with Augustus,
or enemies to Mæcenas ; and this was the poetical
revenge he took : for *genus irritabile vatum*, as Horace
says. When a poet is thoroughly provoked, he will 20
do himself justice, however dear it cost him ; *animam-*
que in vulnere ponit. I think these are not bare imaginations of my own, though I find no trace of them in the
commentators ; but one poet may judge of another by
himself. The vengeance we defer is not forgotten. 25
I hinted before that the whole Roman people were
obliged by Virgil, in deriving them from Troy ; an
ancestry which they affected. We and the French are
of the same humour : they would be thought to descend
from a son, I think, of Hector ; and we would have our 30
Britain both named and planted by a descendant of
Æneas. Spenser favours this opinion what he can.
His Prince Arthur, or whoever he intends by him, is
a Trojan. Thus the hero of Homer was a Grecian,
of Virgil a Roman, of Tasso an Italian. 35

I have transgressed my bounds, and gone further than the moral led me. But if your Lordship is not tired, I am safe enough.

Thus far, I think, my author is defended. But, as Augustus is still shadowed in the person of Æneas, of which I shall say more when I come to the manners which the poet gives his hero, I must prepare that subject by showing how dexterously he managed both the prince and people, so as to displease neither, and to do good to both ; which is the part of a wise and an honest man, and proves that it is possible for a courtier not to be a knave. I shall continue still to speak my thoughts like a free-born subject, as I am ; though such things, perhaps, as no Dutch commentator could, and I am sure no Frenchman durst. I have already told your Lordship my opinion of Virgil, that he was no arbitrary man. Obliged he was to his master for his bounty ; and he repays him with good counsel, how to behave himself in his new monarchy, so as to gain the affections of his subjects, and deserve to be called the Father of his Country. From this consideration it is that he chose, for the ground-work of his poem, one empire destroyed, and another raised from the ruins of it. This was just the parallel. Æneas could not pretend to be Priam's heir in a lineal succession ; for Anchises, the hero's father, was only of the second branch of the royal family ; and Helenus, a son of Priam, was yet surviving, and might lawfully claim before him. It may be, Virgil mentions him on that account. Neither has he forgotten Priamus, in the fifth of his *Æneis*, the son of Polites, youngest son to Priam, who was slain by Pyrrhus, in the Second Book. Æneas had only married Creusa, Priam's daughter, and by her could have no title while any of the male issue were remaining. In this case, the poet gave him the

next title, which is that of an elective king. The
remaining Trojans chose him to lead them forth, and
settle them in some foreign country. Ilioneus, in his
speech to Dido, calls him expressly by the name of
king. Our poet, who all this while had Augustus in 5
his eye, had no desire he should seem to succeed by
any right of inheritance derived from Julius Cæsar
(such a title being but one degree removed from conquest), for what was introduced by force, by force may
be removed. 'Twas better for the people that they 10
should give, than he should take ; since that gift was
indeed no more at bottom than a trust. Virgil gives
us an example of this in the person of Mezentius :
he governed arbitrarily ; he was expelled, and came
to the deserved end of all tyrants. Our author shows 15
us another sort of kingship, in the person of Latinus :
he was descended from Saturn, and, as I remember,
in the third degree. He is described a just and
gracious prince, solicitous for the welfare of his people,
always consulting with his Senate to promote the 20
common good. We find him at the head of them,
when he enters into the council-hall, speaking first,
but still demanding their advice, and steering by it,
as far as the iniquity of the times would suffer him.
And this is the proper character of a King by 25
inheritance, who is born a Father of his Country.
Æneas, though he married the heiress of the crown,
yet claimed no title to it during the life of his father-
in-law. *Pater arma Latinus habeto*, &c. are Virgil's
words. As for himself, he was contented to take care 30
of his country gods, who were not those of Latium ;
wherein our divine author seems to relate to the after-
practice of the Romans, which was to adopt the gods
of those they conquered, or received as members of
their commonwealth. Yet, withal, he plainly touches 35

at the office of the high-priesthood, with which Augustus
was invested, and which made his person more sacred
and inviolable than even the tribunitial power. It was
not therefore for nothing, that the most judicious of all
5 poets made that office vacant by the death of Panthus in
the Second Book of the *Æneis*, for his hero to succeed
in it, and consequently for Augustus to enjoy. I know
not that any of the commentators have taken notice of
that passage. If they have not, I am sure they ought ;
10 and if they have, I am not indebted to them for the
observation. The words of Virgil are very plain :—

Sacra, suosque tibi commendat Troja penates.

As for Augustus, or his uncle Julius, claiming by
descent from Æneas, that title is already out of doors.
15 Æneas succeeded not, but was elected. Troy was fore-
doomed to fall for ever :—

Postquam res Asiæ Priamique evertere gentem
Immeritam visum superis.—ÆNEIS iii. line 1.

Augustus, 'tis true, had once resolved to rebuild that
20 city, and there to make the seat of empire : but Horace
writes an ode on purpose to deter him from that thought ;
declaring the place to be accursed, and that the gods
would as often destroy it as it should be raised. Hereupon the Emperor laid aside a project so ungrateful to
25 the Roman people. But by this, my Lord, we may
conclude that he had still his pedigree in his head, and
had an itch of being thought a divine king, if his poets
had not given him better counsel.

I will pass by many less material objections, for want
30 of room to answer them : what follows next is of great
importance, if the critics can make out their charge ; for
'tis levelled at the manners which our poet gives his
hero, and which are the same which were eminently

seen in his Augustus. Those manners were, piety
to the gods and a dutiful affection to his father, love
to his relations, care of his people, courage and conduct
in the wars, gratitude to those who had obliged him,
and justice in general to mankind. 5

Piety, as your Lordship sees, takes place of all, as the
chief part of his character ; and the word in Latin is
more full than it can possibly be expressed in any
modern language ; for there it comprehends not only
devotion to the gods, but filial love, and tender affection 10
to relations of all sorts. As instances of this, the deities
of Troy, and his own Penates, are made the companions
of his flight : they appear to him in his voyage, and
advise him ; and at last he replaces them in Italy, their
native country. For his father, he takes him on his 15
back : he leads his little son : his wife follows him ;
but, losing his footsteps through fear or ignorance, he
goes back into the midst of his enemies to find her,
and leaves not his pursuit until her ghost appears, to
forbid his further search. I will say nothing of his 20
duty to his father while he lived, his sorrow for his
death, of the games instituted in honour of his memory,
or seeking him, by his command, even after his death,
in the Elysian fields. I will not mention his tenderness
for his son, which everywhere is visible—of his raising 25
a tomb for Polydorus, the obsequies for Misenus, his
pious remembrance of Deiphobus, the funerals of his
nurse, his grief for Pallas, and his revenge taken on
his murderer, whom otherwise, by his natural compassion, he had forgiven : and then the poem had been 30
left imperfect ; for we could have had no certain
prospect of his happiness, while the last obstacle to it
was removed. Of the other parts which compose his
character, as a king or as a general, I need say nothing ;
the whole *Æneis* is one continued instance of some one 35

or other of them ; and where I find anything of them
taxed, it shall suffice me, as briefly as I can, to vindicate
my divine master to your Lordship, and by you to the
reader. But herein Segrais, in his admirable preface
5 to his translation of the *Æneis*, as the author of the
Dauphin's *Virgil* justly calls it, has prevented me.
Him I follow, and what I borrow from him, am ready
to acknowledge to him. For, impartially speaking, the
French are as much better critics than the English, as
10 they are worse poets. Thus we generally allow, that
they better understand the management of a war than
our islanders ; but we know we are superior to them
in the day of battle. They value themselves on their
generals, we on our soldiers. But this is not the
15 proper place to decide that question, if they make it
one. I shall say perhaps as much of other nations,
and their poets, excepting only Tasso ; and hope to
make my assertion good, which is but doing justice
to my country ; part of which honour will reflect on
20 your Lordship, whose thoughts are always just ; your
numbers harmonious, your words chosen, your expressions strong and manly, your verse flowing, and
your turns as happy as they are easy. If you would
set us more copies, your example would make all pre-
25 cepts needless. In the mean time, that little you have
written is owned, and that particularly by the poets
(who are a nation not over lavish of praise to their
contemporaries), as a principal ornament of our language ; but the sweetest essences are always confined
30 in the smallest glasses.

When I speak of your Lordship, 'tis never a digression, and therefore I need beg no pardon for it ; but
take up Segrais where I left him, and shall use him less
often than I have occasion for him ; for his preface is
35 a perfect piece of criticism, full and clear, and digested

into an exact method ; mine is loose, and, as I intended
it, epistolary. Yet I dwell on many things which he
durst not touch ; for 'tis dangerous to offend an arbitrary master ; and every patron who has the power of
Augustus has not his clemency. In short, my Lord, 5
I would not translate him, because I would bring you
somewhat of my own. His notes and observations on
every book are of the same excellency ; and, for the
same reason, I omit the greater part.

He takes notice that Virgil is arraigned for placing 10
piety before valour, and making that piety the chief
character of his hero. I have said already from Bossu,
that a poet is not obliged to make his hero a virtuous
man ; therefore, neither Homer nor Tasso are to be
blamed for giving what predominant quality they 15
pleased to their first character. But Virgil, who designed to form a perfect prince, and would insinuate
that Augustus, whom he calls Æneas in his poem, was
truly such, found himself obliged to make him without
blemish, thoroughly virtuous ; and a thorough virtue 20
both begins and ends in piety. Tasso, without question, observed this before me, and therefore split his
hero in two : he gave Godfrey piety, and Rinaldo fortitude, for their chief qualities or manners. Homer, who
had chosen another moral, makes both Agamemnon 25
and Achilles vicious ; for his design was to instruct in
virtue, by showing the deformity of vice. I avoid repetition of what I have said above. What follows is
translated literally from Segrais.

' Virgil had considered, that the greatest virtues of 30
Augustus consisted in the perfect art of governing his
people ; which caused him to reign for more than forty
years in great felicity. He considered that his emperor
was valiant, civil, popular, eloquent, politic, and religious ; he has given all these qualities to Æneas. But, 35

knowing that piety alone comprehends the whole duty
of man towards the gods, towards his country, and
towards his relations, he judged that this ought to be
his first character, whom he would set for a pattern of
5 perfection.   In reality, they who believe that the praises
which arise from valour are superior to those which
proceed from any other virtues, have not considered
(as they ought), that valour, destitute of other virtues,
cannot render a man worthy of any true esteem.   That
10 quality, which signifies no more than an intrepid
courage, may be separated from many others which
are good, and accompanied with many which are ill.
A man may be very valiant, and yet impious and vicious.
But the same cannot be said of piety, which excludes
15 all ill qualities, and comprehends even valour itself,
with all other qualities which are good.   Can we, for
example, give the praise of valour to a man who should
see his gods profaned, and should want the courage to
defend them ? to a man who should abandon his father,
20 or desert his king, in his last necessity ? '

Thus far Segrais, in giving the preference to piety
before valour.   I will now follow him, where he considers this valour, or intrepid courage, singly in itself ;
and this also Virgil gives to his Æneas, and that in
25 a heroical degree.

Having first concluded, that our poet did for the best
in taking the first character of his hero from that essential virtue on which the rest depend, he proceeds to
tell us that in the ten years' war of Troy he was con-
30 sidered as the second champion of his country, allowing
Hector the first place ; and this, even by the confession
of Homer, who took all occasions of setting up his own
countrymen the Grecians, and of undervaluing the
Trojan chiefs.   But Virgil (whom Segrais forgot to
35 cite) makes Diomede give him a higher character for

strength and courage. His testimony is this, in the
Eleventh Book :—

> . . . *Stetimus tela aspera contra,*
> *Contulimusque manus : experto credite, quantus*
> *In clypeum assurgat, quo turbine torqueat hastam.*   5
> *Si duo præterea tales Idæa tulisset*
> *Terra viros, ultro Inachias venisset ad urbes*
> *Dardanus, et versis lugeret Græcia fatis.*
> *Quicquid apud duræ cessatum est mænia Trojæ,*
> *Hectoris Æneæque manu victoria Graium*   10
> *Hæsit, et in decumum vestigia rettulit annum.*
> *Ambo animis, ambo insignes præstantibus armis :*
> *Hic pietate prior . . .*

I give not here my translation of these verses, though
I think I have not ill succeeded in them, because your
Lordship is so great a master of the original, that
I have no reason to desire you should see Virgil and
me so near together ; but you may please, my Lord, to
take notice, that the Latin author refines upon the
Greek, and insinuates that Homer had done his hero
wrong in giving the advantage of the duel to his own
countryman ; though Diomedes was manifestly the
second champion of the Grecians ; and Ulysses preferred him before Ajax, when he chose him for the
companion of his nightly expedition ; for he had a
headpiece of his own, and wanted only the fortitude
of another, to bring him off with safety, and that he
might compass his design with honour.

The French translator thus proceeds : ' They, who
accuse Æneas for want of courage, either understand
not Virgil, or have read him slightly ; otherwise they
would not raise an objection so easily to be answered.'
Hereupon he gives so many instances of the hero's
valour, that to repeat them after him would tire your
Lordship, and put me to the unnecessary trouble of
transcribing the greatest part of the three last Æneids.

In short, more could not be expected from an Amadis, a Sir Lancelot, or the whole Round Table, than he performs. *Proxima quæque metit gladio*, is the perfect account of a knight-errant. ' If it be replied,' continues
5 Segrais, ' that it was not difficult for him to undertake and achieve such hardy enterprises, because he wore enchanted arms ; that accusation, in the first place, must fall on Homer, ere it can reach Virgil.' Achilles was as well provided with them as Æneas, though he
10 was invulnerable without them. And Ariosto, the two Tasso's, Bernardo and Torquato, even our own Spenser, in a word, all modern poets, have copied Homer as well as Virgil : he is neither the first nor last, but in the midst of them ; and therefore is safe, if they are so.
15 ' Who knows,' says Segrais, ' but that his fated armour was only an allegorical defence, and signified no more than that he was under the peculiar protection of the gods ?—born, as the astrologers will tell us out of Virgil (who was well versed in the Chaldean mysteries),
20 under the favourable influence of Jupiter, Venus, and the Sun.' But I insist not on this, because I know you believe' not there is such an art ; though not only Horace and Persius, but Augustus himself, thought otherwise. But, in defence of Virgil, I dare positively
25 say, that he has been more cautious in this particular than either his predecessor, or his descendants : for Æneas was actually wounded, in the Twelfth of the *Æneis ;* though he had the same God-smith to forge his arms as had Achilles. It seems he was no warluck, as
30 the Scots commonly call such men, who, they say, are iron-free, or lead-free. Yet, after this experiment, that his arms were not impenetrable, when he was cured indeed by his mother's help, because he was that day to conclude the war by the death of Turnus, the poet
35 durst not carry the miracle too far, and restore him

wholly to his former vigour : he was still too weak to
overtake his enemy ; yet we see with what courage he
attacks Turnus, when he faces and renews the combat.
I need say no more ; for Virgil defends himself without
needing my assistance, and proves his hero truly to 5
deserve that name. He was not then a second-rate
champion, as they would have him, who think fortitude
the first virtue in a hero. But, being beaten from this
hold, they will not yet allow him to be valiant, because
he wept more often, as they think, than well becomes 10
a man of courage.

In the first place, if tears are arguments of cowardice,
what shall I say of Homer's hero ? Shall Achilles
pass for timorous because he wept, and wept on less
occasions than Æneas ? Herein Virgil must be granted 15
to have excelled his master. For once both heroes are
described lamenting their lost loves : Briseis was taken
away by force from the Grecians ; Creusa was lost for
ever to her husband. But Achilles went roaring along
the salt sea-shore, and, like a booby, was complaining 20
to his mother, when he should have revenged his injury
by arms. Æneas took a nobler course ; for, having
secured his father and his son, he repeated all his
former dangers, to have found his wife, if she had been
above ground. And here your Lordship may observe 25
the address of Virgil ; it was not for nothing that this
passage was related with all these tender circumstances.
Æneas told it ; Dido heard it. That he had been so
affectionate a husband was no ill argument to the coming
dowager, that he might prove as kind to her. Virgil 30
has a thousand secret beauties, though I have not
leisure to remark them.

Segrais, on this subject of a hero shedding tears,
observes, that historians commend Alexander for weeping when he read the mighty actions of Achilles ; and 35

Julius Cæsar is likewise praised, when, out of the same
noble envy, he wept at the victories of Alexander. But,
if we observe more closely, we shall find that the tears
of Æneas were always on a laudable occasion. Thus
he weeps out of compassion and tenderness of nature,
when, in the temple of Carthage, he beholds the pictures
of his friends, who sacrificed their lives in defence of
their country. He deplores the lamentable end of his
pilot Palinurus, the untimely death of young Pallas
his confederate, and the rest, which I omit. Yet, even
for these tears, his wretched critic dare condemn
him. They make Æneas little better than a kind of
St. Swithin hero, always raining. One of these censors
is bold enough to argue him of cowardice, when, in the
beginning of the First Book, he not only weeps, but
trembles, at an approaching storm—

> *Extemplo Æneæ solvuntur frigore membra :*
> *Ingemit ; et duplices tendens ad sidera palmas*, &c.

But to. this I have answered formerly, that his fear
was not for himself, but for his people. And what can
give a sovereign a better commendation, or recommend
a hero more to the affection of the reader ? They were
threatened with a tempest, and he wept ; he was promised Italy, and therefore he prayed for the accomplishment of that promise. All this in the beginning
of a storm ; therefore he showed the more early piety,
and the quicker sense of compassion. Thus much
I have urged elsewhere in the defence of Virgil ; and,
since, I have been informed by Mr. Moyle, a young
gentleman whom I can never sufficiently commend, that
the Ancients accounted drowning an accursed death ;
so that, if we grant him to have been afraid, he had just
occasion for that fear, both in relation to himself and
to his subjects. I think our adversaries can carry this

argument no further, unless they tell us, that he ought
to have had more confidence in the promise of the gods ;
but how was he assured that he had understood their
oracles aright ?   Helenus might be mistaken ; Phœbus
might speak doubtfully ; even his mother might flatter 5
him, that he might prosecute his voyage, which if it
succeeded happily, he should be the founder of an
empire ; for, that she herself was doubtful of his fortune, is apparent by the address she made to Jupiter
on his behalf ; to which the god makes answer in these 10
words—

> *Parce metu, Cytherea : manent immota tuorum*
> *Fata tibi,* &c.—

notwithstanding which, the goddess, though comforted,
was not assured ; for, even after this, through the course 15
of the whole *Æneis*, she still apprehends the interest
which Juno might make with Jupiter against her son.
For it was a moot point in heaven, whether he could
alter Fate, or not.   And indeed some passages in Virgil
would make us suspect that he was of opinion Jupiter 20
might defer Fate, though he could not alter it ; for, in
the latter end of the Tenth Book, he introduces Juno
begging for the life of Turnus, and flattering her
husband with the power of changing destiny : *Tua,*
qui potes, orsa reflectas !   To which he graciously 25
answers—

> *Si mora præsentis leti, tempusque caduco*
> *Oratur juveni, meque hoc ita ponere sentis,*
> *Tolle fuga Turnum, atque instantibus eripe fatis.*
> *Hactenus indulsisse vacat. Sin altior istis*   30
> *Sub precibus venia ulla latet, totumque moveri*
> *Mutarive putas bellum, spes pascis inanes.*

But, that he could not alter those decrees, the king
of gods himself confesses, in the book above cited,
when he comforts Hercules for the death of Pallas, 35

who had invoked his aid, before he threw his lance
at Turnus—

> . . . *Trojæ sub mœnibus altis,*
> *Tot nati cecidere deum ; quin occidit una*
> 5 *Sarpedon, mea progenies. Etiam sua Turnum*
> *Fata manent, metasque dati pervenit ad œvi.*

Where he plainly acknowledges that he could not save
his own son, or prevent the death which he foresaw.
Of his power to defer the blow, I once occasionally
10 discoursed with that excellent person Sir Robert
Howard, who is better conversant, than any man that
I know, in the doctrine of the Stoics ; and he set me
right, from the concurrent testimony of philosophers
and poets, that Jupiter could not retard the effects of
15 Fate, even for a moment. For, when I cited Virgil,
as favouring the contrary opinion in that verse,

> *Tolle fuga Turnum, atque instantibus eripe fatis* . . .

he replied, and, I think, with exact judgment, that,
when Jupiter gave Juno leave to withdraw Turnus
20 from the present danger, it was because he certainly
foreknew that his fatal hour was not come ; that it was
in Destiny for Juno at that time to save him ; and that
he himself obeyed Destiny, in giving her that leave.

I need say no more in justification of our hero's
25 courage, and am much deceived if ever he be attacked
on this side of his character again. But he is arraigned
with more show of reason by the ladies, who will make
a numerous party against him, for being false to love,
in forsaking Dido. And I cannot much blame them ;
30 for, to say the truth, it is an ill precedent for their
gallants to follow. Yet, if I can bring him off with
flying colours, they may learn experience at her cost,
and, for her sake, avoid a cave, as the worst shelter
they can choose from a shower of rain, especially when
35 they have a lover in their company.

In the first place, Segrais observes with much acuteness, that they who blame Æneas for his insensibility of love when he left Carthage, contradict their former accusation of him, for being always crying, compassionate, and effeminately sensible of those misfortunes 5 which befell others. They give him two contrary characters ; but Virgil makes him of a piece, always grateful, always tender-hearted. But they are impudent enough to discharge themselves of this blunder, by laying the contradiction at Virgil's door. He, say they, 10 has shown his hero with these inconsistent characters, acknowledging and ungrateful, compassionate and hard-hearted, but, at the bottom, fickle and self-interested. For Dido had not only received his weather-beaten troops before she saw him, and given them her pro- 15 tection, but had also offered them an equal share in her dominion—

> *Vultis et his mecum pariter considere regnis ?*
> *Urbem quam statuo, vestra est.*

This was an obligement never to be forgotten ; and 20 the more to be considered, because antecedent to her love. That passion, 'tis true, produced the usual effects, of generosity, gallantry, and care to please ; and thither we refer them. But when she had made all these advances it was still in his power to have 25 refused them ; after the intrigue of the cave (call it marriage, or enjoyment only), he was no longer free to take or leave ; he had accepted the favour, and was obliged to be constant, if he would be grateful.

My Lord, I have set this argument in the best light 30 I can, that the ladies may not think I write booty ; and perhaps it may happen to me, as it did to Dr. Cudworth, who has raised such strong objections against the being of a God, and Providence, that many think he has not answered them. You may please at least 35

to hear the adverse party. Segrais pleads for Virgil,
that no less than an absolute command from Jupiter
could excuse this insensibility of the hero, and this
abrupt departure, which looks so like extreme ingrati-
5 tude. But, at the same time, he does wisely to remember you, that Virgil had made piety the first
character of Æneas ; and this being allowed, as I am
afraid it must, he was obliged, antecedent to all other
considerations, to search an asylum for his Gods in
10 Italy ; for those very Gods, I say, who had promised
to his race the universal empire. Could a pious man
dispense with the commands of Jupiter, to satisfy his
passion ? or take it in the strongest sense, to comply
with the obligations of his gratitude ? Religion, 'tis
15 true, must have moral honesty for its ground-work, or
we shall be apt to suspect its truth ; but an immediate
revelation dispenses with all duties of morality. All
casuists agree that theft is a breach of the moral law ;
yet, if I might presume to mingle things sacred with
20 profane, the Israelites only spoiled the Egyptians, not
robbed them ; because the propriety was transferred,
by a revelation to their law-giver. I confess Dido was
a very infidel in this point ; for she would not believe,
as Virgil makes her say, that ever Jupiter would send
25 Mercury on such an immoral errand. But this needs
no answer, at least no more than Virgil gives it :—

Fata obstant ; placidasque viri Deus obstruit aures.

This notwithstanding, as Segrais confesses, he might
have shown a little more sensibility when he left her ;
30 for that had been according to his character.

But let Virgil answer for himself. He still loved
her, and struggled with his inclinations to obey the
Gods—

... *Curam sub corde premebat,*
35   *Multa gemens, magnoque animum labefactus amore.*

Upon the whole matter, and humanly speaking, I doubt there was a fault somewhere ; and Jupiter is better able to bear the blame, than either Virgil or Æneas. The poet, it seems, had found it out, and therefore brings the deserting hero and the forsaken 5 lady to meet together in the lower regions, where he excuses himself when 'tis too late ; and accordingly she will take no satisfaction, nor so much as hear him. Now Segrais is forced to abandon his defence, and excuses his author by saying that the *Æneis* is an 10 imperfect work, and that death prevented the divine poet from reviewing it ; and for that reason he had condemned it to the fire ; though, at the same time, his two translators must acknowledge that the Sixth Book is the most correct of the whole *Æneis*. Oh, how 15 convenient is a machine sometimes in a heroic poem ! This of Mercury is plainly one ; and Virgil was constrained to use it here, or the honesty of his hero would be ill-defended. And the fair sex, however, if they had the deserter in their power, would certainly have shown 20 him no more mercy than the Bacchanals did Orpheus : for if too much constancy may be a fault sometimes, then want of constancy, and ingratitude after the last favour, is a crime that never will be forgiven. But, of machines, more in their proper place ; where I shall 25 show, with how much judgment they have been used by Virgil ; and, in the mean time, pass to another article of his defence, on the present subject ; where, if I cannot clear the hero, I hope at least to bring off the poet ; for here I must divide their causes. Let 30 Æneas trust to his machine, which will only help to break his fall ; but the address is incomparable. Plato, who borrowed so much from Homer, and yet concluded for the banishment of all poets, would at least have rewarded Virgil before he sent him into exile. But 35

I go further, and say, that he ought to be acquitted, and deserved, beside, the bounty of Augustus, and the gratitude of the Roman people. If, after this, the ladies will stand out, let them remember that the jury is not
5 all agreed ; for Octavia was of his party, and was of the first quality in Rome ; she was present at the reading of the Sixth Æneid : and we know not that she condemned Æneas ; but we are sure she presented the poet for his admirable elegy on her son Marcellus.
10 But let us consider the secret reasons which Virgil had for thus framing this noble episode, wherein the whole passion of love is more exactly described than in any other poet. Love was the theme of his Fourth Book ; and, though it is the shortest of the whole
15 *Æneis*, yet there he has given its beginning, its progress, its traverses, and its conclusion ; and had exhausted so entirely this subject, that he could resume it but very slightly in the eight ensuing books.

She was warmed with the graceful appearance of
20 the hero ; she smothered those sparkles out of decency ; but conversation blew them up into a flame. Then she was forced to make a confidant of her whom she best might trust, her own sister, who approves the passion, and thereby augments it ; then succeeds her public
25 owning it ; and, after that, the consummation. Of Venus and Juno, Jupiter and Mercury, I say nothing ; for they were all machining work ; but, possession having cooled his love, as it increased hers, she soon perceived the change, or at least grew suspicious of
30 a change ; this suspicion soon turned to jealousy, and jealousy to rage ; then she disdains and threatens, and again is humble, and entreats, and, nothing availing, despairs, curses, and at last becomes her own executioner. See here the whole process of that
35 passion, to which nothing can be added. I dare go

no further, lest I should lose the connexion of my discourse.

To love our native country, and to study its benefit and its glory, to be interested in its concerns, is natural to all men, and is indeed our common duty. A poet 5 makes a further step ; for endeavouring to do honour to it, 'tis allowable in him even to be partial in its cause ; for he is not tied to truth, or fettered by the laws of history. Homer and Tasso are justly praised for choosing their heroes out of Greece and Italy ; 10 Virgil indeed made his a Trojan ; but it was to derive the Romans and his own Augustus from him. But all the three poets are manifestly partial to their heroes, in favour of their country ; for Dares Phrygius reports of Hector that he was slain cowardly ; Æneas, according 15 to the best account, slew not Mezentius, but was slain by him ; and the chronicles of Italy tell us little of that Rinaldo d'Este who conquers Jerusalem in Tasso. He might be a champion of the Church ; but we know not that he was so much as present at the siege. To 20 apply this to Virgil, he thought himself engaged in honour to espouse the cause and quarrel of his country against Carthage. He knew he could not please the Romans better, or oblige them more to patronize his poem, than by disgracing the foundress of that city. 25 He shows her ungrateful to the memory of her first husband, doting on a stranger ; enjoyed, and afterwards forsaken, by him. This was the original, says he, of the immortal hatred betwixt the two rival nations. 'Tis true, he colours the falsehood of Æneas by an 30 express command from Jupiter, to forsake the queen who had obliged him ; but he knew the Romans were to be his readers ; and them he bribed, perhaps at the expense of his hero's honesty ; but he gained his cause, however, as pleading before corrupt judges. They 35

were content to see their founder false to love ; for
still he had the advantage of the amour ; it was their
enemy whom he forsook ; and she might have forsaken
him, if he had not got the start of her ; she had already
5 forgotten her vows to her Sichæus ; and *varium et
mutabile semper femina* is the sharpest satire, in the
fewest words, that ever was made on womankind ; for
both the adjectives are neuter, and *animal* must be
understood, to make them grammar.   Virgil does well
10 to put those words into the mouth of Mercury.   *If
a God had not spoken them, neither durst he have
written them, nor I translated them.*   Yet the deity
was forced to come twice on the same errand ; and the
second time, as much a hero as Æneas was, he frighted
15 him.   It seems he feared not Jupiter so much as Dido ;
for your Lordship may observe that, as much intent as
he was upon his voyage, yet he still delayed it, till the
messenger was obliged to tell him plainly, that, if he
weighed not anchor in the night, the queen would be
20 with him in the morning.   *Notumque furens quid femina
possit ;* she was injured ; she was revengeful ; she was
powerful.   The poet had likewise before hinted that her
people were naturally perfidious ; for he gives their
character in their queen, and makes a proverb of *Punica*
25 *fides*, many ages before it was invented.

Thus, I hope, my Lord, that I have made good my
promise, and justified the poet, whatever becomes of
the false knight.   And sure a poet is as much privileged
to lie as an ambassador, for the honour and interest
30 of his country ; at least as Sir Henry Wotton has
defined.

This naturally leads me to the defence of the famous
anachronism, in making Æneas and Dido contemporaries ; for it is certain that the hero lived almost
35 two hundred years before the building of Carthage.

One who imitates Boccalini says that Virgil was accused
before Apollo for this error. The God soon found that
he was not able to defend his favourite by reason ; for the
case was clear : he therefore gave this middle sentence,
that anything might be allowed to his son Virgil, on the 5
account of his other merits ; that, being a monarch, he
had a dispensing power, and pardoned him. But, that
this special act of grace might never be drawn into
example, or pleaded by his puny successors in justification of their ignorance, he decreed for the future, no 10
poet should presume to make a lady die for love two
hundred years before her birth. To moralize this
story, Virgil is the Apollo who has this dispensing
power. His great judgment made the laws of poetry ;
but he never made himself a slave to them ; chronology, 15
at best, is but a cobweb-law, and he broke through it
with his weight. They who will imitate him wisely,
must choose, as he did, an obscure and a remote era,
where they may invent at pleasure, and not be easily
contradicted. Neither he, nor the Romans, had ever 20
read the Bible, by which only his false computation of
times can be made out against him. This Segrais says
in his defence, and proves it from his learned friend
Bochartus, whose letter on this subject he has printed
at the end of the Fourth Æneid, to which I refer your 25
Lordship and the reader. Yet the credit of Virgil was
so great, that he made this fable of his own invention
pass for an authentic history, or at least as credible as
anything in Homer. Ovid takes it up after him, even
in the same age, and makes an ancient heroine of 30
Virgil's new-created Dido ; dictates a letter for her,
just before her death, to the ungrateful fugitive ; and,
very unluckily for himself, is for measuring a sword
with a man so much superior in force to him, on the
same subject. I think I maybe judge of this, because 35

I have translated both. The famous author of the *Art
of Love* has nothing of his own ; he borrows all from
a greater master in his own profession ; and, which is
worse, improves nothing which he finds. Nature fails
5 him ; and, being forced to his old shift, he has recourse
to witticism. This passes indeed with his soft admirers,
and gives him the preference to Virgil in their esteem.
But let them like for themselves, and not prescribe to
others : for our author needs not their admiration.
10   The motives that induced Virgil to coin this fable,
I have shewed already ; and have also begun to show
that he might make this anachronism, by superseding
the mechanic rules of poetry, for the same reason
that a monarch may dispense with or suspend his own
15 laws, when he finds it necessary so to do, especially if
those laws are not altogether fundamental. Nothing is
to be called a fault in poetry, says Aristotle, but what
is against the art ; therefore a man may be an admirable
poet without being an exact chronologer. Shall we
20 dare, continues Segrais, to condemn Virgil for having
made a fiction against the order of time, when we commend Ovid and other poets, who have made many of
their fictions against the order of Nature ? For what else
are the splendid miracles of the *Metamorphoses* ? Yet
25 these are beautiful as they are related, and have also
deep learning and instructive mythologies couched
under them : but to give, as Virgil does in this episode,
the original cause of the long wars betwixt Rome and
Carthage, to draw truth out of fiction after so probable
30 a manner, with so much beauty, and so much for the
honour of his country, was proper only to the divine wit
of Maro ; and Tasso, in one of his *Discourses*, admires
him for this particularly. 'Tis not lawful, indeed, to
contradict a point of history which is known to all the
35 world, as, for example, to make Hannibal and Scipio

contemporaries with Alexander ; but, in the dark recesses of antiquity, a great poet may and ought to feign
such things as he finds not there, if they can be brought
to embellish that subject which he treats. On the other
side, the pains and diligence of ill poets is but thrown 5
away, when they want the genius to invent and feign
agreeably. But, if the fictions be delightful (which they
always are, if they be natural), if they be of a piece ; if
the beginning, the middle, and the end be in their due
places, and artfully united to each other, such works 10
can never fail of their deserved success. And such is
Virgil's episode of Dido and Æneas ; where the sourest
critic must acknowledge that if he had deprived his
Æneis of so great an ornament, because he found no
traces of it in antiquity, he had avoided their unjust 15
censure, but had wanted one of the greatest beauties of
his poem. I shall say more of this in the next article
of their charge against him, which is want of invention.
In the meantime, I may affirm, in honour of this episode,
that it is not only now esteemed the most pleasing 20
entertainment of the *Æneis*, but was so accounted in
his own age, and before it was mellowed into that reputation which time has given it ; for which I need
produce no other testimony than that of Ovid, his
contemporary :   25

> *Nec pars ulla magis legitur de corpore toto,*
> *Quam non legitimo fœdere junctus amor.*

Where, by the way, you may observe, my Lord, that
Ovid, in those words, *Non legitimo fœdere junctus amor,*
will by no means allow it to be a lawful marriage 30
betwixt Dido and Æneas. He was in banishment
when he wrote those verses, which I cite from his letter
to Augustus : ' You, Sir,' says he, ' have sent me into
exile for writing my *Art of Love,* and my wanton
Elegies ; yet your own poet was happy in your good 35

graces, though he brought Dido and Æneas into a cave,
and left them there not over honestly together. May
I be so bold to ask your Majesty, is it a greater fault
to teach the art of unlawful love, than to show it in the
5 action ? ' But was Ovid, the court-poet, so bad a courtier as to find no other plea to excuse himself than by
a plain accusation of his master ? Virgil confessed it
was a lawful marriage betwixt the lovers, that Juno, the
Goddess of Matrimony, had ratified it by her presence ;
10 for it was her business to bring matters to that issue.
That the ceremonies were short, we may believe ; for
Dido was not only amorous, but a widow. Mercury
himself, though employed on a quite contrary errand, yet
owns it a marriage by an *innuendo : pulchramque uxo-*
15 *rius urbem Exstruis.* He calls Æneas not only a husband, but upbraids him for being a fond husband, as
the word *uxorius* implies. Now mark a little, if your
Lordship pleases, why Virgil is so much concerned to
make this marriage (for he seems to be the father of the
20 bride himself, and to give her to the bridegroom) : it
was to make way for the divorce which he intended
afterwards ; for he was a finer flatterer than Ovid ; and
I more than conjecture that he had in his eye the
divorce which not long before had passed betwixt the
25 Emperor and Scribonia. He drew this dimple in the
cheek of Æneas, to prove Augustus of the same family
by so remarkable a feature in the same place. Thus,
as we say in our homespun English proverb, he killed
two birds with one stone ; pleased the Emperor, by
30 giving him the resemblance of his ancestor, and gave
him such a resemblance as was not scandalous in that
age. For, to leave one wife, and take another, was but
a matter of gallantry at that time of day among the
Romans. *Neque hæc in fœdera veni* is the very excuse
35 which Æneas makes, when he leaves his lady : ' I made

no such bargain with you at our marriage, to live
always drudging on at Carthage : my business was
Italy ; and I never made a secret of it. If I took my
pleasure, had not you your share of it ? I leave you
free, at my departure, to comfort yourself with the next 5
stranger who happens to be shipwrecked on your coast.
Be as kind a hostess as you have been to me ; and you
can never fail of another husband. In the meantime,
I call the Gods to witness, that I leave your shore
unwillingly ; for, though Juno made the marriage, yet 10
Jupiter commands me to forsake you.' This is the
effect of what he saith, when it is dishonoured out of
Latin verse into English prose. If the poet argued not
aright, we must pardon him for a poor blind heathen,
who knew no better morals.   15

I have detained your Lordship longer than I intended
on this objection ; which would indeed weigh something
in a spiritual court, but I am not to defend our poet
there. The next, I think, is but a cavil, though the
cry is great against him, and hath continued from the 20
time of Macrobius to this present age. I hinted it
before. They lay no less than want of invention to
his charge—a capital crime, I must acknowledge ; for
a poet is a maker, as the word signifies ; and he who
cannot make, that is, invent, has his name for nothing. 25
That which makes this accusation look so strange at the
first sight, is, that he has borrowed so many things from
Homer, Apollonius Rhodius, and others who preceded
him. But, in the first place, if invention is to be taken
in so strict a sense that the matter of a poem must be 30
wholly new, and that in all its parts, then Scaliger has
made out, says Segrais, that the history of Troy was
no more the invention of Homer than of Virgil. There
was not an old woman, or almost a child, but had it in
their mouths, before the Greek poet or his friends 35

digested it into this admirable order in which we read
it. At this rate, as Solomon hath told us, there is
nothing new beneath the sun. Who then can pass
for an inventor, if Homer, as well as Virgil, must be
5 deprived of that glory ? Is Versailles the less a new
building, because the architect of that palace hath imitated others which were built before it ? Walls, doors,
and windows, apartments, offices, rooms of convenience
and magnificence, are in all great houses. So descrip-
10 tions, figures, fables, and the rest, must be in all heroic
poems ; they are the common materials of poetry,
furnished from the magazine of nature ; every poet
hath as much right to them, as every man hath to air
or water.

15   *Quid prohibetis aquas ? Usus communis aquarum est.*

But the argument of the work, that is to say, its principal action, the œconomy and disposition of it ; these
are the things which distinguish copies from originals.
The poet who borrows nothing from others is yet to be
20 born ; he and the Jews' Messias will come together.
There are parts of the *Æneis* which resemble some
parts both of the *Ilias* and of the *Odysseis ;* as, for
example, Æneas descended into Hell, and Ulysses
had been there before him ; Æneas loved Dido, and
25 Ulysses loved Calypso ; in few words, Virgil hath
imitated Homer's *Odysseis* in his first six books, and,,
in his six last, the *Ilias*. But from hence can we infer
that the two poets write the same history ? Is there no
invention in some other parts of Virgil's *Æneis ?* The
30 disposition of so many various matters, is not that his
own ? From what book of Homer had Virgil his episode
of Nisus and Euryalus, of Mezentius and Lausus ?
From whence did he borrow his design of bringing
Æneas into Italy ? of establishing the Roman Empire
35 on the foundations of a Trojan colony ? to say nothing

of the honour he did his patron, not only in his descent
from Venus, but in making him so like her in his best
features,that the Goddess might have mistaken Augustus
for her son. He had indeed the story from common
fame, as Homer had his from the Egyptian priestess. 5
Æneadum genetrix was no more unknown to Lucretius
than to him. But Lucretius taught him not to form his
hero, to give him piety or valour for his manners, and
both in so eminent a degree, that, having done what was
possible for man to save his king and country, his mother 10
was forced to appear to him, and restrain his fury, which
hurried him to death in their revenge. But the poet
made his piety more successful ; he brought off his
father and his son ; and his Gods witnessed to his devotion, by putting themselves under his protection, to 15
be replaced by him in their promised Italy. Neither
the invention nor the conduct of this great action were
owing to Homer, or any other poet. 'Tis one thing to
copy, and another thing to imitate from Nature. The
copier is that servile imitator, to whom Horace gives 20
no better a name than that of animal ; he will not so
much as allow him to be a man. Raphael imitated
Nature ; they who copy one of Raphael's pieces imitate
but him ; for his work is their original. They translate
him, as I do Virgil ; and fall as short of him, as I of 25
Virgil. There is a kind of invention in the imitation
of Raphael ; for, though the thing was in Nature, yet
the idea of it was his own. Ulysses travelled ; so did
Æneas : but neither of them were the first travellers ;
for Cain went into the land of Nod before they were 30
born : and neither of the poets ever heard of such
a man. If Ulysses had been killed at Troy, yet Æneas
must have gone to sea, or he could never have arrived
in Italy. But the designs of the two poets were as
different as the courses of their heroes ; one went home, 35

and the other sought a home. To return to my first
similitude : suppose Apelles and Raphael had each of
them painted a burning Troy, might not the modern
painter have succeeded as well as the ancient, though
5 neither of them had seen the town on fire ? For the
draughts of both were taken from the ideas which they
had of Nature. Cities had been burnt before either of
them were in being. But, to close the simile as I begun
it ; they would not have designed after the same manner.
10 Apelles would have distinguished Pyrrhus from the rest
of all the Grecians, and shewed him forcing his entrance
into Priam's palace ; there he had set him in the fairest
light, and given him the chief place of all his figures ;
because he was a Grecian, and he would do honour to
15 his country. Raphael,who was an Italian, and descended
from the Trojans, would have made Æneas the hero of
his piece ; and perhaps not with his father on his back,
his son in one hand, his bundle of gods in the other,
and his wife following (for an act of piety is not half so
20 graceful in a picture as an act of courage) : he would
rather have drawn him killing Androgeos, or some
other, hand to hand ; and the blaze of the fires should
have darted full upon his face, to make him conspicuous
amongst his Trojans. This, I think, is a just comparison
25 betwixt the two poets, in the conduct of their several
designs. Virgil cannot be said to copy Homer ; the
Grecian had only the advantage of writing first. If it
be urged, that I have granted a resemblance in some
parts, yet therein Virgil has excelled him. For what
30 are the tears of Calypso for being left, to the fury and
death of Dido ? Where is there the whole process of
her passion and all its violent effects to be found, in the
languishing episode of the *Odysseis ?* If this be to
copy, let the critics shew us the same disposition,
35 features, or colouring, in their original. The like may

be said of the Descent to Hell, which was not of
Homer's invention neither ; he had it from the story
of Orpheus and Eurydice.   But to what end did
Ulysses make that journey ?   Æneas undertook it by
the express commandment of his father's ghost ; there 5
he was to show him all the succeeding heroes of his
race, and, next to Romulus (mark, if you please, the
address of Virgil), his own patron, Augustus Cæsar.
Anchises was likewise to instruct him how to manage
the Italian war, and how to conclude it with his honour ; 10
that is, in other words, to lay the foundations of that
Empire which Augustus was to govern.   This is the
noble invention of our author ; but it has been copied
by so many sign-post daubers, that now 'tis grown
fulsome, rather by their want of skill, than by the 15
commonness.

In the last place, I may safely grant that, by reading
Homer, Virgil was taught to imitate his invention ;
that is, to imitate like him ; which is no more than if
a painter studied Raphael, that he might learn to 20
design after his manner.   And thus I might imitate
Virgil, if I were capable of writing an heroic poem,
and yet the invention be my own : but I should endeavour to avoid a servile copying.   I would not give
the same story under other names, with the same char- 25
acters, in the same order, and with the same sequel ;
for every common reader to find me out at the first
sight for a plagiary, and cry : ' This I read before in
Virgil, in a better language, and in better verse : this
is like Merry Andrew on the low rope, copying lubberly 30
the same tricks which his master is so dexterously performing on the high.'

I will trouble your Lordship but with one objection
more, which I know not whether I found in Le Fèvre,
or Valois ; but I am sure I have read it in another 35

French critic, whom I will not name, because I think
it is not much for his reputation. Virgil, in the heat
of action—suppose, for example, in describing the fury
of his hero in a battle, when he is endeavouring to raise
5 our concernments to the highest pitch—turns short on
the sudden into some similitude, which diverts, say
they, your attention from the main subject, and mis-
spends it on some trivial image. He pours cold water
into the caldron, when his business is to make it boil.

10   This accusation is general against all who would be
thought heroic poets ; but I think it touches Virgil less
than any. He is too great a master of his art, to make
a blot which may so easily be hit. Similitudes, as I have
said, are not for tragedy, which is all violent, and where
15 the passions are in a perpetual ferment ; for there they
deaden where they should animate ; they are not of the
nature of dialogue, unless in comedy : a metaphor is
almost all the stage can suffer, which is a kind of similitude comprehended in a word. But this figure has
20 a contrary effect in heroic poetry ; there it is employed
to raise the admiration, which is its proper business ;
and admiration is not of so violent a nature as fear or
hope, compassion or horror, or any concernment we can
have for such or such a person on the stage. Not but
25 I confess that similitudes and descriptions, when drawn
into an unreasonable length, must needs nauseate the
reader. Once, I remember, and but once, Virgil makes
a similitude of fourteen lines ; and his description of
Fame is about the same number. He is blamed for
30 both ; and I doubt not but he would have contracted
them, had he lived to have reviewed his work ; but
faults are no precedents. This I have observed of his
similitudes in general, that they are not placed, as our
unobserving critics tell us, in the heat of any action,
35 but commonly in its declining. When he has warmed

us in his description as much as possibly he can, then,
lest that warmth should languish, he renews it by some
apt similitude, which illustrates his subject, and yet palls
not his audience.   I need give your Lordship but one
example of this kind, and leave the rest to your obser- 5
vation, when next you review the whole *Æneis* in the
original, unblemished by my rude translation.   'Tis in
the First Book, where the poet describes Neptune com-
posing the ocean, on which Æolus had raised a tempest
without his permission.   He had already chidden the 10
rebellious winds for obeying the commands of their
usurping master ; he had warned them from the seas ;
he had beaten down the billows with his mace, dispelled
the clouds, restored the sunshine, while Triton and
Cymothoë were heaving the ships from off the quick- 15
sands, before the poet would offer at a similitude for
illustration :—

> *Ac, veluti magno in populo cum sæpe coorta est*
> *Seditio, sævitque animis ignobile vulgus,*
> *Jamque faces et saxa volant ; furor arma ministrat ;*   20
> *Tum, pietate gravem ac meritis si forte virum quem*
> *Conspexere, silent, arrectisque auribus adstant ;*
> *Ille regit dictis animos, et pectora mulcet ;*
> *Sic cunctus pelagi cecidit fragor, æquora postquam*
> *Prospiciens genitor, cæloque invectus aperto,*   25
> *Flectit equos, curruque volans dat lora secundo.*

This is the first similitude which Virgil makes in this
poem, and one of the longest in the whole ; for which
reason I the rather cite it.   While the storm was in its
fury, any allusion had been improper ; for the poet 30
could have compared it to nothing more impetuous
than itself ; consequently he could have made no illustration.   If he could have illustrated, it had been an
ambitious ornament out of season, and would have
diverted our concernment : *nunc non erat hisce locus ;* 35
and therefore he deferred it to its proper place.

These are the criticisms of most moment which have
been made against the *Æneis* by the Ancients or
Moderns. As for the particular exceptions against
this or that passage, Macrobius and Pontanus have
5 answered them already. If I desired to appear more
learned than I am, it had been as easy for me to have
taken their objections and solutions, as it is for a country
parson to take the expositions of the fathers out of
Junius and Tremellius, or not to have named the
10 authors from whence I had them ; for so Ruæus, otherwise a most judicious commentator on Virgil's works,
has used Pontanus, his greatest benefactor ; of whom
he is very silent ; and I do not remember that he once
cites him.

15   What follows next is no objection ; for that implies
a fault : and it had been none in Virgil, if he had
extended the time of his action beyond a year. At
least Aristotle has set no precise limits to it. Homer's,
we know, was within two months : Tasso, I am sure,
20 exceeds not a summer ; and, if I examined him, perhaps
he might be reduced into a much less compass. Bossu
leaves it doubtful whether Virgil's action were within
the year, or took up some months beyond it. Indeed,
the whole dispute is of no more concernment to the
25 common reader, than it is to a ploughman, whether
February this year had 28 or 29 days in it. But, for
the satisfaction of the more curious (of which number
I am sure your Lordship is one), I will translate what
I think convenient out of Segrais, whom perhaps you
30 have not read ; for he has made it highly probable
that the action of the *Æneis* began in the spring,
and was not extended beyond the autumn. And we
have known campaigns that have begun sooner, and
have ended later.

35   Ronsard, and the rest whom Segrais names, who are

of opinion that the action of this poem takes up almost
a year and half, ground their calculation thus. Anchises
died in Sicily at the end of winter, or beginning of the
spring. Æneas, immediately after the interment of his
father, puts to sea for Italy. He is surprised by the 5
tempest described in the beginning of the First Book ;
and there it is that the scene of the poem opens, and
where the action must commence. He is driven by
this storm on the coasts of Afric ; he stays at Carthage
all that summer, and almost all the winter following, sets 10
sail again for Italy just before the beginning of the
spring, meets with contrary winds, and makes Sicily
the second time. This part of the action completes the
year. Then he celebrates the anniversary of his father's
funerals, and shortly after arrives at Cumes ; and from 15
thence his time is taken up in his first treaty with
Latinus, the overture of the war, the siege of his camp
by Turnus, his going for succours to relieve it, his
return, the raising of the siege by the first battle, the
twelve days' truce, the second battle, the assault of 20
Laurentum, and the single fight with Turnus ; all which,
they say, cannot take up less than four or five months
more ; by which account we cannot suppose the entire
action to be contained in a much less compass than a year
and half.   25

Segrais reckons another way ; and his computation
is not condemned by the learned Ruæus, who compiled
and published the commentaries on our poet which we
call the *Dauphin's Virgil*.

He allows the time of year when Anchises died to be 30
in the latter end of winter, or the beginning of the
spring : he acknowledges that, when Æneas is first
seen at sea afterwards, and is driven by the tempest on
the coast of Afric, is the time when the action is naturally
to begin : he confesses, further, that Æneas left Carthage 35

in the latter end of winter ; for Dido tells him in express
terms, as an argument for his longer stay,

Quinetiam hiberno moliris sidere classem.

But, whereas Ronsard's followers suppose that, when
5 Æneas had buried his father, he set sail immediately for
Italy (though the tempest drove him on the coast of
Carthage), Segrais will by no means allow that supposition, but thinks it much more probable that he remained
in Sicily till the midst of July, or the beginning of
10 August ; at which time he places the first appearance
of his hero on the sea ; and there opens the action of
the poem.   From which beginning, to the death of
Turnus, which concludes the action, there need not be
supposed above ten months of intermediate time : for,
15 arriving at Carthage in the latter end of summer, staying
there the winter following, departing thence in the very
beginning of the spring, making a short abode in Sicily
the second time, landing in Italy, and making the war,
may be reasonably judged the business but of ten [1]
20 months.   To this the Ronsardians reply, that, having
been for seven years before in quest of Italy, and having
no more to do in Sicily than to inter his father—after
that office was performed, what remained for him, but,
without delay, to pursue his first adventure ?   To
25 which Segrais answers, that the obsequies of his
father, according to the rites of the Greeks and
Romans, would detain him for many days ; that a
longer time must be taken up in the refitting of his
ships after so tedious a voyage, and in refreshing his
30 weather-beaten soldiers on a friendly coast.   These
indeed are but suppositions on both sides ; yet those
of Segrais seem better grounded : for the feast of Dido,
when she entertained Æneas first, has the appearance

---

[1] ' three,' ed. 1697.

of a summer's night, which seems already almost ended
when he begins his story ; therefore the love was made
in autumn : the hunting followed properly when the
heats of that scorching country were declining ; the
winter was passed in jollity, as the season and their 5
love required ; and he left her in the latter end of
winter, as is already proved. This opinion is fortified
by the arrival of Æneas at the mouth of Tiber ; which
marks the season of the spring ; that season being
perfectly described by the singing of the birds saluting 10
the dawn, and by the beauty of the place, which
the poet seems to have painted expressly in the
Seventh Æneid—

> *Aurora in roseis fulgebat lutea bigis,*
> *Cum venti posuere. . . .* 15
> *. . . Variæ, circumque supraque,*
> *Assuetæ ripis volucres, et fluminis alveo,*
> *Æthera mulcebant cantu. . . .*

The remainder of the action required but three
months more : for, when Æneas went for succour to the 20
Tuscans, he found their army in a readiness to march,
and wanting only a commander : so that, according to
this calculation, the *Æneis* takes not up above a year
complete, and may be comprehended in less compass.

This, amongst other circumstances treated more at 25
large by Segrais, agrees with the rising of Orion, which
caused the tempest described in the beginning of the
First Book. By some passages in the *Pastorals*, but
more particularly in the *Georgics*, our poet is found
to be an exact astronomer, according to the know- 30
ledge of that age. Now Ilioneus (whom Virgil twice
employs in embassies, as the best speaker of the
Trojans) attributes that tempest to Orion, in his speech
to Dido—

> *Cum, subito assurgens fluctu, nimbosus Orion.—* 35

He must mean either the heliacal or achronical rising
of that sign. The heliacal rising of a constellation is
when it comes from under the rays of the sun, and
begins to appear before daylight ; the achronical rising,
5 on the contrary, is when it appears at the close of day,
and in opposition to the sun's diurnal course.

The heliacal rising of Orion is at present computed
to be about the sixth of July ; and about that time
it is that he either causes or presages tempests on
10 the seas.

Segrais has observed further, that,when Anna counsels
Dido to stay Æneas during the winter, she speaks also
of Orion—

Dum pelago desævit hiems, et aquosus Orion.

15 If therefore Ilioneus, according to our supposition,
understand the heliacal rising of Orion, Anna must
mean the achronical, which the different epithets given
to that constellation seem to manifest. Ilioneus calls
him *nimbosus ;* Anna, *aquosus.* He is tempestuous in
20 the summer, when he rises heliacally, and rainy in the
winter, when he rises achronically. Your Lordship
will pardon me for the frequent repetition of these cant
words, which I could not avoid in this abbreviation of
Segrais, who, I think, deserves no little commendation
25 in this new criticism.

I have yet a word or two to say of Virgil's machines,
from my own observation of them. He has imitated
those of Homer, but not copied them. It was established, long before this time, in the Roman religion
30 as well as in the Greek, that there were Gods ; and
both nations, for the most part, worshipped the same
Deities ; as did also the Trojans, from whom the
Romans, I suppose, would rather be thought to derive
the rites of their religion, than from the Grecians ;
35 because they thought themselves descended from them.

Each of those Gods had his proper office, and the
chief of them their particular attendants. Thus
Jupiter had in propriety Ganymede and Mercury, and
Juno had Iris. It was not then for Virgil to create
new ministers : he must take what he found in his 5
religion. It cannot therefore be said, that he borrowed
them from Homer, any more than Apollo, Diana, and
the rest, whom he uses as he finds occasion for them,
as the Grecian poet did ; but he invents the occasions
for which he uses them. Venus, after the destruction 10
of Troy, had gained Neptune entirely to her party ;
therefore we find him busy in the beginning of the
Æneis, to calm the tempest raised by Æolus, and
afterwards conducting the Trojan fleet to Cumes in
safety, with the loss only of their pilot, for whom he 15
bargains. I name those two examples amongst a hundred which I omit ; to prove that Virgil, generally
speaking, employed his machines in performing those
things which might possibly have been done without
them. What more frequent than a storm at sea, upon 20
the rising of Orion ? What wonder, if, amongst so
many ships, there should one be overset, which was
commanded by Orontes, though half the winds had
not been there which Æolus employed ? Might not
Palinurus, without a miracle, fall asleep, and drop into 25
the sea, having been over-wearied with watching, and
secure of a quiet passage, by his observation of the
skies ? At least Æneas, who knew nothing of the
machine of Somnus, takes it plainly in this sense—

> *O nimium cælo et pelago confise sereno,* 30
> *Nudus in ignota, Palinure, jacebis arena.*

But machines sometimes are specious things to amuse
the reader, and give a colour of probability to things
otherwise incredible. And besides it soothed the
vanity of the Romans, to find the Gods so visibly 35

concerned in all the actions of their predecessors.
We, who are better taught by our religion, yet own
every wonderful accident, which befalls us for the best,
to be brought to pass by some special providence of
5 Almighty God, and by the care of guardian Angels :
and from hence I might infer, that no heroic poem can
be writ on the Epicurean principles. Which I could
easily demonstrate, if there were need to prove it, or
I had leisure.

10　When Venus opens the eyes of her son Æneas,
to behold the Gods who combated against Troy in
that fatal night when it was surprised, we share the
pleasure of that glorious vision (which Tasso has not
ill copied in the sacking of Jerusalem) : but the Greeks
15 had done their business, though neither Neptune, Juno,
nor Pallas had given them their divine assistance. The
most crude machine which Virgil uses is in the episode
of Camilla, where Opis, by the command of her mistress,
kills Aruns. The next is in the Twelfth Æneid, where
20 Venus cures her son Æneas. But in the last of these
the poet was driven to a necessity ; for Turnus was to
be slain that very day ; and Æneas, wounded as he was,
could not have engaged him in single combat, unless
his hurt had been miraculously healed. And the poet
25 had considered that the dittany which she brought
from Crete could not have wrought so speedy an
effect without the juice of ambrosia which she
mingled with it. After all, that his machine might
not seem too violent, we see the hero limping after
30 Turnus. The wound was skinned ; but the strength
of his thigh was not restored. But what reason had
our author to wound Æneas at so critical a time ?
and how came the cuisses to be worse tempered than
the rest of his armour, which was all wrought by Vulcan
35 and his journeymen ? These difficulties are not easily

to be solved without confessing that Virgil had not life
enough to correct his work ; though he had reviewed
it, and found those errors, which he resolved to mend :
but, being prevented by death, and not willing to leave
an imperfect work behind him, he ordained, by his last 5
testament, that his *Æneis* should be burned. As for
the death of Aruns, who was shot by a goddess, the
machine was not altogether so outrageous as the
wounding Mars and Venus by the sword of Diomede.
Two divinities, one would have thought, might have 10
pleaded their prerogative of impassibility, or at least
not to have been wounded by any mortal hand ; beside
that the ἰχώρ, which they shed, was so very like our
common blood, that it was not to be distinguished
from it, but only by the name and colour. As for 15
what Horace says in his *Art of Poetry*, that no
machines are to be used, unless on some extraordinary occasion,

Nec deus intersit, nisi dignus vindice nodus—

that rule is to be applied to the theatre, of which he 20
is then speaking ; and means no more than this, that,
when the knot of the play is to be untied, and no
other way is left for making the discovery ; then, and
not otherwise, let a God descend upon a rope, and
clear the business to the audience : but this has no re- 25
lation to the machines which are used in an epic poem.

In the last place, for the *Dira*, or flying pest, which,
flapping on the shield of Turnus, and fluttering about
his head, disheartened him in the duel, and presaged
to him his approaching death, I might have placed 30
it more properly amongst the objections : for the
critics, who lay want of courage to the charge of
Virgil's hero, quote this passage as a main proof
of their assertion. They say our author had not only

secured him before the duel, but also, in the beginning
of it, had given him the advantage in impenetrable
arms, and in his sword ; for that of Turnus was not his
own, which was forged by Vulcan for his father, but a
5 weapon which he had snatched in haste, and by mistake, belonging to his charioteer Metiscus ; that, after
all this, Jupiter, who was partial to the Trojan, and
distrustful of the event, though he had hung the
balance, and given it a jog of his hand to weigh down
10 Turnus, thought convenient to give the Fates a col-
lateral security, by sending the screech-owl to discourage
him.   For which they quote these words of Virgil,

> . . . *Non me tua turbida virtus*
> *Terret, ait : di me terrent, et Jupiter hostis.*

15 In answer to which, I say, that this machine is one of
those which the poet uses only for ornament, and not
out of necessity.   Nothing can be more beautiful or
more poetical than his description of the three *Diræ*,
or the setting of the balance, which our Milton has
20 borrowed from him, but employed to a different end :
for, first, he makes God Almighty set the scales for
St. Michael and Satan, when he knew no combat was
to follow ;   then he makes the good angel's scale
descend, and the Devil's mount, quite contrary to
25 Virgil, if I have translated the three verses according
to my author's sense—

> *Jupiter ipse duas æquato examine lances*
> *Sustinet ; et fata imponit diversa duorum ;*
> *Quem damnet labor, et quo vergat pondere letum—*

30 for I have taken these words, *quem damnet labor,* in the
sense which Virgil gives them in another place,—
damnabis tu quoque votis,—to signify a prosperous event.
Yet I dare not condemn so great a genius as Milton :
for I am much mistaken if he alludes not to the text

in Daniel, where Belshazzar was put into the balance
and found too light. This is digression ; and I return
to my subject. I said above, that these two machines
of the balance and the *Dira* were only ornamental, and
that the success of the duel had been the same without 5
them : for, when Æneas and Turnus stood fronting
each other before the altar, Turnus looked dejected,
and his colour faded in his face, as if he desponded
of the victory before the fight ; and not only he, but all
his party, when the strength of the two champions was 10
judged by the proportion of their limbs, concluded it
was *impar pugna*, and that their chief was over-matched :
whereupon Juturna (who was of the same opinion) took
this opportunity to break the treaty and renew the war.
Juno herself had plainly told the nymph before-hand 15
that her brother was to fight

Imparibus fatis, nec dis nec viribus æquis ;

so that there was no need of an apparition to fright
Turnus : he had the presage within himself of his
impending destiny. The *Dira* only served to confirm 20
him in his first opinion, that it was his destiny to die
in the ensuing combat ; and in this sense are those
words of Virgil's to be taken,

. . . Non me tua turbida virtus
Terret, ait : di me terrent, et Jupiter hostis. 25

I doubt not but the adverb *solum* is to be understood ;
' 'Tis not your valour only that gives me this concernment ; but I find also, by this portent, that Jupiter is
my enemy.' For Turnus fled before, when his first
sword was broken, till his sister supplied him with a 30
better ; which indeed he could not use, because Æneas
kept him at a distance with his spear. I wonder Ruæus
saw not this, where he charges his author so unjustly,
for giving Turnus a second sword to no purpose. How

could he fasten a blow, or make a thrust, when he was not suffered to approach ? Besides, the chief errand of the *Dira* was to warn Juturna from the field ; for she could have brought the chariot again, when she saw
5 her brother worsted in the duel. I might further add, that Æneas was so eager of the fight, that he left the city, now almost in his possession, to decide his quarrel with Turnus by the sword ; whereas Turnus had manifestly declined the combat, and suffered his sister to
10 convey him as far from the reach of his enemy as she could. I say, not only suffered her, but consented to it ; for 'tis plain he knew her, by these words :—

> *O soror, et dudum agnovi, cum prima per artem*
> *Fœdera turbasti, teque hæc in bella dedisti ;*
15 > *Et nunc necquicquam fallis dea. . . .*

I have dwelt so long on this subject, that I must contract what I have to say in reference to my translation, unless I would swell my Preface into a volume, and make it formidable to your Lordship, when you see so
20 many pages yet behind. And, indeed what I have already written, either in justification or praise of Virgil, is against myself, for presuming to copy, in my coarse English, the thoughts and beautiful expressions of this inimitable poet, who flourished in an age when
25 his language was brought to its last perfection, for which it was particularly owing to him and Horace. I will give your Lordship my opinion, that those two friends had consulted each other's judgment, wherein they should endeavour to excel ; and they seem to have
30 pitched on propriety of thought, elegance of words, and harmony of numbers. According to this model, Horace writ his *Odes* and *Epodes :* for his *Satires* and *Epistles,* being intended wholly for instruction, required another style :
35 > *Ornari res ipsa negat, contenta doceri :*

and therefore, as he himself professes, are *sermoni pro-piora*, nearer prose than verse. But Virgil, who never attempted the lyric verse, is everywhere elegant, sweet, and flowing in his hexameters. His words are not only chosen, but the places in which he ranks them for 5 the sound. He who removes them from the station wherein their master set them, spoils the harmony. What he says of the Sibyl's prophecies may be as properly applied to every word of his : they must be read in order as they lie ; the least breath discomposes 10 them ; and somewhat of their divinity is lost. I cannot boast that I have been thus exact in my verses ; but I have endeavoured to follow the example of my master, and am the first Englishman, perhaps, who made it his design to copy him in his numbers, his choice of words, 15 and his placing them for the sweetness of the sound. On this last consideration I have shunned the *cæsura* as much as possibly I could : for, wherever that is used, it gives a roughness to the verse ; of which we can have little need in a language which is overstocked 20 with consonants. Such is not the Latin, where the vowels and consonants are mixed in proportion to each other : yet Virgil judged the vowels to have somewhat of an over-balance, and therefore tempers their sweet-ness with *cæsuras*. Such difference there is in tongues, 25 that the same figure, which roughens one, gives majesty to another : and that was it which Virgil studied in his verses. Ovid uses it but rarely ; and hence it is that his versification cannot so properly be called sweet, as luscious. The Italians are forced upon it once or twice 30 in every line, because they have a redundancy of vowels in their language. Their metal is so soft, that it will not coin without alloy to harden it. On the other side, for the reason already named, 'tis all we can do to give sufficient sweetness to our language : we must not only 35

choose our words for elegance, but for sound ; to perform which, a mastery in the language is required ; the
poet must have a magazine of words, and have the art
to manage his few vowels to the best advantage, that
5 they may go the further. He must also know the
nature of the vowels, which are more sonorous, and
which more soft and sweet, and so dispose them as his
present occasions require : all which, and a thousand
secrets of versification beside, he may learn from Virgil,
10 if he will take him for his guide. If he be above
Virgil, and is resolved to follow his own *verve*, (as the
French call it,) the proverb will fall heavily upon him :
Who teaches himself, has a fool for his master.

Virgil employed eleven years upon his *Æneis ;* yet
15 he left it, as he thought himself, imperfect ; which when
I seriously consider, I wish that, instead of three years,
which I have spent in the translation of his works, I
had four years more allowed me to correct my errors,
that I might make my version somewhat more tolerable
20 than it is. For a poet cannot have too great a reverence for his readers, if he expects his labours should
survive him. Yet I will neither plead my age nor sickness, in excuse of the faults which I have made : that
I wanted time, is all that I have to say ; for some of my
25 subscribers grew so clamorous, that I could no longer
defer the publication. I hope, from the candour of your
Lordship, and your often experienced goodness to
me, that, if the faults are not too many, you will make
allowances with Horace—

30   . . . *si plura nitent in carmine, non ego paucis*
            Offendar maculis, quas aut incuria fudit,
            Aut humana parum cavit natura.—

You may please also to observe, that there is not,
to the best of my remembrance, one vowel gaping on
35 another for want of a *cæsura*, in this whole poem : but,

where a vowel ends a word, the next begins either with
a consonant, or what is its equivalent ; for our *W* and
H aspirate, and our diphthongs, are plainly such.   The
greatest latitude I take is in the letter *Y*, when it concludes a word, and the first syllable of the next begins 5
with a vowel.   Neither need I have called this a latitude, which is only an explanation of this general rule,
that no vowel can be cut off before another when we
cannot sink the pronunciation of it ; as *he, she, me,
I,* etc.   Virgil thinks it sometimes a beauty to imitate the 10
licence of the Greeks, and leave two vowels opening on
each other, as in that verse of the Third *Pastoral,*

> *Et succus pecori, et lac subducitur agnis.*

But *nobis non licet esse tam disertis,* at least if we
study to refine our numbers.   I have long had by me 15
the materials of an English *Prosodia,* containing all the
mechanical rules of versification, wherein I have treated,
with some exactness, of the feet, the quantities, and the
pauses.   The French and Italians know nothing of the
two first ; at least their best poets have not practised 20
them.   As for the pauses, Malherbe first brought them
into France within this last century ; and we see how
they adorn their Alexandrines.   But, as Virgil pro-
pounds a riddle, which he leaves unsolved—

> *Dic, quibus in terris, inscripti nomina regum*   25
> *Nascuntur flores, et Phyllida solus habeto—*

so I will give your Lordship another, and leave the
exposition of it to your acute judgment.   I am sure
there are few who make verses, have observed the
sweetness of these two lines in *Cooper's Hill*—   30

> Though deep, yet clear ; though gentle, yet not dull ;
> Strong without rage ; without o'erflowing, full.

And there are yet fewer who can find the reason of that

sweetness. I have given it to some of my friends in conversation ; and they have allowed the criticism to be just. But, since the evil of false quantities is diffi- cult to be cured in any modern language ; since the
5 French and the Italians, as well as we, are yet ignorant what feet are to be used in Heroic Poetry ; since I have not strictly observed those rules myself, which I can teach others ; since I pretend to no dictatorship among my fellow-poets ; since, if I should instruct some of
10 them to make well-running verses, they want genius to give them strength as well as sweetness ; and, above all, since your Lordship has advised me not to publish that little which I know, I look on your counsel as your command, which I shall observe inviolably, till
15 you shall please to revoke it, and leave me at liberty to make my thoughts public. In the meantime, that I may arrogate nothing to myself, I must acknowledge that Virgil in Latin, and Spenser in English, have been my masters. Spenser has also given me the boldness
20 to make use sometimes of his Alexandrine line, which we call, though improperly, the Pindaric, because Mr. *Cowley* has often employed it in his *Odes*. It adds a certain majesty to the verse, when it is used with judgment, and stops the sense from overflowing
25 into another line. Formerly the French, like us, and the Italians, had but five feet, or ten syllables, in their heroic verse ; but, since Ronsard's time as I suppose, they found their tongue too weak to support their epic poetry, without the addition of another foot. That
30 indeed has given it somewhat of the run and measure of a trimeter ; but it runs with more activity than strength : their language is not strung with sinews, like our English ; it has the nimbleness of a greyhound, but not the bulk and body of a mastiff. Our men and
35 our verses overbear them by their weight ; and *Pondere,*

non numero, is the British motto. The French have
set up purity for the standard of their language ; and
a masculine vigour is that of ours. Like their tongue is
the genius of their poets, light and trifling in comparison of the English ; more proper for sonnets, madri- 5
gals, and elegies, than heroic poetry. The turn on
thoughts and words is their chief talent ; but the Epic
Poem is too stately to receive those little ornaments.
The painters draw their nymphs in thin and airy habits ;
but the weight of gold and of embroideries is reserved 10
for queens and goddesses. Virgil is never frequent in
those turns, like Ovid, but much more sparing of them
in his *Æneis* than in his *Pastorals* and *Georgics*.

Ignoscenda quidem, scirent si ignoscere manes.

That turn is beautiful indeed ; but he employs it in 15
the story of Orpheus and Eurydice, not in his great
poem. I have used that licence in his *Æneis* sometimes ; but I own it as my fault. 'Twas given to those
who understand no better. 'Tis like Ovid's

Semivirumque bovem, semibovemque virum. 20

The poet found it before his critics, but it was a
darling sin, which he would not be persuaded to reform.
The want of genius, of which I have accused the
French, is laid to their charge by one of their own
great authors, though I have forgotten his name, and 25
where I read it. If rewards could make good poets,
their great master has not been wanting on his part
in his bountiful encouragements : for he is wise enough
to imitate Augustus, if he had a Maro. The triumvir
and proscriber had descended to us in a more hideous 30
form than they now appear, if the Emperor had not
taken care to make friends of him and Horace. I
confess, the banishment of Ovid was a blot in his

escutcheon : yet he was only banished ; and who knows
but his crime was capital, and then his exile was
a favour ?   Ariosto, who, with all his faults, must be
acknowledged a great poet, has put these words into
5 the mouth of an Evangelist : but whether they will pass
for gospel now, I cannot tell.

> *Non fu si santo ni benigno Augusto,*
> *Come la tuba di Virgilio suona ;*
> *L'haver havuto in poesia buon gusto,*
> 10 *La proscrittione imqua gli perdona.*

But Heroic Poetry is not of the growth of France,
as it might be of England, if it were cultivated. Spenser
wanted only to have read the rules of Bossu ; for no
man was ever born with a greater genius, or had more
15 knowledge to support it. But the performance of the
French is not equal to their skill ; and hitherto we have
wanted skill to perform better. Segrais, whose preface
is so wonderfully good, yet is wholly destitute of elevation, though his version is much better than that of
20 the two brothers, or any of the rest who have attempted
Virgil. Hannibal Caro is a great name amongst the
Italians ; yet his translation of the *Æneis* is most
scandalously mean, though he has taken the advantage
of writing in blank verse, and freed himself from the
25 shackles of modern rhyme, if it be modern ; for Le Clerc
has told us lately, and I believe has made it out, that
David's Psalms were written in as arrant rhyme as they
are translated. Now, if a Muse cannot run when she
is unfettered, it is a sign she has but little speed.
30 I will not make a digression here, though I am strangely
tempted to it ; but will only say, that he who can write
well in rhyme may write better in blank verse. Rhyme
is certainly a constraint even to the best poets, and
those who make it with most ease ; though perhaps
35 I have as little reason to complain of that hardship as

any man, excepting Quarles and Withers. What it
adds to sweetness, it takes away from sense ; and he
who loses the least by it may be called a gainer. It
often makes us swerve from an author's meaning ; as,
if a mark be set up for an archer at a great distance, 5
let him aim as exactly as he can, the least wind will
take his arrow, and divert it from the white. I return
to our Italian translator of the *Æneis*. He is a foot-
poet, he lacqueys by the side of Virgil at the best, but
never mounts behind him. Doctor Morelli, who is no 10
mean critic in our poetry, and therefore may be presumed to be a better in his own language, has confirmed
me in this opinion by his judgment, and thinks, withal,
that he has often mistaken his master's sense. I would
say so, if I durst, but am afraid I have committed the 15
same fault more often, and more grossly ; for I have
forsaken Ruæus (whom generally I follow) in many
places, and made expositions of my own in some, quite
contrary to him ; of which I will give but two examples, because they are so near each other in the Tenth 20
Æneid.

. . . Sorti Pater æquus utrique :

Pallas says it to Turnus, just before they fight. Ruæus
thinks that the word *Pater* is to be referred to Evander,
the father of Pallas. But how could he imagine that 25
it was the same thing to Evander, if his son were slain,
or if he overcame ? The poet certainly intended Jupiter,
the common father of mankind ; who, as Pallas hoped,
would stand an impartial spectator of the combat, and
not be more favourable to Turnus than to him. The 30
second is not long after it, and both before the duel
is begun. They are the words of Jupiter, who comforts
Hercules for the death of Pallas, which was immediately to ensue, and which Hercules could not hinder
(though the young hero had addressed his prayers to 35

him for his assistance) because the Gods cannot controul
Destiny. The verse follows :—

Sic ait ; atque oculos Rutulorum rejicit arvis,—

which the same Ruæus thus construes : Jupiter, after
5 he had said this, immediately turns his eyes to the
Rutulian fields, and beholds the duel. I have given
this place another exposition :—that he turned his eyes
from the field of combat, that he might not behold
a sight so unpleasing to him. The word *rejicit*, I know,
10 will admit of both senses ; but Jupiter, having confessed
that he could not alter Fate, and being grieved he
could not, in consideration of Hercules, it seems to
me that he should avert his eyes, rather than take
pleasure in the spectacle. But of this I am not so
15 confident as the other, though I think I have followed
Virgil's sense.

What I have said, though it has the face of arrogance,
yet is intended for the honour of my country ; and
therefore I will boldly own, that this English translation
20 has more of Virgil's spirit in it than either the French
or the Italian. Some of our countrymen have translated
episodes and other parts of Virgil, with great success ;
as particularly your Lordship, whose version of *Orpheus
and Eurydice* is eminently good. Amongst the dead
25 authors, the *Silenus* of my Lord Roscommon cannot
be too much commended. I say nothing of Sir John
Denham, Mr. Waller, and Mr. Cowley ; 'tis the utmost
of my ambition to be thought their equal, or not to
be much inferior to them, and some others of the living.
30 But 'tis one thing to take pains on a fragment, and
translate it perfectly ; and another thing to have the
weight of a whole author on my shoulders. They who
believe the burthen light, let them attempt the Fourth,
Sixth, or Eighth *Pastoral ;* the First or Fourth *Georgic ;*
35 and, amongst the *Æneids*, the Fourth, the Fifth, the

Seventh, the Ninth, the Tenth, the Eleventh, or the
Twelfth ; for in these I think I have succeeded best.

Long before I undertook this work, I was no stranger
to the original. I had also studied Virgil's design, his
disposition of it, his manners, his judicious management 5
of the figures, the sober retrenchments of his sense,
which always leaves somewhat to gratify our imagination, on which it may enlarge at pleasure ; but, above
all, the elegance of his expressions, and the harmony
of his numbers. For, as I have said in a former dis- 10
sertation, the words are, in Poetry, what the colours
are in Painting ; if the design be good, and the draught
be true, the colouring is the first beauty that strikes
the eye. Spenser and Milton are the nearest, in
English, to Virgil and Horace in the Latin ; and I have 15
endeavoured to form my style by imitating their masters.
I will further own to you, my Lord, that my chief
ambition is to please those readers who have discern-
ment enough to prefer Virgil before any other poet
in the Latin tongue. Such spirits as he desired to 20
please, such would I choose for my judges, and would
stand or fall by them alone. Segrais has distinguished
the readers of poetry, according to their capacity of
judging, into three classes (he might have said the same
of writers too, if he had pleased) : in the lowest form 25
he places those whom he calls *les petits esprits ;* such
things as are our upper-gallery audience in a playhouse,
who like nothing but the husk and rind of wit ; prefer
a quibble, a conceit, an epigram, before solid sense and
elegant expression. These are mob readers : if Virgil 30
and Martial stood for Parliament-men, we know already
who would carry it. But, though they make the greatest
appearance in the field, and cry the loudest, the best
on't is, they are but a sort of French Huguenots, or
Dutch boors, brought over in herds, but not naturalized ; 35

who have not land of two pounds *per annum* in Parnassus, and therefore are not privileged to poll. Their
authors are of the same level, fit to represent them on
a mountebank's stage, or to be masters of the cere-
5 monies in a bear-garden. Yet these are they who have
the most admirers. But it often happens, to their
mortification, that, as their readers improve their stock
of sense (as they may by reading better books, and by
conversation with men of judgment), they soon forsake
10 them : and when the torrent from the mountains falls
no more, the swelling writer is reduced into his shallow
bed, like the Mançanares at Madrid with scarce water
to moisten his own pebbles. There are a middle sort
of readers (as we hold there is a middle state of souls),
15 such as have a further insight than the former, yet have
not the capacity of judging right ; for I speak not of
those who are bribed by a party, and know better, if
they were not corrupted ; but I mean a company of warm
young men, who are not yet arrived so far as to discern
20 the difference betwixt fustian, or ostentatious sentences,
and the true sublime. These are above liking Martial,
or Owen's Epigrams, but they would certainly set Virgil
below Statius or Lucan. I need not say their poets
are of the same taste with their admirers. They affect
25 greatness in all they write ; but 'tis a bladdered greatness, like that of the vain man whom Seneca describes ;
an ill habit of body, full of humours, and swelled with
dropsy. Even these too desert their authors, as their
judgment ripens. The young gentlemen themselves
30 are commonly misled by their pedagogue at school,
their tutor at the university, or their governor in their
travels : and many of those three sorts are the most
positive blockheads in the world. How many of those
flatulent writers have I known, who have sunk in their
35 reputation, after seven or eight editions of their works !

for indeed they are poets only for young men. They had great success at their first appearance ; but, not being of God (as a wit said formerly), they could not stand.

I have already named two sorts of judges ; but Virgil 5 wrote for neither of them : and, by his example, I am not ambitious of pleasing the lowest or the middle form of readers.

He chose to please the most judicious : souls of the highest rank, and truest understanding. These are few 10 in number ; but whoever is so happy as to gain their approbation can never lose it, because they never give it blindly. Then they have a certain magnetism in their judgment, which attracts others to their sense. Every day they gain some new proselyte, and in time 15 become the Church. For this reason, a well-weighed judicious poem, which at its first appearance gains no more upon the world than to be just received, and rather not blamed than much applauded, insinuates itself by insensible degrees into the liking of the reader : 20 the more he studies it, the more it grows upon him ; every time he takes it up, he discovers some new graces in it. And whereas poems which are produced by the vigour of imagination only have a gloss upon them at the first which time wears off, the works of judgment 25 are like the diamond ; the more they are polished, the more lustre they receive. Such is the difference betwixt Virgil's *Æneis* and Marini's *Adone*. And, if I may be allowed to change the metaphor, I would say, that Virgil is like the Fame which he describes— 30

Mobilitate viget, viresque acquirit eundo.

Such a sort of reputation is my aim, though in a far inferior degree, according to my motto in the title-page : *Sequiturque patrem non passibus æquis :* and therefore I appeal to the highest court of judicature, like that of 35 the peers, of which your Lordship is so great an ornament.

Without this ambition, which I own, of desiring to please the *judices natos*, I could never have been able to
5 have done anything at this age, when the fire of poetry is commonly extinguished in other men.   Yet Virgil has given me the example of Entellus for my encouragement : when he was well heated, the younger champion could not stand before him.   And we find the elder
10 contended not for the gift, but for the honour : *nec dona moror.*   For Dampier has informed us, in his *Voyages*, that the air of the country which produces gold is never wholesome.

I had long since considered that the way to please
15 the best judges is not to translate a poet literally; and Virgil least of any other : for, his peculiar beauty lying in his choice of words, I am excluded from it by the narrow compass of our heroic verse, unless I would make use of monosyllables only, and those clogged with
20 consonants, which are the dead weight of our mother-tongue.   'Tis possible, I confess, though it rarely happens, that a verse of monosyllables may sound harmoniously ; and some examples of it I have seen. My first line of the *Æneis* is not harsh—

25   Arms, and the Man I sing, who forc'd by Fate, &c.

But a much better instance may be given from the last line of Manilius, made English by our learned and judicious Mr. Creech—

Nor could the World have borne so fierce a Flame—

30 where the many liquid consonants are placed so art-fully, that they give a pleasing sound to the words, though they are all of one syllable.

'Tis true, I have been sometimes forced upon it in other places of this work : but I never did it out of

choice ; I was either in haste, or Virgil gave me no
occasion for the ornament of words ; for it seldom
happens but a monosyllable line turns verse to prose ;
and even that prose is rugged and unharmonious.
Philarchus, I remember, taxes Balzac for placing 5
twenty monosyllables in file, without one dissyllable
betwixt them. The way I have taken is not so strait
as metaphrase, nor so loose as paraphrase : some
things too I have omitted, and sometimes have added of
my own. Yet the omissions, I hope, are but of circum- 10
stances, and such as would have no grace in English ;
and the additions, I also hope, are easily deduced from
Virgil's sense. They will seem (at least I have the
vanity to think so), not stuck into him, but growing out
of him. He studies brevity more than any other poet : 15
but he had the advantage of a language wherein much
may be comprehended in a little space. We, and all
the modern tongues, have more articles and pronouns,
besides signs of tenses and cases, and other barbarities
on which our speech is built by the faults of our fore- 20
fathers. The Romans founded theirs upon the Greek :
and the Greeks, we know, were labouring many hundred years upon their language, before they brought it
to perfection. They rejected all those signs, and cut
off as many articles as they could spare ; comprehend- 25
ing in one word what we are constrained to express in
two ; which is one reason why we cannot write so concisely as they have done. The word *pater*, for example,
signifies not only *a* father, but *your* father, *my* father,
his or *her* father, all included in a word.   30

This inconvenience is common to all modern tongues ;
and this alone constrains us to employ more words
than the ancients needed. But having before observed
that Virgil endeavours to be short, and at the same
time elegant, I pursue the excellence and forsake the 35

brevity : for there he is like ambergris, a rich perfume,
but of so close and glutinous a body, that it must be
opened with inferior scents of musk or civet, or the
sweetness will not be drawn out into another language.
5   On the whole matter, I thought fit to steer betwixt
the two extremes of paraphrase and literal translation ;
to keep as near my author as I could, without losing all
his graces, the most eminent of which are in the beauty
of his words ; and those words, I must add, are always
10 figurative. Such of these as would retain their elegance in our tongue, I have endeavoured to graff on it ;
but most of them are of necessity to be lost, because
they will not shine in any but their own. Virgil has
sometimes two of them in a line ; but the scantiness of
15 our heroic verse is not capable of receiving more than
one ; and that too must expiate for many others which
have none. Such is the difference of the languages, or
such my want of skill in choosing words. Yet I may
presume to say, and I hope with as much reason as
20 the French translator, that, taking all the materials of
this divine author, I have endeavoured to make Virgil
speak such English as he would himself have spoken,
if he had been born in England, and in this present
age. I acknowledge, with Segrais, that I have not
25 succeeded in this attempt according to my desire : yet
I shall not be wholly without praise, if in some sort
I may be allowed to have copied the clearness, the
purity, the easiness, and the magnificence of his style.
But I shall have occasion to speak further on this sub-
30 ject before I end the Preface.

   When I mentioned the Pindaric line, I should have
added, that I take another licence in my verses : for
I frequently make use of triplet rhymes, and for the
same reason, because they bound the sense. And
35 therefore I generally join these two licences together,

and make the last verse of the triplet a Pindaric : for, besides the majesty which it gives, it confines the sense within the barriers of three lines, which would languish if it were lengthened into four. Spenser is my example for both these privileges of English verses ; and Chap- 5 man has followed him in his translation of Homer. Mr. Cowley has given into them after both ; and all succeeding writers after him. I regard them now as the *Magna Charta* of heroic poetry, and am too much an Englishman to lose what my ancestors have gained 10 for me. Let the French and Italians value themselves on their regularity ; strength and elevation are our standard. I said before, and I repeat it, that the affected purity of the French has unsinewed their heroic verse. The language of an epic poem is almost wholly 15 figurative : yet they are so fearful of a metaphor, that no example of Virgil can encourage them to be bold with safety. Sure they might warm themselves by that sprightly blaze, without approaching it so close as to singe their wings ; they may come as near it as their 20 master. Not that I would discourage that purity of diction in which he excels all other poets. But he knows how far to extend his franchises, and advances to the verge, without venturing a foot beyond it. On the other side, without being injurious to the memory 25 of our English Pindar, I will presume to say, that his metaphors are sometimes too violent, and his language is not always pure. But at the same time I must excuse him ; for through the iniquity of the times he was forced to travel, at an age when, instead of learning 30 foreign languages, he should have studied the beauties of his mother-tongue, which, like all other speeches, is to be cultivated early, or we shall never write it with any kind of elegance. Thus, by gaining abroad, he lost at home ; like the painter in the *Arcadia*, who, going to 35

see a skirmish, had his arms lopped off, and returned,
says Sir Philip Sidney, well instructed how to draw
a battle, but without a hand to perform his work.

There is another thing in which I have presumed to
5 deviate from him and Spenser. They both make hemistichs (or half verses), breaking off in the middle of a line.
I confess there are not many such in the *Fairy Queen ;*
and even those few might be occasioned by his unhappy
choice of so long a stanza. Mr. Cowley had found out
10 that no kind of staff is proper for a heroic poem, as
being all too lyrical : yet, though he wrote in couplets,
where rhyme is freer from constraint, he frequently
affects half verses ; of which we find not one in Homer,
and I think not in any of the Greek poets, or the Latin,
15 excepting only Virgil ; and there is no question but he
thought he had Virgil's authority for that licence. But,
I am confident, our poet never meant to leave him, or
any other, such a precedent : and I ground my opinion
on these two reasons : first, we find no example of
20 a hemistich in any of his *Pastorals* or *Georgics ;* for
he had given the last finishing strokes to both these
poems : but his *Æneis* he left so incorrect, at least so
short of that perfection at which he aimed, that we know
how hard a sentence he passed upon it : and, in the
25 second place, I reasonably presume, that he intended
to have filled up all those hemistichs, because in one of
them we find the sense imperfect—

Quem tibi jam Troja . . .

which some foolish grammarian has ended for him with
30 a half line of nonsense—

. . . peperit fumante Creusa :

for Ascanius must have been born some years before
the burning of that city ; which I need not prove. On
the other side, we find also, that he himself filled up one

line in the Sixth Æneid, the enthusiasm seizing him while
he was reading to Augustus—

> *Misenum Æolidem, quo non præstantior alter*
> *Ære ciere viros . .*

to which he added, in that transport, *Martemque accen-* 5
dere cantu : and never was any line more nobly finished ;
for the reasons which I have given in the *Book of Paint-*
ing. On these considerations I have shunned hemistichs ; not being willing to imitate Virgil to a fault,
like Alexander's courtiers, who affected to hold their 10
necks awry, because he could not help it. I am confident your Lordship is by this time of my opinion, and
that you will look on those half lines hereafter as the
imperfect products of a hasty Muse ; like the frogs and
serpents in the Nile ; part of them kindled into life, and 15
part a lump of unformed unanimated mud.

I am sensible that many of my whole verses are as
imperfect as those halves, for want of time to digest
them better : but give me leave to make the excuse of
Boccace, who, when he was upbraided that some of his 20
novels had not the spirit of the rest, returned this answer,
that Charlemain, who made the Paladins, was never
able to raise an army of them. The leaders may be
heroes, but the multitude must consist of common
men. 25

I am also bound to tell your Lordship, in my own
defence, that, from the beginning of the First *Georgic*
to the end of the last *Æneid*, I found the difficulty of
translation growing on me in every succeeding book.
For Virgil, above all poets, had a stock, which I may 30
call almost inexhaustible, of figurative, elegant, and
sounding words : I, who inherit but a small portion of
his genius, and write in a language so much inferior to
the Latin, have found it very painful to vary phrases,
when the same sense returns upon me. Even he him- 35

self, whether out of necessity or choice, has often expressed the same thing in the same words, and often
repeated two or three whole verses which he had used
before. Words are not so easily coined as money ; and
5 yet we see that the credit not only of banks but of ex-
chequers cracks, when little comes in, and much goes
out. Virgil called upon me in every line for some new
word : and I paid so long, that I was almost bankrupt ;
so that the latter end must needs be more burdensome
10 than the beginning or the middle ; and, consequently,
the Twelfth Æneid cost me double the time of the First
and Second. What had become of me, if Virgil had
taxed me with another book ? I had certainly been
reduced to pay the public in hammered money, for want
15 of milled ; that is, in the same old words which I had
used before : and the receivers must have been forced
to have taken any thing, where there was so little to be
had.

Besides this difficulty (with which I have struggled,
20 and made a shift to pass it over), there is one remaining,
which is insuperable to all translators. We are bound
to our author's sense, though with the latitudes already
mentioned ; for I think it not so sacred, as that one
iota must not be added or diminished, on pain of an
25 *Anathema*. But slaves we are, and labour on another
man's plantation ; we dress the vineyard, but the wine
is the owner's : if the soil be sometimes barren, then
we are sure of being scourged : if it be fruitful, and our
care succeeds, we are not thanked ; for the proud reader
30 will only say, the poor drudge has done his duty. But
this is nothing to what follows ; for, being obliged to
make his sense intelligible, we are forced to untune our
own verses, that we may give his meaning to the reader.
He, who invents, is master of his thoughts and words :
35 he can turn and vary them as he pleases, till he renders

them harmonious ; but the wretched translator has no
such privilege : for, being tied to the thoughts, he must
make what music he can in the expression ; and, for
this reason, it cannot always be so sweet as that of the
original. There is a beauty of sound, as Segrais has 5
observed, in some Latin words, which is wholly lost in
any modern language. He instances in that *mollis
amaracus*, on which Venus lays Cupid, in the First
Æneid. If I should translate it *sweet marjoram*, as the
word signifies, the reader would think I had mistaken 10
Virgil : for those village words, as I may call them, give
us a mean idea of the thing ; but the sound of the Latin
is so much more pleasing, by the just mixture of the
vowels with the consonants, that it raises our fancies to
conceive somewhat more noble than a common herb, and 15
to spread roses under him, and strew lilies over him ;
a bed not unworthy the grandson of the goddess.

If I cannot copy his harmonious numbers, how shall
I imitate his noble flights, where his thoughts and words
are equally sublime ? *Quem*   20

> *. . . quisquis studet æmulari,*
> *. . . cæratis ope Dædalea*
> *Nititur pennis, vitreo daturus*
> *Nomina ponto.*

What modern language, or what poet, can express 25
the majestic beauty of this one verse, amongst a thousand others ?

> *Aude, hospes, contemnere opes, et te quoque dignum*
> *Finge deo. . . .*

For my part, I am lost in the admiration of it : I con- 30
temn the world when I think on it, and myself when
I translate it.

Lay by Virgil, I beseech your Lordship, and all my
better sort of judges, when you take up my version ;
and it will appear a passable beauty when the original 35

Muse is absent. But, like Spenser's false Florimel
made of snow, it melts and vanishes when the true one
comes in sight. I will not excuse, but justify myself,
for one pretended crime, with which I am liable to be
5 charged by false critics, not only in this translation, but
in many of my original poems ; that I latinize too much.
'Tis true, that, when I find an English word significant
and sounding, I neither borrow from the Latin, nor any
other language ; but, when I want at home, I must seek
10 abroad.

If sounding words are not of our growth and manufacture, who shall hinder me to import them from a
foreign country ? I carry not out the treasure of the
nation, which is never to return ; but what I bring from
15 Italy, I spend in England : here it remains, and here it
circulates ; for, if the coin be good, it will pass from one
hand to another. I trade both with the living and the
dead, for the enrichment of our native language. We
have enough in England to supply our necessity ; but,
20 if we will have things of magnificence and splendour,
we must get them by commerce. Poetry requires
ornament ; and that is not to be had from our old
Teuton monosyllables : therefore, if I find any elegant
word in a classic author, I propose it to be naturalized,
25 by using it myself ; and, if the public approves of it, the
bill passes. But every man cannot distinguish between
pedantry and poetry : every man, therefore, is not fit to
innovate. Upon the whole matter, a poet must first be
certain that the word he would introduce is beautiful in
30 the Latin, and is to consider, in the next place, whether
it will agree with the English idiom : after this, he
ought to take the opinion of judicious friends, such as
are learned in both languages : and, lastly, since no
man is infallible, let him use this licence very sparingly;
35 for if too many foreign words are poured in upon us, it

looks as if they were designed not to assist the natives, but to conquer them.

I am now drawing towards a conclusion, and suspect your Lordship is very glad of it. But permit me first to own what helps I have had in this undertaking. The 5 late Earl of Lauderdail sent me over his new translation of the *Æneis*, which he had ended before I engaged in the same design. Neither did I then intend it : but, some proposals being afterwards made me by my bookseller, I desired his Lordship's leave that I might accept 10 them, which he freely granted ; and I have his letter yet to show for that permission. He resolved to have printed his work ; which he might have done two years before I could publish mine ; and had performed it if death had not prevented him. But, having his manu- 15 script in my hands, I consulted it as often as I doubted of my author's sense ; for no man understood Virgil better than that learned Nobleman. His friends, I hear, have yet another and more correct copy of that translation by them, which, had they pleased to have given 20 the public, the judges must have been convinced that I have not flattered him. Besides this help, which was not inconsiderable, Mr. Congreve has done me the favour to review the *Æneis*, and compare my version with the original. I shall never be ashamed to own, 25 that this excellent young man has shewed me many faults, which I have endeavoured to correct. 'Tis true, he might have easily found more, and then my translation had been more perfect.

Two other worthy friends of mine, who desire to 30 have their names concealed, seeing me straitened in my time, took pity on me, and gave me the *Life of Virgil*, the two *Prefaces* to the *Pastorals* and the *Georgics*, and all the arguments in prose to the whole translation ; which, perhaps, has caused a report, that the two first 35

poems are not mine. If it had been true, that I had
taken their verses for my own, I might have gloried in
their aid, and, like Terence, have fathered [1] the opinion
that Scipio and Lælius joined with me. But the same
5 style being continued through the whole, and the same
laws of versification observed, are proofs sufficient, that
this is one man's work : and your Lordship is too well
acquainted with my manner, to doubt that any part of it
is another's.

10   That your Lordship may see I was in earnest when
I promised to hasten to an end, I will not give the
reasons why I writ not always in the proper terms of
navigation, land-service, or in the cant of any profession. I will only say, that Virgil has avoided those
15 proprieties, because he writ not to mariners, soldiers,
astronomers, gardeners, peasants, etc., but to all in
general, and in particular to men and ladies of the first
quality, who have been better bred than to be too nicely
knowing in the terms. In such cases, it is enough for
20 a poet to write so plainly, that he may be understood
by his readers ; to avoid impropriety, and not affect to
be thought learned in all things.

I have omitted the four preliminary lines of the First
Æneid, because I think them inferior to any four others
25 in the whole poem, and consequently believe they are
not Virgil's. There is too great a gap betwixt the
adjective *vicina* in the second line, and the substantive
arva in the latter end of the third, which keeps his
meaning in obscurity too long, and is contrary to the
30 clearness of his style.

Ut quamvis avido

is too ambitious an ornament to be his ; and

Gratum opus agricolis,

[1] farther'd, ed. 1697.

are all words unnecessary, and independent of what he
had said before.

> . . . *Horrentia Martis*
> *Arma* . . .

is worse than any of the rest. *Horrentia* is such a flat 5
epithet, as Tully would have given us in his verses.
It is a mere filler, to stop a vacancy in the hexameter,
and connect the preface to the work of Virgil. Our
author seems to sound a charge, and begins like the
clangour of a trumpet—   10

> *Arma, virumque cano, Trojæ qui primus ab oris*

scarce a word without an *r*, and the vowels, for the
greater part, sonorous. The prefacer began with *Ille
ego*, which he was constrained to patch up in the fourth
line with *at nunc*, to make the sense cohere ; and, if 15
both those words are not notorious botches, I am much
deceived, though the French translator thinks otherwise. For my own part, I am rather of the opinion
that they were added by Tucca and Varius, than retrenched.   20

I know it may be answered, by such as think Virgil
the author of the four lines, that he asserts his title to
the *Æneis* in the beginning of his work, as he did to
the two former in the last lines of the Fourth Georgic.
I will not reply otherwise to this, than by desiring them 25
to compare these four lines with the four others, which
we know are his, because no poet but he alone could
write them. If they cannot distinguish creeping from
flying, let them lay down Virgil, and take up Ovid *de
Ponto*, in his stead. My master needed not the assist- 30
ance of that preliminary poet to prove his claim. His
own majestic mien discovers him to be the king,
amidst a thousand courtiers. It was a superfluous
office ; and, therefore, I would not set those verses in

the front of Virgil, but have rejected them to my own
preface.

> I, who before, with Shepherds in the Groves,
> Sung to my oaten Pipe, their rural Loves,
> 5   And, issuing thence, compell'd the neighbouring Field
> A plenteous Crop of rising Corn to yield,
> Manur'd the Glebe, and stock'd the fruitful Plain,
> (A Poem grateful to the greedy Swain), &c.

If there be not a tolerable line in all these six, the
10 prefacer gave me no occasion to write better. This is
a just apology in this place ; but I have done great
wrong to Virgil in the whole translation : want of time,
the inferiority of our language, the inconvenience of
rhyme, and all the other excuses I have made, may
15 alleviate my fault, but cannot justify the boldness of my
undertaking. What avails it me to acknowledge freely,
that I have not been able to do him right in any line ?
For even my own confession makes against me ; and
it will always be returned upon me, ' Why then did you
20 attempt it ? ' To which no other answer can be made,
than that I have done him less injury than any of his
former libellers.

What they called his picture, had been drawn at
length, so many times, by the daubers of almost all
25 nations, and still so unlike him, that I snatched up the
pencil with disdain ; being satisfied beforehand, that
I could make some small resemblance of him, though
I must be content with a worse likeness. A Sixth
Pastoral, a *Pharmaceutria*, a single *Orpheus*, and some
30 other features, have been exactly taken : but those
holiday authors writ for pleasure ; and only shewed us
what they could have done, if they would have taken
pains to perform the whole.

Be pleased, my Lord, to accept, with your wonted
35 goodness, this unworthy present which I make you.

I have taken off one trouble from you, of defending it,
by acknowledging its imperfections : and, though some
part of them are covered in the verse, (as Erichthonius
rode always in a chariot, to hide his lameness,) such of
them as cannot be concealed, you will please to connive 5
at, though, in the strictness of your judgment, you cannot pardon.   If Homer was allowed to nod sometimes
in so long a work, it will be no wonder if I often fall
asleep.   You took my *Aureng-zebe* into your protection,
with all his faults : and I hope here cannot be so many, 10
because I translate an author who gives me such
examples of correctness.   What my jury may be, I know
not ; but it is good for a criminal to plead before a
favourable judge : if I had said partial, would your Lordship have forgiven me ?   or will you give me leave to 15
acquaint the world, that I have many times been
obliged to your bounty since the Revolution ?   Though
I never was reduced to beg a charity, nor ever had the
impudence to ask one, either of your Lordship, or your
noble kinsman the Earl of Dorset, much less of any 20
other ; yet, when I least expected it, you have both
remembered me : so inherent it is in your family not
to forget an old servant.   It looks rather like ingratitude on my part, that, where I have been so often
obliged, I have appeared so seldom to return my 25
thanks, and where I was also so sure of being well
received.   Somewhat of laziness was in the case, and
somewhat too of modesty, but nothing of disrespect or
of unthankfulness.   I will not say that your Lordship
has encouraged me to this presumption, lest, if my 30
labours meet with no success in public, I may expose
your judgment to be censured.   As for my own enemies,
I shall never think them worth an answer ; and, if your
Lordship has any, they will not dare to arraign you for
want of knowledge in this art, till they can produce 35

somewhat better of their own, than your *Essay on Poetry*.
'Twas on this consideration, that I have drawn out my
Preface to so great a length. Had I not addressed
to a poet and a critic of the first magnitude, I had
5 myself been taxed for want of judgment, and shamed
my patron for want of understanding. But neither will
you, my Lord, so soon be tired as any other, because
the discourse is on your art ; neither will the learned
reader think it tedious, because it is *ad Clerum*. At least,
10 when he begins to be weary, the church doors are open.
That I may pursue the allegory with a short prayer,
after a long sermon :

May you live happily and long, for the service of
your Country, the encouragement of good Letters, and
15 the ornament of Poetry ; which cannot be wished more
earnestly by any man, than by

Your Lordship's most humble,

Most obliged, and most obedient Servant,

JOHN DRYDEN.

POSTSCRIPT TO THE READER

20   WHAT Virgil wrote in the vigour of his age, in plenty
and at ease, I have undertaken to translate in my
declining years ; struggling with wants, oppressed with
sickness, curbed in my genius, liable to be misconstrued
in all I write ; and my judges, if they are not very
25 equitable, already prejudiced against me, by the lying
character which has been given them of my morals.
Yet steady to my principles, and not dispirited with my
afflictions, I have, by the blessing of God on my
endeavours, overcome all difficulties, and, in some

measure, acquitted myself of the debt which I owed the
public when I undertook this work. In the first place,
therefore, I thankfully acknowledge to the Almighty
Power the assistance He has given me in the beginning, the prosecution, and conclusion of my present 5
studies, which are more happily performed than I could
have promised to myself, when I laboured under such
discouragements. For, what I have done, imperfect as
it is for want of health and leisure to correct it, will
be judged in after-ages, and possibly in the present, to 10
be no dishonour to my native country, whose language
and poetry would be more esteemed abroad, if they
were better understood. Somewhat (give me leave to
say) I have added to both of them in the choice of
words, and harmony of numbers, which were wanting, 15
especially the last, in all our poets, even in those who,
being endued with genius, yet have not cultivated their
mother-tongue with sufficient care ; or, relying on the
beauty of their thoughts, have judged the ornament of
words, and sweetness of sound, unnecessary. One is 20
for raking in Chaucer (our English Ennius) for antiquated words, which are never to be revived, but when
sound or significancy is wanting in the present language.
But many of his deserve not this redemption, any more
than the crowds of men who daily die, or are slain 25
for sixpence in a battle, merit to be restored to life, if
a wish could revive them. Others have no ear for
verse, nor choice of words, nor distinction of thoughts ;
but mingle farthings with their gold, to make up the
sum. Here is a field of satire opened to me : but, 30
since the Revolution, I have wholly renounced that
talent. For who would give physic to the great, when
he is uncalled ?—to do his patient no good, and en-
danger himself for his prescription ? Neither am
I ignorant, but I may justly be condemned for many 35

of those faults of which I have too liberally arraigned
others.

                        . . . *Cynthius aurem*
Vellit, et admonuit . . .

5   'Tis enough for me, if the Government will let me
pass unquestioned.   In the meantime, I am obliged, in
gratitude, to return my thanks to many of them, who
have not only distinguished me from others of the same
party, by a particular exception of grace, but, without
10 considering the man, have been bountiful to the poet :
have encouraged Virgil to speak such English as I
could teach him, and rewarded his interpreter for the
pains he has taken in bringing him over into Britain,
by defraying the charges of his voyage.   Even Cer-
15 berus, when he had received the sop, permitted Æneas
to pass freely to Elysium.   Had it been offered me, and
I had refused it, yet still some gratitude is due to such
who were willing to oblige me ; but how much more to
those from whom I have received the favours which
20 they have offered to one of a different persuasion !
Amongst whom I cannot omit naming the Earls of
Derby and of Peterborough.   To the first of these
I have not the honour to be known ; and therefore his
liberality was as much unexpected as it was undeserved.
25 The present Earl of Peterborough has been pleased
long since to accept the tenders of my service : his
favours are so frequent to me, that I receive them
almost by prescription.   No difference of interests or
opinion has been able to withdraw his protection from
30 me ; and I might justly be condemned for the most
unthankful of mankind, if I did not always preserve for
him a most profound respect and inviolable gratitude.
I must also add, that, if the last *Æneid* shine amongst
its fellows, 'tis owing to the commands of Sir William
35 Trumball, one of the principal Secretaries of State, who

recommended it, as his favourite, to my care ; and for his sake particularly, I have made it mine. For who would confess weariness, when he enjoined a fresh labour ? I could not but invoke the assistance of a Muse, for this last office.   5

> *Extremum hunc, Arethusa . . .*
> *. . . Negat quis carmina Gallo ?*

Neither am I to forget the noble present which was made me by Gilbert Dolben, Esq., the worthy son of the late Archbishop of York, who, when I began this 10 work, enriched me with all the several editions of Virgil, and all the commentaries of those editions in Latin ; amongst which, I could not but prefer the Dauphin's [1], as the last, the shortest, and the most judicious. Fabrini I had also sent me from Italy ; but 15 either he understands Virgil very imperfectly, or I have no knowledge of my author.

Being invited by that worthy gentleman, Sir William Bowyer, to Denham Court, I translated the First *Georgic* at his house, and the greatest part of the last 20 *Æneid*. A more friendly entertainment no man ever found. No wonder, therefore, if both those versions surpass the rest, and own the satisfaction I received in his converse, with whom I had the honour to be bred in Cambridge, and in the same college. The Seventh 25 Æneid was made English at Burleigh, the magnificent abode of the Earl of Exeter. In a village belonging to his family I was born ; and under his roof I endeavoured to make that *Æneid* appear in English with as much lustre as I could ; though my author has not given the 30 finishing strokes either to it, or to the Eleventh, as I perhaps could prove in both, if I durst presume to criticise my master.

The *Dolphins*, ed. 1697.

By a letter from William Walsh, of Abberley, Esq.
(who has so long honoured me with his friendship, and
who, without flattery, is the best critic of our nation),
I have been informed, that his Grace the Duke of
5 Shrewsbury has procured a printed copy of the *Pastorals, Georgics*, and first six *Æneids*, from my bookseller,
and has read them in the country, together with my
friend. This noble person having been pleased to give
them a commendation, which I presume not to insert,
10 has made me vain enough to boast of so great a favour,
and to think I have succeeded beyond my hopes ; the
character of his excellent judgment, the acuteness of his
wit, and his general knowledge of good letters, being
known as well to all the world, as the sweetness of his
15 disposition, his humanity, his easiness of access, and
desire of obliging those who stand in need of his protection, are known to all who have approached him, and
to me in particular, who have formerly had the honour
of his conversation. Whoever has given the world the
20 translation of part of the Third *Georgic*, which he calls
The Power of Love, has put me to sufficient pains to
make my own not inferior to his ; as my Lord Roscommon's *Silenus* had formerly given me the same trouble.
The most ingenious Mr. Addison of Oxford has also
25 been as troublesome to me as the other two, and on
the same account. After his *Bees*, my latter swarm is
scarcely worth the hiving. Mr. Cowley's *Praise of a
Country Life* is excellent, but is rather an imitation of
Virgil than a version. That I have recovered, in some
30 measure, the health which I had lost by too much
application to this work, is owing, next to God's mercy,
to the skill and care of Dr. Guibbons and Dr. Hobbs,
the two ornaments of their profession, whom I can only
pay by this acknowledgment. The whole Faculty has
35 always been ready to oblige me ; and the only one of

them, who endeavoured to defame me, had it not in his
power. I desire pardon from my readers for saying so
much in relation to myself, which concerns not them ;
and, with my acknowledgments to all my subscribers,
have only to add, that the few Notes which follow are 5
par manière d'acquit, because I had obliged myself by
articles to do somewhat of that kind. These scattering
observations are rather guesses at my author's meaning
in some passages, than proofs that so he meant. The
unlearned may have recourse to any poetical dictionary 10
in English, for the names of persons, places, or fables,
which the learned need not : but that little which I say
is either new or necessary ; and the first of these qualifications never fails to invite a reader, if not to please
him.   15

PREFACE

TO THE FABLES

[1700]

'TIS with a Poet, as with a man who designs to build, and is very exact, as he supposes, in casting up the cost beforehand; but, generally speaking, he is mistaken in his account, and reckons short of the expense 5 he first intended. He alters his mind as the work proceeds, and will have this or that convenience more, of which he had not thought when he began. So has it happened to me; I have built a house, where I intended but a lodge; yet with better success than 10 a certain nobleman, who, beginning with a dog-kennel, never lived to finish the palace he had contrived.

From translating the First of Homer's *Iliads*, (which I intended as an essay to the whole work,) I proceeded to the translation of the Twelfth Book of Ovid's *Meta-* 15 *morphoses*, because it contains, among other things, the causes, the beginning, and ending, of the Trojan war. Here I ought in reason to have stopped; but the speeches of Ajax and Ulysses lying next in my way, I could not balk 'em. When I had compassed them, 20 I was so taken with the former part of the Fifteenth Book, (which is the masterpiece of the whole *Metamorphoses*,) that I enjoined myself the pleasing task of rendering it into English. And now I found, by the

number of my verses, that they began to swell into
a little volume ; which gave me an occasion of looking
backward on some beauties of my author, in his former
books : there occurred to me the *Hunting of the Boar,*
Cinyras and Myrrha, the good-natured story of *Baucis* 5
and Philemon, with the rest, which I hope I have
translated closely enough, and given them the same
turn of verse which they had in the original ; and this,
I may say, without vanity, is not the talent of every
poet.   He who has arrived the nearest to it, is the 10
ingenious and learned Sandys, the best versifier of the
former age ; if I may properly call it by that name,
which was the former part of this concluding century.
For Spenser and Fairfax both flourished in the reign
of Queen Elizabeth ; great masters in our language, 15
and who saw much farther into the beauties of our
numbers than those who immediately followed them.
Milton was the poetical son of Spenser, and Mr. Waller
of Fairfax ; for we have our lineal descents and clans
as well as other families.   Spenser more than once 20
insinuates, that the soul of Chaucer was transfused into
his body ; and that he was begotten by him two hundred
years after his decease.   Milton has acknowledged to
me, that Spenser was his original ; and many besides
myself have heard our famous Waller own, that he 25
derived the harmony of his numbers from *Godfrey*
of Bulloign, which was turned into English by Mr.
Fairfax.

But to return : having done with Ovid for this time,
it came into my mind, that our old English poet, 30
Chaucer, in many things resembled him, and that with
no disadvantage on the side of the modern author,
as I shall endeavour to prove when I compare them ;
and as I am, and always have been, studious to promote
the honour of my native country, so I soon resolved 35

to put their merits to the trial, by turning some of the *Canterbury Tales* into our language, as it is now refined ; for by this means both the poets being set in the same light, and dressed in the same English habit, story to
5 be compared with story, a certain judgment may be made betwixt them by the reader, without obtruding my opinion on him. Or if I seem partial to my countryman, and predecessor in the laurel, the friends of antiquity are not few ; and, besides many of the
10 learned, Ovid has almost all the *Beaux*, and the whole Fair Sex, his declared patrons. Perhaps I have assumed somewhat more to myself than they allow me, because I have adventured to sum up the evidence ; but the readers are the jury, and their privilege remains
15 entire, to decide according to the merits of the cause ; or, if they please, to bring it to another hearing before some other court. In the mean time, to follow the thrid of my discourse (as thoughts, according to Mr. Hobbes, have always some connexion,) so from
20 Chaucer I was led to think on Boccace, who was not only his contemporary, but also pursued the same studies ; wrote novels in prose, and many works in verse ; particularly is said to have invented the octave rhyme, or stanza of eight lines, which ever since has
25 been maintained by the practice of all Italian writers who are, or at least assume the title of heroic poets. He and Chaucer, among other things, had this in common, that they refined their mother-tongues ; but with this difference, that Dante had begun to file their
30 language, at least in verse, before the time of Boccace, who likewise received no little help from his master Petrarch ; but the reformation of their prose was wholly owing to Boccace himself, who is yet the standard of purity in the Italian tongue, though many of his phrases
35 are become obsolete, as in process of time it must

needs happen. Chaucer (as you have formerly been told by our learned Mr. Rymer) first adorned and amplified our barren tongue from the Provençal [1], which was then the most polished of all the modern languages; but this subject has been copiously treated [5] by that great critic, who deserves no little commendation from us his countrymen. For these reasons of time, and resemblance of genius, in Chaucer and Boccace, I resolved to join them in my present work; to which I have added some original papers of my own, [10] which whether they are equal or inferior to my other poems, an author is the most improper judge; and therefore I leave them wholly to the mercy of the reader. I will hope the best, that they will not be condemned; but if they should, I have the excuse of [15] an old gentleman, who, mounting on horseback before some ladies, when I was present, got up somewhat heavily, but desired of the fair spectators, that they would count fourscore and eight before they judged him. By the mercy of God, I am already come within [20] twenty years of his number, a cripple in my limbs, but what decays are in my mind, the reader must determine. I think myself as vigorous as ever in the faculties of my soul, excepting only my memory, which is not impaired to any great degree; and if I lose not [25] more of it, I have no great reason to complain. What judgment I had, increases rather than diminishes; and thoughts, such as they are, come crowding in so fast upon me, that my only difficulty is to choose or to reject, to run them into verse, or to give them the [30] other harmony of prose: I have so long studied and practised both, that they are grown into a habit, and become familiar to me. In short, though I may lawfully plead some part of the old gentleman's excuse,

[1] *Provencall*, ed. 1700.

yet I will reserve it till I think I have greater need,
and ask no grains of allowance for the faults of this
my present work, but those which are given of course
to human frailty. I will not trouble my reader with
5 the shortness of time in which I writ it, or the several
intervals of sickness. They who think too well of their
own performances, are apt to boast in their prefaces
how little time their works have cost them, and what
other business of more importance interfered ; but the
10 reader will be as apt to ask the question, why they
allowed not a longer time to make their works more
perfect ? and why they had so despicable an opinion
of their judges as to thrust their indigested stuff upon
them, as if they deserved no better ?
15   With this account of my present undertaking, I conclude the first part of this discourse : in the second part,
as at a second sitting, though I alter not the draught,
I must touch the same features over again, and change
the dead-colouring of the whole. In general I will only
20 say, that I have written nothing which savours of immorality or profaneness ; at least, I am not conscious to
myself of any such intention. If there happen to be
found an irreverent expression, or a thought too wanton,
they are crept into my verses through my inadvertency :
25 if the searchers find any in the cargo, let them be
staved or forfeited, like counterbanded goods ; at least,
let their authors be answerable for them, as being but
imported merchandise, and not of my own manufacture.
On the other side, I have endeavoured to choose such
30 fables, both ancient and modern, as contain in each of
them some instructive moral, which I could prove by
induction, but the way is tedious ; and they leap foremost
into sight, without the reader's trouble of looking after
them. I wish I could affirm with a safe conscience,
35 that I had taken the same care in all my former writ-

ings ; for it must be owned, that supposing verses are
never so beautiful or pleasing, yet, if they contain anything which shocks religion or good manners, they are
at best what Horace says of good numbers without
good sense, *Versus inopes rerum nugæque canoræ*. Thus 5
far, I hope, I am right in court, without renouncing
to my other right of self-defence, where I have been
wrongfully accused, and my sense wire-drawn into
blasphemy or bawdry, as it has often been by a religious
lawyer, in a late pleading against the stage ; in which 10
he mixes truth with falsehood, and has not forgotten
the old rule of calumniating strongly, that something
may remain.

I resume the thrid of my discourse with the first of
my translations, which was the first *Iliad* of Homer. If 15
it shall please God to give me longer life, and moderate
health, my intentions are to translate the whole *Ilias* ;
provided still that I meet with those encouragements
from the public, which may enable me to proceed in my
undertaking with some cheerfulness. And this I dare 20
assure the world beforehand, that I have found, by trial,
Homer a more pleasing task than Virgil, though I say
not the translation will be less laborious ; for the Grecian
is more according to my genius than the Latin poet.
In the works of the two authors we may read their 25
manners, and natural inclinations, which are wholly
different. Virgil was of a quiet, sedate temper ; Homer
was violent, impetuous, and full of fire. The chief
talent of Virgil was propriety of thoughts, and ornament
of words : Homer was rapid in his thoughts, and took 30
all the liberties, both of numbers and of expressions,
which his language, and the age in which he lived,
allowed him. Homer's invention was more copious,
Virgil's more confined ; so that if Homer had not led
the way, it was not in Virgil to have begun heroic 35

poetry ; for nothing can be more evident, than that the
Roman poem is but the second part of the *Ilias* ; a continuation of the same story, and the persons already
formed.   The manners of Æneas are those of Hector,
5 superadded to those which Homer gave him.   The
adventures of Ulysses in the *Odysseis* are imitated in
the first Six Books of Virgil's *Æneis* ; and though the
accidents are not the same, (which would have argued
him of a servile copying, and total barrenness of in-
10 vention,) yet the seas were the same in which both
the heroes wandered ; and Dido cannot be denied to
be the poetical daughter of Calypso.   The six latter
Books of Virgil's poem are the four-and-twenty *Iliads*
contracted ; a quarrel occasioned by a lady, a single
15 combat, battles fought, and a town besieged.   I say
not this in derogation to Virgil, neither do I contradict
anything which I have formerly said in his just praise ;
for his episodes are almost wholly of his own invention,
and the form which he has given to the telling makes
20 the tale his own, even though the original story had
been the same.   But this proves, however, that Homer
taught Virgil to design ; and if invention be the first
virtue of an epic poet, then the Latin poem can only be
allowed the second place.   Mr. Hobbes, in the preface
25 to his own bald translation of the *Ilias*, (studying
poetry as he did mathematics, when it was too late,)
Mr. Hobbes, I say, begins the praise of Homer where
he should have ended it.   He tells us, that the first
beauty of an epic poem consists in diction ; that is, in
30 the choice of words, and harmony of numbers.   Now
the words are the colouring of the work, which, in the
order of nature, is last to be considered.   The design,
the disposition, the manners, and the thoughts, are all
before it : where any of those are wanting or imperfect,
35 so much wants or is imperfect in the imitation of human

life, which is in the very definition of a poem. Words,
indeed, like glaring colours, are the first beauties that
arise and strike the sight ; but, if the draught be false
or lame, the figures ill disposed, the manners obscure
or inconsistent, or the thoughts unnatural, then the 5
finest colours are but daubing, and the piece is a beautiful monster at the best. Neither Virgil nor Homer
were deficient in any of the former beauties ; but in this
last, which is expression, the Roman poet is at least
equal to the Grecian, as I have said elsewhere : supply- 10
ing the poverty of his language by his musical ear, and
by his diligence.

But to return : our two great poets being so different
in their tempers, one choleric and sanguine, the other
phlegmatic and melancholic ; that which makes them 15
excel in their several ways is, that each of them has
followed his own natural inclination, as well in forming
the design, as in the execution of it. The very heroes
shew their authors : Achilles is hot, impatient, revengeful— 20

> *Impiger, iracundus, inexorabilis, acer, &c.,*

Æneas patient, considerate, careful of his people, and
merciful to his enemies ; ever submissive to the will of
heaven—

> *quo fata trahunt retrahuntque, sequamur.* 25

I could please myself with enlarging on this subject,
but am forced to defer it to a fitter time. From all
I have said, I will only draw this inference, that the
action of Homer, being more full of vigour than that of
Virgil, according to the temper of the writer, is of con- 30
sequence more pleasing to the reader. One warms you
by degrees ; the other sets you on fire all at once, and
never intermits his heat. 'Tis the same difference
which Longinus makes betwixt the effects of eloquence

in Demosthenes and Tully ; one persuades, the other
commands. You never cool while you read Homer,
even not in the Second Book (a graceful flattery to his
countrymen) ; but he hastens from the ships, and con-
5 cludes not that book till he has made you an amends
by the violent playing of a new machine. From thence
he hurries on his action with variety of events, and
ends it in less compass than two months. This vehem-
ence of his, I confess, is more suitable to my temper ;
10 and therefore I have translated his First Book with
greater pleasure than any part of Virgil ; but it was
not a pleasure without pains. The continual agitations
of the spirits must needs be a weakening of any constitution, especially in age ; and many pauses are required
15 for refreshment betwixt the heats ; the *Iliad* of itself
being a third part longer than all Virgil's works together.

This is what I thought needful in this place to say
of Homer. I proceed to Ovid and Chaucer ; consider-
20 ing the former only in relation to the latter. With
Ovid ended the golden age of the Roman tongue ; from
Chaucer the purity of the English tongue began. The
manners of the poets were not unlike. Both of them
were well-bred, well-natured, amorous, and libertine,
25 at least in their writings, it may be also in their lives.
Their studies were the same, philosophy and philology.
Both of them were knowing in astronomy ; of which
Ovid's books of the Roman Feasts, and Chaucer's
Treatise of the Astrolabe, are sufficient witnesses. But
30 Chaucer was likewise an astrologer, as were Virgil,
Horace, Persius, and Manilius. Both writ with wonderful facility and clearness ; neither were great inventors :
for Ovid only copied the Grecian fables, and most of
Chaucer's stories were taken from his Italian contem-
35 poraries, or their predecessors. Boccace his *Decameron*

was first published, and from thence our Englishman
has borrowed many of his *Canterbury Tales* : yet that of
Palamon and Arcite was written, in all probability, by
some Italian wit, in a former age, as I shall prove
hereafter. The tale of Grizild was the invention of 5
Petrarch ; by him sent to Boccace, from whom it came
to Chaucer. *Troilus and Cressida* was also written by
a Lombard author, but much amplified by our English
translator, as well as beautified ; the genius of our
countrymen in general being rather to improve an 10
invention than to invent themselves, as is evident not
only in our poetry, but in many of our manufactures.
I find I have anticipated already, and taken up from
Boccace before I come to him : but there is so much
less behind ; and I am of the temper of most kings, who 15
love to be in debt, are all for present money, no matter
how they pay it afterwards : besides, the nature of a
preface is rambling, never wholly out of the way, nor in
it. This I have learned from the practice of honest
Montaigne, and return at my pleasure to Ovid and 20
Chaucer, of whom I have little more to say.

Both of them built on the inventions of other men ;
yet since Chaucer had something of his own, as the
Wife of Bath's Tale, the *Cock and the Fox*, which I have
translated, and some others, I may justly give our 25
countryman the precedence in that part ; since I can
remember nothing of Ovid which was wholly his. Both
of them understood the manners ; under which name
I comprehend the passions, and, in a larger sense, the
descriptions of persons, and their very habits. For an 30
example, I see Baucis and Philemon as perfectly before
me, as if some ancient painter had drawn them ; and all
the Pilgrims in the *Canterbury Tales*, their humours,
their features, and the very dress, as distinctly as if
I had supped with them at the Tabard in Southwark. 35

Yet even there too the figures of Chaucer are much more lively, and set in a better light ; which though I have not time to prove, yet I appeal to the reader, and am sure he will clear me from partiality. The thoughts and words remain to be considered, in the comparison of the two poets, and I have saved myself one-half of the labour, by owning that Ovid lived when the Roman tongue was in its meridian ; Chaucer, in the dawning of our language : therefore that part of the comparison stands not on an equal foot, any more than the diction of Ennius and Ovid, or of Chaucer and our present English. The words are given up as a post not to be defended in our poet, because he wanted the modern art of fortifying. The thoughts remain to be considered : and they are to be measured only by their propriety ; that is, as they flow more or less naturally from the persons described, on such and such occasions. The vulgar judges, which are nine parts in ten of all nations, who call conceits and jingles wit, who see Ovid full of them, and Chaucer altogether without them, will think me little less than mad for preferring the Englishman to the Roman. Yet, with their leave, I must presume to say, that the things they admire are only glittering trifles, and so far from being witty, that in a serious poem they are nauseous, because they are unnatural. Would any man who is ready to die for love, describe his passion like Narcissus ? Would he think of *inopem me copia fecit*, and a dozen more of such expressions, poured on the neck of one another, and signifying all the same thing ? If this were wit, was this a time to be witty, when the poor wretch was in the agony of death ? This is just John Littlewit in *Bartholomew Fair*, who had a conceit (as he tells you) left him in his misery ; a miserable conceit. On these occasions the poet should endeavour to raise pity ; but, instead of this, Ovid is tickling you to laugh. Virgil never made use of such machines when he was moving you to commiserate the death of Dido : he would not destroy what he was building. Chaucer makes Arcite violent in his love, and unjust in the pursuit of it ; yet, when he came 5 to die, he made him think more reasonably : he repents not of his love, for that had altered his character ; but acknowledges the injustice of his proceedings, and resigns Emilia to Palamon. What would Ovid have done on this occasion ? He would certainly have made 10 Arcite witty on his deathbed ; he had complained he was further off from possession, by being so near, and a thousand such boyisms, which Chaucer rejected as below the dignity of the subject. They who think otherwise, would, by the same reason, prefer Lucan and 15 Ovid to Homer and Virgil, and Martial to all four of them. As for the turn of words, in which Ovid particularly excels all poets, they are sometimes a fault, and sometimes a beauty, as they are used properly or improperly ; but in strong passions always to be 20 shunned, because passions are serious, and will admit no playing. The French have a high value for them ; and, I confess, they are often what they call delicate, when they are introduced with judgment ; but Chaucer writ with more simplicity, and followed Nature more 25 closely, than to use them. I have thus far, to the best of my knowledge, been an upright judge betwixt the parties in competition, not meddling with the design nor the disposition of it ; because the design was not their own ; and in the disposing of it they were equal. It 30 remains that I say somewhat of Chaucer in particular.

In the first place, as he is the father of English poetry, so I hold him in the same degree of veneration as the Grecians held Homer, or the Romans Virgil. He is a perpetual fountain of good sense ; learn'd in all 35

sciences ; and, therefore, speaks properly on all subjects. As he knew what to say, so he knows also when
to leave off ; a continence which is practised by few
writers, and scarcely by any of the ancients, excepting
5 Virgil and Horace. One of our late great poets is
sunk in his reputation, because he could never forgive
any conceit which came in his way ; but swept like
a drag-net, great and small. There was plenty enough,
but the dishes were ill sorted ; whole pyramids of sweet-
10 meats, for boys and women ; but little of solid meat, for
men. All this proceeded not from any want of knowledge, but of judgment. Neither did he want that in
discerning the beauties and faults of other poets, but
only indulged himself in the luxury of writing ; and
15 perhaps knew it was a fault, but hoped the reader would
not find it. For this reason, though he must always be
thought a great poet, he is no longer esteemed a good
writer ; and for ten impressions, which his works have
had in so many successive years, yet at present a
20 hundred books are scarcely purchased once a twelve-
month ; for, as my last Lord Rochester said, though
somewhat profanely, *Not being of God, he could not
stand*.

Chaucer followed Nature everywhere, but was never
25 so bold to go beyond her ; and there is a great difference of being *poeta* and *nimis poeta*, if we may believe
Catullus, as much as betwixt a modest behaviour and
affectation. The verse of Chaucer, I confess, is not
harmonious to us ; but 'tis like the eloquence of one
30 whom Tacitus commends, it was *auribus istius temporis
accommodata :* they who lived with him, and some time
after him, thought it musical ; and it continues so even
in our judgment, if compared with the numbers of
Lidgate and Gower, his contemporaries : there is the
35 rude sweetness of a Scotch tune in it, which is natural

and pleasing, though not perfect. 'Tis true, I cannot
go so far as he who published the last edition of him ;
for he would make us believe the fault is in our ears,
and that there were really ten syllables in a verse where
we find but nine : but this opinion is not worth con- 5
futing ; 'tis so gross and obvious an error, that common
sense (which is a rule in everything but matters of
Faith and Revelation) must convince the reader, that
equality of numbers, in every verse which we call *heroic,*
was either not known, or not always practised, in 10
Chaucer's age. It were an easy matter to produce
some thousands of his verses, which are lame for want
of half a foot, and sometimes a whole one, and which
no pronunciation can make otherwise. We can only
say, that he lived in the infancy of our poetry, and that 15
nothing is brought to perfection at the first. We must
be children before we grow men. There was an Ennius,
and in process of time a Lucilius, and a Lucretius,
before Virgil and Horace ; even after Chaucer there
was a Spenser, a Harrington, a Fairfax, before Waller 20
and Denham were in being ; and our numbers were in
their nonage till these last appeared. I need say little
of his parentage, life, and fortunes ; they are to be found
at large in all the editions of his works. He was employed abroad, and favoured, by Edward the Third, 25
Richard the Second, and Henry the Fourth, and was
poet, as I suppose, to all three of them. In Richard's
time, I doubt, he was a little dipt in the rebellion of
the Commons ; and being brother-in-law to John of
Ghant, it was no wonder if he followed the fortunes 30
of that family ; and was well with Henry the Fourth
when he had deposed his predecessor. Neither is it to
be admired, that Henry, who was a wise as well as
a valiant prince, who claimed by succession, and was
sensible that his title was not sound, but was rightfully 35

in Mortimer, who had married the heir of York ; it was
not to be admired, I say, if that great politician should
be pleased to have the greatest Wit of those times in
his interests, and to be the trumpet of his praises.
5 Augustus had given him the example, by the advice
of Mæcenas, who recommended Virgil and Horace to
him ; whose praises helped to make him popular while
he was alive, and after his death have made him precious to posterity. As for the religion of our poet, he
10 seems to have some little bias towards the opinions of
Wickliff, after John of Ghant his patron ; somewhat
of which appears in the tale of *Piers Plowman* : yet
I cannot blame him for inveighing so sharply against
the vices of the clergy in his age : their pride, their
15 ambition, their pomp, their avarice, their worldly interest, deserved the lashes which he gave them, both
in that, and in most of his *Canterbury Tales*. Neither
has his contemporary Boccace spared them : yet both
those poets lived in much esteem with good and holy
20 men in orders ; for the scandal which is given by
particular priests reflects not on the sacred function.
Chaucer's Monk, his Canon, and his Friar, took not
from the character of his Good Parson. A satirical poet
is the check of the laymen on bad priests. We are only
25 to take care, that we involve not the innocent with the
guilty in the same condemnation. The good cannot be
too much honoured, nor the bad too coarsely used ; for
the corruption of the best becomes the worst. When
a clergyman is whipped, his gown is first taken off, by
30 which the dignity of his order is secured. If he be
wrongfully accused, he has his action of slander ; and
'tis at the poet's peril if he transgress the law. But
they will tell us, that all kind of satire, though never so
well deserved by particular priests, yet brings the whole
35 order into contempt. Is then the peerage of England

anything dishonoured when a peer suffers for his treason ? If he be libelled, or any way defamed, he has his *scandalum magnatum* to punish the offender. They who use this kind of argument, seems to be conscious to themselves of somewhat which has deserved the poet's lash, and are less concerned for their public capacity than for their private ; at least there is pride at the bottom of their reasoning. If the faults of men in orders are only to be judged among themselves, they are all in some sort parties ; for, since they say the honour of their order is concerned in every member of it, how can we be sure that they will be impartial judges ? How far I may be allowed to speak my opinion in this case, I know not ; but I am sure a dispute of this nature caused mischief in abundance betwixt a King of England and an Archbishop of Canterbury ; one standing up for the laws of his land, and the other for the honour (as he called it) of God's Church ; which ended in the murder of the prelate, and in the whipping of his Majesty from post to pillar for his penance. The learned and ingenious Dr. Drake has saved me the labour of inquiring into the esteem and reverence which the priests have had of old ; and I would rather extend than diminish any part of it : yet I must needs say, that when a priest provokes me without any occasion given him, I have no reason, unless it be the charity of a Christian, to forgive him : *prior læsit* is justification sufficient in the civil law. If I answer him in his own language, self-defence, I am sure must be allowed me ; and if I carry it further, even to a sharp recrimination, somewhat may be indulged to human frailty. Yet my resentment has not wrought so far, but that I have followed Chaucer, in his character of a holy man, and have enlarged on that subject with some pleasure ; reserving to myself the right, if I shall think fit here-

after, to describe another sort of priests, such as are
more easily to be found than the Good Parson ; such as
have given the last blow to Christianity in this age, by
a practice so contrary to their doctrine. But this will
5 keep cold till another time. In the meanwhile, I take
up Chaucer where I left him.

He must have been a man of a most wonderful
comprehensive nature, because, as it has been truly
observed of him, he has taken into the compass of his
10 *Canterbury Tales* the various manners and humours (as
we now call them) of the whole English nation, in his
age. Not a single character has escaped him. All his
pilgrims are severally distinguished from each other ;
and not only in their inclinations, but in their very
15 physiognomies and persons. Baptista Porta could not
have described their natures better, than by the marks
which the poet gives them. The matter and manner of
their tales, and of their telling, are so suited to their
different educations, humours, and callings, that each of
20 them would be improper in any other mouth. Even
the grave and serious characters are distinguished by
their several sorts of gravity : their discourses are such
as belong to their age, their calling, and their breeding ;
such as are becoming of them, and of them only. Some
25 of his persons are vicious, and some virtuous ; some
are unlearn'd, or (as Chaucer calls them) lewd, and some
are learn'd. Even the ribaldry of the low characters
is different : the Reeve, the Miller, and the Cook, are
several men, and distinguished from each other as much
30 as the mincing Lady-Prioress and the broad-speaking,
gap-toothed Wife of Bath. But enough of this ; there
is such a variety of game springing up before me, that
I am distracted in my choice, and know not which to
follow. 'Tis sufficient to say according to the proverb,
35 that here is God's plenty. We have our forefathers

and great-grand-dames all before us, as they were in
Chaucer's days ; their general characters are still remaining in mankind, and even in England, though they
are called by other names than those of Monks, and
Friars, and Canons, and Lady Abbesses, and Nuns ; 5
for mankind is ever the same, and nothing lost out of
Nature, though everything is altered. May I have
leave to do myself the justice, (since my enemies will
do me none, and are so far from granting me to be
a good poet, that they will not allow me so much as to 10
be a Christian, or a moral man), may I have leave, I say,
to inform my reader, that I have confined my choice to
such tales of Chaucer as savour nothing of immodesty.
If I had desired more to please than to instruct, the
Reeve, the Miller, the Shipman, the Merchant, the 15
Sumner, and, above all, the Wife of Bath, in the *Prologue*
to her *Tale*, would have procured me as many friends
and readers, as there are *beaux* and ladies of pleasure
in the town. But I will no more offend against good
manners : I am sensible as I ought to be of the scandal 20
I have given by my loose writings ; and make what
reparation I am able, by this public acknowledgment.
If anything of this nature, or of profaneness, be crept
into these poems, I am so far from defending it, that
I disown it. *Totum hoc indictum volo.* Chaucer makes 25
another manner of apology for his broad speaking, and
Boccace makes the like ; but I will follow neither of
them. Our countryman, in the end of his Characters,
before the *Canterbury Tales*, thus excuses the ribaldry,
which is very gross, in many of his novels : 30

> *But firste, I pray you, of your courtesy,*
> *That ye ne arrete it nought my villany,*
> *Though that I plainly speak in this mattere*
> *To tellen you her words, and eke her chere :*
> *Ne though I speak her words properly,* 35
> *For this ye known as well as I,*

Who shall tellen a tale after a man
He mote rehearse as nye, as ever He can :
Everich word of it ben in his charge,
All speke he, never so rudely, ne large :
5 *Or else he mote tellen his tale untrue,*
Or feine things, or find words new :
He may not spare, altho he were his brother,
He mote as wel say o word as another.
Crist spake himself ful broad in holy Writ,
10 *And well I wote no Villany is it.*
Eke Plato saith, who so can him rede,
The words mote been Cousin to the dede.

    Yet if a man should have enquired of Boccace or of
Chaucer, what need they had of introducing such char-
15 acters, where obscene words were proper in their mouths,
but very undecent to be heard ; I know not what answer
they could have made ; for that reason, such tales shall
be left untold by me. You have here a *Specimen* of
Chaucer's language, which is so obsolete, that his sense
20 is scarce to be understood ; and you have likewise more
than one example of his unequal numbers, which were
mentioned before. Yet many of his verses consist of
ten syllables, and the words not much behind our present English : as for example, these two lines, in the
25 description of the Carpenter's young wife :

    Wincing she was, as is a jolly Colt,
    Long as a Mast, and upright as a Bolt.

    I have almost done with Chaucer, when I have an-
swered some objections relating to my present work.
30 I find some people are offended that I have turned these
tales into modern English ; because they think them
unworthy of my pains, and look on Chaucer as a dry,
old-fashioned wit, not worth reviving [1]. I have often
heard the late Earl of Leicester say, that Mr. Cowley
35 himself was of that opinion ; who, having read him over

        [1] *receiving*, ed. 1700.

at my Lord's request, declared he had no taste of him.
I dare not advance my opinion against the judgment of
so great an author ; but I think it fair, however, to leave
the decision to the public. Mr. Cowley was too modest
to set up for a dictator ; and being shocked perhaps 5
with his old style, never examined into the depth of his
good sense. Chaucer, I confess, is a rough diamond,
and must first be polished ere he shines. I deny not
likewise, that, living in our early days of poetry, he
writes not always of a piece ; but sometimes mingles 10
trivial things with those of greater moment. Sometimes
also, though not often, he runs riot, like Ovid, and knows
not when he has said enough. But there are more
great wits besides Chaucer, whose fault is their excess
of conceits, and those ill sorted. An author is not to 15
write all he can, but only all he ought. Having observed
this redundancy in Chaucer, (as it is an easy matter for
a man of ordinary parts to find a fault in one of greater,)
I have not tied myself to a literal translation ; but have
often omitted what I judged unnecessary, or not of dig- 20
nity enough to appear in the company of better thoughts.
I have presumed farther in some places, and added
somewhat of my own where I thought my author was
deficient, and had not given his thoughts their true
lustre, for want of words in the beginning of our lan- 25
guage. And to this I was the more emboldened, because
(if I may be permitted to say it of myself) I found I had
a soul congenial to his, and that I had been conversant
in the same studies. Another poet, in another age, may
take the same liberty with my writings ; if at least they 30
live long enough to deserve correction. It was also
necessary sometimes to restore the sense of Chaucer,
which was lost or mangled in the errors of the press.
Let this example suffice at present : in the story of
Palamon and Arcite, where the temple of Diana is 35

described, you find these verses, in all the editions of
our author :

> *There saw I* Danè *turned unto a Tree,*
> *I mean not the Goddess* Diane,
> 5   *But* Venus *Daughter, which that hight* Danè.

Which after a little consideration I knew was to be
reformed into this sense, that Daphne the daughter of
Peneus was turned into a tree. I durst not make thus
bold with Ovid, lest some future Milbourne should arise,
10 and say, I varied from my author, because I understood
him not.

But there are other judges, who think I ought not to
have translated Chaucer into English, out of a quite
contrary notion : they suppose there is a certain venera-
15 tion due to his old language ; and that it is little less
than profanation and sacrilege to alter it. They are
farther of opinion, that somewhat of his good sense will
suffer in this transfusion, and much of the beauty of his
thoughts will infallibly be lost, which appear with more
20 grace in their old habit. Of this opinion was that excellent person whom I mentioned, the late Earl of Leicester,
who valued Chaucer as much as Mr. Cowley despised
him. My Lord dissuaded me from this attempt, (for
I was thinking of it some years before his death,) and
25 his authority prevailed so far with me, as to defer my
undertaking while he lived, in deference to him : yet
my reason was not convinced with what he urged against
it. If the first end of a writer be to be understood, then,
as his language grows obsolete, his thoughts must grow
30 obscure—

> *Multa renascentur, quæ nunc cecidere ; cadentque*
> *Quæ nunc sunt in honore vocabula, si volet usus,*
> *Quem penes arbitrium est et jus et norma loquendi.*

When an ancient word for its sound and significancy
35 deserves to be revived, I have that reasonable venera-

tion for antiquity to restore it. All beyond this is superstition. Words are not like landmarks, so sacred as never to be removed ; customs are changed, and even statutes are silently repealed, when the reason ceases for which they were enacted. As for the other part of 5 the argument, that his thoughts will lose of their original beauty by the innovation of words ; in the first place, not only their beauty, but their being is lost, where they are no longer understood, which is the present case. I grant that something must be lost in all transfusion, 10 that is, in all translations ; but the sense will remain, which would otherwise be lost, or at least be maimed, when it is scarce intelligible, and that but to a few. How few are there who can read Chaucer, so as to understand him perfectly ? And if imperfectly, then 15 with less profit, and no pleasure. 'Tis not for the use of some old Saxon friends, that I have taken these pains with him : let them neglect my version, because they have no need of it. I made it for their sakes who understand sense and poetry as well as they, when 20 that poetry and sense is put into words which they understand. I will go farther, and dare to add, that what beauties I lose in some places, I give to others which had them not originally : but in this I may be partial to myself ; let the reader judge, and I submit to 25 his decision. Yet I think I have just occasion to complain of them, who because they understand Chaucer, would deprive the greater part of their countrymen of the same advantage, and hoard him up, as misers do their grandam gold, only to look on it themselves, and 30 hinder others from making use of it. In sum, I seriously protest, that no man ever had, or can have, a greater veneration for Chaucer than myself. I have translated some part of his works, only that I might perpetuate his memory, or at least refresh it, amongst my countrymen. 35

If I have altered him anywhere for the better, I must at the same time acknowledge, that I could have done nothing without him. *Facile est inventis addere* is no great commendation ; and I am not so vain to think 5 I have deserved a greater. I will conclude what I have to say of him singly, with this one remark : A lady of my acquaintance, who keeps a kind of correspondence with some authors of the fair sex in France, has been informed by them, that Mademoiselle de Scudery, who 10 is as old as Sibyl, and inspired like her by the same God of Poetry, is at this time translating Chaucer into modern French. From which I gather, that he has been formerly translated into the old Provençal ; for how she should come to understand old English, I know 15 not. But the matter of fact being true, it makes me think that there is something in it like fatality ; that, after certain periods of time, the fame and memory of great Wits should be renewed, as Chaucer is both in France and England. If this be wholly chance, 'tis 20 extraordinary ; and I dare not call it more, for fear of being taxed with superstition.

Boccace comes last to be considered, who, living in the same age with Chaucer, had the same genius, and followed the same studies. Both writ novels, and each 25 of them cultivated his mother tongue. But the greatest resemblance of our two modern authors being in their familiar style, and pleasing way of relating comical adventures, I may pass it over, because I have translated nothing from Boccace of that nature. In the 30 serious part of poetry, the advantage is wholly on Chaucer's side ; for though the Englishman has borrowed many tales from the Italian, yet it appears, that those of Boccace were not generally of his own making, but taken from authors of former ages, and by him only 35 modelled ; so that what there was of invention, in either

of them, may be judged equal. But Chaucer has
refined on Boccace, and has mended the stories, which
he has borrowed, in his way of telling ; though prose
allows more liberty of thought, and the expression is
more easy when unconfined by numbers. Our country- 5
man carries weight, and yet wins the race at disadvantage. I desire not the reader should take my word ;
and, therefore, I will set two of their discourses, on the
same subject, in the same light, for every man to judge
betwixt them. I translated Chaucer first, and, amongst 10
the rest, pitched on the Wife of Bath's Tale ; not daring,
as I have said, to adventure on her *Prologue*, because
'tis too licentious. There Chaucer introduces an old
woman, of mean parentage, whom a youthful knight, of
noble blood, was forced to marry, and consequently 15
loathed her. The crone being in bed with him on the
wedding-night, and finding his aversion, endeavours to
win his affection by reason, and speaks a good word for
herself, (as who could blame her ?) in hope to mollify
the sullen bridegroom. She takes her topics from the 20
benefits of poverty, the advantages of old age and ugliness, the vanity of youth, and the silly pride of ancestry
and titles, without inherent virtue, which is the true
nobility. When I had closed Chaucer, I returned to
Ovid, and translated some more of his fables ; and, by 25
this time, had so far forgotten the Wife of Bath's Tale,
that, when I took up Boccace, unawares I fell on the
same argument, of preferring virtue to nobility of blood
and titles, in the story of *Sigismonda* ; which I had
certainly avoided, for the resemblance of the two dis- 30
courses, if my memory had not failed me. Let the
reader weigh them both ; and, if he thinks me partial to
Chaucer, 'tis in him to right Boccace.

I prefer, in our countryman, far above all his other
stories, the noble poem of Palamon and Arcite, which is 35

of the epic kind, and perhaps not much inferior to the
Ilias, or the *Æneis*. The story is more pleasing than
either of them, the manners as perfect, the diction as
poetical, the learning as deep and various, and the
5 disposition full as artful : only it includes a greater
length of time, as taking up seven years at least ; but
Aristotle has left undecided the duration of the action ;
which yet is easily reduced into the compass of a year,
by a narration of what preceded the return of Palamon
10 to Athens. I had thought, for the honour of our narration, and more particularly for his, whose laurel, though
unworthy, I have worn after him, that this story was of
English growth, and Chaucer's own : but I was unde-
ceived by Boccace ; for, casually looking on the end of
15 his seventh *Giornata*, I found Dioneo, (under which
name he shadows himself,) and Fiametta, (who represents his mistress, the natural daughter of Robert, King
of Naples,) of whom these words are spoken : *Dioneo e
Fiametta gran pezza cantarono insieme d'Arcita, e di*
20 *Palemone ;* by which it appears, that this story was
written before the time of Boccace ; but the name of its
author being wholly lost, Chaucer is now become an
original ; and I question not but the poem has received
many beauties, by passing through his noble hands.
25 Besides this tale, there is another of his own invention,
after the manner of the Provençals, called *The Flower
and the Leaf*, with which I was so particularly pleased,
both for the invention and the moral, that I cannot
hinder myself from recommending it to the reader.
30 As a corollary to this preface, in which I have done
justice to others, I owe somewhat to myself : not that
I think it worth my time to enter the lists with one
M——, or one B——, but barely to take notice, that
such men there are, who have written scurrilously
35 against me, without any provocation. M——, who is

in orders, pretends, amongst the rest, this quarrel to
me, that I have fallen foul on priesthood : if I have,
I am only to ask pardon of good priests, and am afraid
his part of the reparation will come to little. Let him
be satisfied, that he shall not be able to force himself 5
upon me for an adversary. I contemn him too much to
enter into competition with him. His own translations
of Virgil have answered his criticisms on mine. If (as
they say, he has declared in print) he prefers the
version of Ogilby to mine, the world has made him the 10
same compliment ; for 'tis agreed on all hands, that he
writes even below Ogilby. That, you will say, is not
easily to be done ; but what cannot M—— bring about ?
I am satisfied, however, that, while he and I live together, I shall not be thought the worst poet of the age. 15
It looks as if I had desired him underhand to write so
ill against me ; but upon my honest word I have not
bribed him to do me this service, and am wholly guilt-
less of his pamphlet. 'Tis true, I should be glad if
I could persuade him to continue his good offices, and 20
write such another critique on anything of mine ; for
I find, by experience, he has a great stroke with the
reader, when he condemns any of my poems, to make
the world have a better opinion of them. He has taken
some pains with my poetry ; but nobody will be per- 25
suaded to take the same with his. If I had taken to
the Church (as he affirms, but which was never in my
thoughts) I should have had more sense, if not more
grace, than to have turned myself out of my benefice,
by writing libels on my parishioners. But his account 30
of my manners and my principles are of a piece with
his cavils and his poetry ; and so I have done with him
for ever.

As for the City Bard, or Knight Physician, I hear his
quarrel to me is, that I was the author of *Absalom and* 35

Achitophel, which, he thinks, is a little hard on his
fanatic patrons in London.

But I will deal the more civilly with his two poems,
because nothing ill is to be spoken of the dead ; and
5 therefore peace be to the *Manes* of his *Arthurs*. I will
only say, that it was not for this noble Knight that
I drew the plan of an epic poem on *King Arthur*, in my
preface to the translation of Juvenal. The Guardian
Angels of kingdoms were machines too ponderous for
10 him to manage ; and therefore he rejected them, as
Dares did the whirl-bats of Eryx when they were thrown
before him by Entellus : yet from that preface he
plainly took his hint ; for he began immediately upon
the story, though he had the baseness not to acknow-
15 ledge his benefactor, but instead of it, to traduce me in
a libel.

I shall say the less of Mr. Collier, because in many
things he has taxed me justly ; and I have pleaded
guilty to all thoughts and expressions of mine, which
20 can be truly argued of obscenity, profaneness, or immorality, and retract them. If he be my enemy, let him
triumph ; if he be my friend, as I have given him no
personal occasion to be otherwise, he will be glad of my
repentance. It becomes me not to draw my pen in the
25 defence of a bad cause, when I have so often drawn it
for a good one. Yet it were not difficult to prove, that
in many places he has perverted my meaning by his
glosses, and interpreted my words into blasphemy and
bawdry, of which they were not guilty. Besides that,
30 he is too much given to horse-play in his raillery, and
comes to battle like a dictator from the plough. I will
not say, *The Zeal of God's House has eaten him up* ; but
I am sure it has devoured some part of his good
manners and civility. It might also be doubted, whether
35 it were altogether zeal which prompted him to this

rough manner of proceeding ; perhaps it became not
one of his function to rake into the rubbish of ancient
and modern plays ; a divine might have employed his
pains to better purpose, than in the nastiness of Plautus
and Aristophanes, whose examples, as they excuse not 5
me, so it might be possibly supposed, that he read them
not without some pleasure. They who have written
commentaries on those poets, or on Horace, Juvenal,
and Martial, have explained some vices, which without
their interpretation had been unknown to modern 10
times. Neither has he judged impartially betwixt the
former age and us. There is more bawdry in one play
of Fletcher's, called *The Custom of the Country*, than in
all ours together. Yet this has been often acted on the
stage in my remembrance. Are the times so much 15
more reformed now, than they were five-and-twenty
years ago ? If they are, I congratulate the amendment
of our morals. But I am not to prejudice the cause of
my fellow-poets, though I abandon my own defence :
they have some of them answered for themselves, and 20
neither they nor I can think Mr. Collier so formidable
an enemy that we should shun him. He has lost
ground at the latter end of the day, by pursuing his
point too far, like the Prince of Condé at the battle of
Senneph : from immoral plays to no plays, *ab abusu ad* 25
usum, non valet consequentia. But being a party, I am
not to erect myself into a judge. As for the rest of
those who have written against me, they are such
scoundrels, that they deserve not the least notice to
be taken of them. B —— and M —— are only dis- 30
tinguished from the crowd by being remembered to
their infamy :

> . . . *Demetri, teque Tigelli,*
> *Discipulorum inter jubeo plorare cathedras.*

NOTES

DEDICATION OF THIRD MISCELLANY (1693).

Lord Radcliffe, eldest son of Francis Earl of Derwentwater.
P. 2, l. 31. *the best poet.* Lord Dorset *to Mr. Edward Howard
on his incomparable, incomprehensible Poem, called the British
Princes* :

       ' Wit like tierce-claret, when 't begins to pall,
       Neglected lies, and 's of no use at all,
       But in its full perfection of decay,
       Turns vinegar and comes again in play.'

    l. 35. *Thus the corruption of a poet is the generation of a critic* ;
v. sup. p. 119, l. 13. This has often been repeated : ' the readiest-
made critics are cut-down poets ' (Landor's *Porson*). Cf. Pope,
Essay on Criticism, and Disraeli, *Lothair*.

    Zoilus. Cf. Longinus, c. 9 τοὺς ἐκ Κίρκης συομορφουμένους οὓς ὁ
Ζωΐλος ἔφη χοιρίδια κλαίοντα.

    P. 3, l. 11. *he who endeavoured to defame Virgil.* Cf. Teuffel,
Latin Literature, § 225, 3. Servius on *Ecl.* 2, 22, *hunc versum male
distinguens Vergiliomastix vituperat.* Carvilius Pictor wrote an
Aeneidomastix.

    l. 27. *to fall on Lucan.* Petronius, *Satyr.* cc. 118–124.

    l. 31. *Scaliger*, on Homer : *Poetices Liber V qui et Criticus* ;
cap. 3, *Homeri et Virgilii Loca* ; beginning *Homeri epitheta saepe
frigida, aut puerilia, aut locis inepta.* Vida had before this rebuked
the impertinences of Homer, especially in his similes :

    ' Sed non Ausonii recte foedissima musca
    Militis aequarit numerum, cum plurima mulctram
    Pervolitat, neque enim in Latio magno ore sonantem
    Arma ducesque decet tam viles decidere in res.'
                               (Poetic. ii.)

Hypercritic. *Hypercriticus* is the title of Scaliger's Sixth Book,
in which the passage on Claudian occurs, c. 5 ; already quoted
by Dryden.

    P. 4, l. 11. *Lucan.* Scaliger, *op. cit.* vi. c. 6 : ' Proinde ut nimis
fortasse libere dicam, interdum mihi latrare, non canere videtur.'

    l. 23. *non ingeniis.* ' Ingeniis non ille favet plauditque
sepultis,' Hor. *Ep.* ii. 1, 88.

P. 5, l. 28. *seemingly courted.* Cf. Rymer's plan for a tragedy
called *The Invincible Armado* on the model of the *Persae* of
Aeschylus : ' If Mr. *Dryden* might try his Pen on this Subject,
doubtless to an Audience that heartily love their Countrey, and
glory in the Vertue of their Ancestors, his imitation of *Aeschylus*
would have better success, and would *Pit, Box,* and *Gallery,* far
beyond anything now in possession of the Stage, however wrought
up by the unimitable *Shakespear* ' (*Short View of Tragedy,* 1693,
p. 17). Rymer is too fond of allusions to *Bayes* in *The Rehearsal* ;
his quotation of the phrase ' Pit, Box, and Gallery,' was unplea-
sant in this context.

P. 6, l. 4. *the quantum mutatus* ; a reference to the *Epistle Dedi-
catory* of Rymer's *Short View* (to Lord Dorset) : ' Three, indeed,
of the Epick (the two by *Homer* and *Virgil's Æneids*) are reckon'd
in the degree of Perfection : But amongst the Tragedies, only the
Oedipus of *Sophocles.* That, by *Corneille,* and by others, of a
Modern Cut, *quantum Mutatus* ! '

l. 21. *Perrault* : his *Parallèle des Anciens et des Modernes*
appeared, the first volume, in 1688 ; the third volume, containing
the fourth *Dialogue* (*en ce qui regarde la Poësie*), in 1692. One
sentence from this latter may be taken in illustration—' puisque
nos bons Romans, comme l'Astrée, où il y a dix fois plus d'invention que dans l'Iliade, le Cleopatre, le Cyrus, le Clelie et plusieurs
autres, n'ont aucun des défauts que j'ay remarquez dans les
ouvrages des anciens Poëtes, mais ont de mesme que nos poëmes
en vers une infinité de beautez toutes nouvelles ' (*op. cit.* p. 149).

P. 7, l. 14. *an underplot.* Cf. Dedication of *Spanish Friar.*

l 27. *scriptions.* The reference has not yet been traced.

l. 30. Horace, *Sat* i. 10, 8 ' et est quaedam tamen hic quoque
virtus.'

P. 8, l. 18. *the daughter of a King.* Lady Radcliffe was the
daughter of King Charles II and Mary Davies.

P. 9, l. 17. *propriety* ; see above, vol. i. p. 190, l. 12.

l. 24. *Mr. Chapman* :

<blockquote>
' —— so the brake
That those translators stuck in, that affect
  Their word for word traductions (where they lose
The free grace of their natural dialect,
  And shame their authors with a forced glose)
I laugh to see.'—(*To the Reader,* before his *Iliads.*)
</blockquote>

P. 10, l. 2. *by the so-much-admired Sandys.* See p. 100, l. 2, and
note, and *Preface to Ovid's Epistles,* 1680, vol. i. p. 230.

l. 31. *turns, both on the words and on the thought.* See note on
p. 108, l. 17, below.

P. 11, l. 34. *Musas colere*, again : see p. 103, l. 9.

P. 12, l. 13. *two fragments of Homer.* Congreve translated Priam's Lamentation and Petition to Achilles, for the Body of his Son Hector, and the Lamentations of Hecuba, Andromache, and Helen, over the dead Body of Hector.

l. 31. *runs off her bias* ; said of a bowl that does not run true.

P. 14, l. 25. *Sir Samuel Tuke* : ' A modest man may praise what 's not his own.' *Prologue to the Adventures of Five Hours* (1663) ; see above, p. 60, l. 17.

A DISCOURSE CONCERNING THE ORIGINAL AND PROGRESS OF SATIRE (1693).

P. 15, l. 10. *Titus* : . . . *amor ac deliciae generis humani* ; Suetonius.

P. 16, l. 12. *Descartes.* The ' reformation ' is the qualification of the statement by prefixing ' I think.'

P. 18, l. 13. *Themistocles.* Herodotus, viii. 123.

ll. 30, 31. *the best good man* :
' For pointed Satire I would Buckhurst choose
The best good man, with the worst-natur'd Muse.'
(Rochester, *Allusion to the Tenth Satire of the First Book of Horace.*)

P. 19, l. 22. *he affects the metaphysics.* Probably the origin of Dr. Johnson's ' metaphysical poets ' ; ' writers of the metaphysical race,' in the *Life of Cowley.*

P. 21, l. 25. *shot at rovers* : ' to shoot *at rovers*,' in archery, is to shoot with an elevation, at a distant mark.

l. 30. *my betters*, especially Sir William Davenant.

P. 23, ll. 16, 17. *dipped in the bath*, i. e. in the chemist's bath, used for gilding.

l. 18. *the sceptres.* ' The four sceptres were placed saltierwise upon the reverse of guineas, till the gold coinage of his present majesty ' (*Scott*).

P. 24, l. 34. *Martial says of him* ; viii. 18. See note on vol. i· p. 42, l. 8.

P. 25, l. 17. *some particular ages*, &c. See *Essay of Dramatic Poesy*, vol. i. p. 36, ' every age has a kind of universal genius . . . the work then being pushed on by many hands must of necessity go forward.'

P. 26, l. 16. *Boileau.* See above note on vol. i. p. 181, l. 25.

P. 27, ll. 9–13. *Tasso . . . confesses himself to have been too lyrical.*
Tasso sent his *Jerusalem* as it was written, in instalments, to
Scipione Gonzaga : many of the accompanying letters were
published as *Lettere Poetiche* in an Appendix to the first edition of
his *Discorsi*, 1587. One of these, dated 15 *aprile* 1575, speaks of
the episode of Olindo and Sofronia, and of Armida, with a kind of
apology : ' Ben è vero, ch' in quanto a l'episodio d' Olindo voglio
indulgere genio et principi, poichè non v' è altro luogo ove tras-
porlo ; ma di questo non parli Vostra Signoria con essi loro cosi
a la libera. Credo che in molti luoghi troveranno forse alquanto di
vaghezza soverchia, ed in particolare ne l' arti di Armida che
sono nel quarto : ma cio non mi da tanto fastidio quanto il
conoscere che 'l trapasso, ch' è nel quinto canto, da Armida a la
contenzione di Rinaldo e di Gernando, e 'l ritorno d'Armida non
è fatta con molta arte ; e 'l modo con che s'uniscono queste due
materie è più tosto da romanzo che da poema eroico, come quello
che lega solamente co 'l legame del tempo e co 'l legame d'un
istante, a mio giudicio assai debol legame.' Tasso returns to the
subject in later letters to Scipione Gonzaga, Sept. 2 and Oct. 4,
1575, and on Ap. 3 [1576] he writes : ' Io ho già condannato con
irrevocabil sentenza alla morte l'episodio di Sofronia, *e perch' in
vero era troppo lirico*, e perch' al Signor Barga e a gli altri pareva
poco connesso, e troppo presto, al giudicio unito de' quali non
ho voluto contrafare, e molto più per dare manco occasione ai
Frati, che sia possibile.' The episode was omitted in the revised
version, *Gerusalemme Conquistata*, 1593. Dryden had read
Tasso's letters ; he may have been reminded of this passage by
Segrais in the Preface to his *Traduction de l' Eneïde* (1668), p. 47 :
' . . . le Tasse, qui ayant connu que son debut par l'Episode
d'Olinde et de Sophronie avoit quelque chose d'une affectation
qui estoit au dessous de la grandeur de son esprit, et qui luy fit
confesser depuis que cet embellissement n'estoit pas en sa place,
s'excusoit dans le commencement en disant que cette faute estoit
un charme pour le Prince qu'il regardoit comme son Mecene, et
qu'il faloit la laisser pour l'amour de luy.' Dryden may also have
been thinking of Rapin's censure of Tasso (see above, p. 190) :
' Et cette proportion que demande Aristote n'est pas seulement
dans la quantité des parties, mais aussi dans la qualité. En quoy
le Tasse est fort defectueux, qui mêle dans son Poëme le caractere
badin avec le serieux, et toute la force et la majesté de la Poësie
heroïque à la delicatesse de l'Eclogue et de la Poësie Lyrique.'
(*Reflexions sur la Poëtique*, p. 148.)

    l. 25. *Owen's Epigrams.* John Owen (*c.* 1560–1622), Fellow
of New College ; his first instalment of Epigrams was published

in 1606, *Joannis Audoeni Epigrammatum Libri Tres* ; in 1624 there were eleven books in all, which went through many editions.

P. 28, l. 4. *St. Lewis* ; by Father Pierre Lemoyne (1602–1672) : *Saint Louis ou la Sainte Couronne reconquise sur les infidèles* (1653).

l. 4. *Pucelle* ; by Jean Chapelain (1595–1674) : *La Pucelle ou la France delivrée : Poëme heroïque par M. Chapelain* (1656).

l. 5. *Alaric* ; by M. de Scudéry (1601–1667) : *Alaric ou Rome Vaincue ; Poëme heroïque* (1654).

P. 29, l. 17. *he runs into a flat of thought.* See above, *Second Miscellany*, vol. i. p. 268, l. 7.

l. 34. *Hannibal Caro.* See above, *Second Miscellany*, vol. i. p. 256, l. 19.

P. 30, l. 11. *bias.* See *Third Miscellany*, p. 12, l. 31.

P. 32, l. 1. *the machines of our Christian religion.* Boileau, *L'Art Poétique*, iii. 193 :

> ' C'est donc bien vainement que nos Auteurs deceus,
> Bannissant de leurs vers ces ornemens receus,
> Pensent faire agir Dieu, ses Saints et ses Prophetes
> Comme ces Dieux éclos du cerveau des Poëtes :
> Mettent à chaque pas le Lecteur en Enfer :
> N'offrent rien qu'Astaroth, Belzebuth, Lucifer.
> De la foy d'un Chrestien les mysteres terribles
> D'ornemens égayés ne sont point susceptibles.'

This was directed against Desmarests de Saint Sorlin, the author of *Clovis*. The question of ' machines ' was about this time (1693) being discussed with some liveliness between Boileau and Perrault in connexion with their Odes on the Taking of Namur. Compare Dryden's letter to Dennis, published by Dennis in 1696, written perhaps in March, 1694 (Letter xi. in Scott's *Dryden*, vol. xviii.) : ' If I undertake the translation of Virgil, the little I can perform will shew at least that no man is fit to write after him in a barbarous modern tongue. Neither will his machines be of any service to a Christian poet. We see how ineffectually they have been tried by Tasso and by Ariosto. It is using them too dully, if we only make devils of his Gods : as if, for example, I would raise a storm, and make use of Æolus, with this only difference of calling him Prince of the Air ; what invention of mine would there be in this ? or who would not see Virgil through me ; only the same trick played over again by a bungling juggler ? Boileau has well observed, that 'tis an easy matter in a Christian poem for God to bring the Devil to reason. I think I have given a better hint for new machines in my Preface to Juvenal ; where I have particularly recommended two subjects, one of King Arthur's conquest of the Saxons, and the other of the Black Prince in his conquest of Spain. But the Guardian Angels of Monarchies and Kingdoms are not to be touched by every hand : a man must be deeply conversant in the Platonic philosophy to deal with them ; and therefore I may reasonably expect, that no poet of our age will presume to handle those machines, for fear of discovering his own ignorance ; or if he should, he might perhaps be ingrateful enough not to own me for his benefactor.'

P. 32, l. 5 *the two victorious Monarchies.* The term ' Fifth-Monarchy man ' is, perhaps, the last vestige of the theory of the four successive Empires, Assyrian, Persian, Grecian, and Roman, which was derived from the visions of the Book of Daniel. Compare St. Augustine, *De Civ. Dei*, xx. 23 ; Sir David Lyndsay, *The Monarchie* ; and H. Fisher, *The Medieval Empire*, i. p. 19.

P. 34, l. 1. *philosophy and the mechanics.* Philosophy again in the general sense common in English ; see *Essay of Dramatic Poesy*, p. 36, l. 37.

l. 15. *Platonic philosophy.* Referred to again in the letter to Dennis, in the same context. Dryden was thinking of the Platonic opinion about daemons as intermediary between Heaven and Earth: Plat. *Symp.* 202 E ; Apuleius, *De Deo Socratis* ; St. Augustine, *De Civitate Dei*, viii. This doctrine was sometimes applied to the aerial spirits, as by Chaucer in the *House of Fame*, ii. 421 :

> ' For in this regioun, certein,
> Dwelleth many a citezein
> Of which that speketh dan Plato.'

It was also used of the Angels. The idea of tutelar Angels was familiar with the Platonists of Dryden's time. Cf. Henry More, *Defence of the Cabbala* (1662), p. 48 : ' So that it is not improbable but that as the great Angel of the Covenant (he whom Philo calls τῶν ἀγγέλων πρεσβύτατον, τὸν ἀρχάγγελον, λόγον, ἀρχήν, ὄνομα θεοῦ, that is, *the Eldest of the Angels, the Archangel, the Word, the Beginning, the name of God, which is Jehovah*) I say, that as he gave Laws to his charge, so the *Tutelar Angels* of other nations might be Instructers of those that they raised up to be Law-givers to their charge ; Though in processe of time the Nations that were at first under the Government of good Angels, by their lewdnesse and disobedience, might make themselves obnoxious to the power and delusion of those ἀπατεῶνες δαίμονες, as they are called, *deceitful and tyrannical Devils.*'

l. 29. *The prince of the Persians.* See the Book of Daniel, ch. x. 13 : ' But the prince of the kingdom of Persia withstood me one and twenty days : but, lo, Michael, one of the chief princes, came to help me ' . . . ; and 20, ' Then said he, Knowest thou wherefore I came unto thee ? and now will I return to fight with the prince of Persia : and when I am gone forth, lo, the prince of Grecia shall come.' Dryden does not say, though he doubtless remembered, what a magnificent adaptation of this had been made by Cowley in his *Discourse by way of Vision, concerning the Government of Oliver Cromwell* : ' I think I should have gone on, but that I was interrupted by a strange and terrible Apparition, for there appeared to me (arising out of the Earth, as I conceived) the figure of a Man taller than a Giant, or, indeed, the shadow of any Giant in the evening. . . . He held in his right hand a sword that was yet bloody, and nevertheless the motto of it was *Pax quaeritur Bello*, and in his left hand a thick book, upon the back of which was written in letters of Gold, *Acts, Ordinances, Protestations, Covenants, Engagements, Declarations, Remonstrances,* &c. Though this sudden, unusual, and dreadful Object might have quelled a greater courage than mine, yet so it pleased God (for there is nothing bolder than a man in a vision) that I was not at all daunted, but asked him resolutely and briefly, What art thou ? And he said I am called the North-west Principality, his Highness the Protector of the Common-wealth of England, Scotland, and Ireland, and the Dominions belonging thereunto ; for I am that Angel to whom the Almighty has committed the government of these three Kingdoms which thou seest from this place,' &c.

P. 36, l. 10. *Virgil.* The most Platonic passages in Virgil, and those of which Dryden was probably thinking, are the 4th *Eclogue* and the 6th Book of the *Aeneid.*

P. 37, l. 21. *the Intelligence of the Sun.* To every Sphere of the Heavens there is assigned an Intelligence, or Intelligences, which are angels : see Dante, *Convivio* ii. c. 5 ; *Paradiso* ii. 127–129 ; and Toynbee, *Dante Dictionary,* s. v. *Cielo.* Allusions are frequent ; e. g. Sir Thomas Browne, *Religio Medici* i., ' the swing of that wheel not moved by intelligences ' ; and Donne, speaking of souls and bodies,

> ' our bodies why do we forbear ?
> They are ours, though not we ; we are
> The Intelligences, they the Spheres.'

P. 38, l. 5. *King Arthur conquering the Saxons.* This was Milton's subject, *Mansus* 78 :

> ' O mihi si mea sors talem concedat amicum,
> Phoebaeos decorasse viros qui tam bene norit,
> Siquando indigenas revocabo in carmina reges,
> Arturumque etiam sub terris bella moventem,
> Aut dicam invictae sociali foedere mensae
> Magnanimos heroas, et (O modo spiritus adsit !)
> Frangam Saxonicas Britonum sub Marte phalanges.'

P. 38, l. 10. *Don Pedro the Cruel.* Don Pedro of Castile is referred to in the *Vindication of the Duke of Guise*, ten years earlier, with Mariana as authority. ' It is Mariana, I think (but am not certain), that makes the following relation, and let the noble family of Trimmers read their own future in it.' The ' relation ' shows that Dryden's projected poem might have been enlivened with modern applications to English politics, besides those which he indicates in this account of his design.

P. 39, l. 33. *Ne, forte, pudori. A. P.* 406.

P. 41, l. 1. *Ut sibi quivis. A. P.* 240.

l. 16. *Coena dubia.* Terence, *Phorm.* ii. 2, 28 ; Hor. *Sat.* ii. 2, 77 ; ' fine confused feeding.'

P. 43, l. 31. *Vida De Arte Poetica* (1527) was generally recognized as an authority. Pope, *Essay on Criticism*, 704 :

　　' A Raphael painted and a Vida sung—
　　Immortal Vida : on whose honour'd brow
　　The Poet's bays and Critic's ivy grow,' &c.

P. 44, l. 10. *Casaubon. De satyrica Graecorum poesi et Romanorum satyra* ; Parisiis, 1605.

l. 10. *Heinsius. Danielis Heinsii de Satyra Horatiana*, in his edition of Horace, 1612.

l. 10. *Rigaltius.* Nicolas Rigault edited Juvenal, 1616.

l. 10. *Dacier.* His translation of Horace (*Œuvres d'Horace*) was published in the years 1681–1689 : from his short essay on Satire (*Preface sur les Satires d'Horace*, t. vi. 1687) Dryden took a number of points and references. It was published in English in 1692 in Gildon's *Miscellany Poems*, and in 1695 as an appendix to Le Bossu's *Treatise of the Epick Poem*, along with Fontenelle on Pastoral.

l. 11. *the Dauphin's* Juvenal : ' cum interpretatione et notis Lud. Pratei,' 1684.

P. 52, l. 5. *Silli.* Mentioned by Heinsius and Dacier, as well as Casaubon.

P. 53, l. 15. *Satira quidem tota nostra est, Inst. Orat.* x. 1, 93.'

l. 18. *Graecis intacti*, &c. Hor. *Sat.* i. 10, 66.

l. 26. σάθυ ; for σάθη. So in Scaliger, *Poet.* i. 12 : ' σάθυ salacitatem dixere veteres ' ; and so also (a quotation from Scaliger) in the Preface to the Dauphin's Juvenal.

P. 54, l. 16. *premices*, to be added to the list of Dryden's French words.

l. 28. *olla, or hotchpotch* : spelt *oleo* in the *Essay of Dramatic Poesy*, p. 60, l. 30.

l. 30. *tacked bills* : when a measure was tacked to a money-bill, so as to force its acceptance in the House of Lords.

P. 55, l. 28. *Tarsians.* This reference is from Casaubon, *op. cit.* i. c. 4—' extemporale genus dicendi Tarsensibus proprium fuisse, tam in soluta quam in astricta numeris oratione ' ; with quotations from Strabo xiv., and Diogenes Laertius, iv. 58.

l. 30. *Scaramucha.* The Italian comedy had been much in favour in Paris from the time of Charles IX ; the most famous of all Scaramouches, Tiberio Fiorelli, was still alive when Dryden was writing this essay. See Baschet, *Les Comédiens italiens à la Cour de France.*

P. 57, l. 6. *says Livy* : all this from Dacier.

P. 59, l. 24. *Exodiarii* ; from Casaubon, Heinsius, and Dacier. Casaubon, ii. c. 1 : ' Scholiastes antiquus Juvenalis [in *Sat.* iii. v. 175] Exodiarius apud veteres in fine ludorum intrabat, quod ridiculum foret : ut quicquid lacrymarum atque tristitiae coegissent ex tragicis affectibus, huius spectaculi visus detergeret.'

P. 62, l. 3. *Quid ? cum est Lucilius ausus,* &c. Hor. *Sat.* ii. 1, 62.

l. 34. *Diomedes the grammarian.* See Casaubon, *op. cit.* ii. c. 3.

P. 64, l. 2. *Dousa,* i. e. van der Does. Janus Dousa, poet and commentator (1545–1604), had two sons who were scholars ; the second, Franciscus Dousa, edited the fragments of Lucilius.

l. 18. *Varronian Satire.* All this from Casaubon, ii. c. 2, whom Dacier copied.

l. 27. *Quintilian,* x. 1.

P. 65, l. 15. *Tully, in his* Academics, i. 2, quoted by Casaubon, *l. c.*

l. 29. *philology* : cf Preface to *Fables,* p. 254, l. 26.

P. 66, l. 2. σπουδογέλοιοι, ' blending jest with earnest.' Casaubon, *l. c.*, on Menippus quotes Strabo xvi. ἐκ τῶν Γαδάρων ἦν Μελέαγρος καὶ Μένιππος ὁ σπουδογέλοιος. The examples of Varronian satire noted by Casaubon are those of Petronius, Seneca, Lucian, Julian, Martianus Capella, and Boetius.

l. 31. *Petronius Arbiter.* ' That bungling supplement to Petronius ' ; ' that scandal to all forgeries ' ; Bentley on *Phalaris.* (*Pet. Arb. Satyricon cum fragmentis Albae Graecae recuperatis anno* 1688. Col. Arg. 1691 ; Budae 1697.)

P. 67, l. 4. *the mock deification* : 'Αποκολοκύντωσις, *or the Translation of the Emperor among the Pumpkins.*

l. 7. *Barclay's* Euphormio. See above, note on vol. i. p. 6, l. 10. *Euphormionis Lusinini Satyricon* began to be published in 1603 ; the first part was dedicated to King James. Five parts, with a key, &c., were published in 1629.

l. 7. *a volume of German authors* ; most probably the *Epistolae Obscurorum Virorum.*

P. 69, ll. 28–31. Casaubon's *Persius* was published in 1605 ; Stelluti's at Rome in 1630 (text, Italian translation in blank verse, and commentary in Italian).

P. 70, l. 13. *scabrous*, in the sense of *rough*.

l. 21. *a Scotch gentleman* ; David Wedderburn of Aberdeen, whose edition of *Persius*, with a commentary, was published in 8vo at Amsterdam, 1664 (Scott).

P. 73, l. 28. *Holyday*. Barten Holyday, D.D., of Christ Church, some time archdeacon of Oxford (1593–1661), published his *Persius* in 1616 ; his *Juvenal* was not published till 1673, along with the fourth edition of *Persius*. Holyday was the author of Τεχνογαμία, *or the Marriages of the Arts, a Comedie*, 1618, 4° ; acted in Christ Church Hall on Feb. 13, 1618, and again at Woodstock in 1621 before the king, who tried in vain to get away before the end of the entertainment.

P. 74, l. 7. *Aeschines*. *Ctes.* 167 ταῦτα δὲ τί ἐστιν, ὦ κίναδος ; ῥήματα ἢ θαύματα ;

l. 22. χελώνης. Suidas is quoted for this proverb by Stephanus, s. v. ἢ δεῖ χελώνης κρέα φαγεῖν ἢ μὴ φαγεῖν ; quoniam sc. ὀλίγα βρωθέντα στρόφους ποιεῖ πολλὰ δὲ καθαίρει. Not *snail*, but *turtle* is the subject of the prescription.

P. 76, l. 25. *Bishop of Salisbury* : Burnet. 'The Satyrical Poets, *Horace, Juvenal*, and *Persius*, may contribute wonderfully to give a man a Detestation of Vice, and a Contempt of the common Methods of mankind ; which they have set out in such true Colours, that they must give a very generous Sense to those who delight in reading them often. Persius his Second Satyr may well pass for one of the best Lectures in Divinity.' (*A Discourse of the Pastoral Care*, written by the Right Reverend Father in God Gilbert Lord Bishop of Sarum ; London, 1692 ; p. 162.)

P. 77, l. 35. *a witty friend of mine*. Wycherley, whose father refused to pay his debts.

P. 83, ll. 5–7. *Petronius . . . ne sententiae*, &c., c. 118.

P. 85, l. 3. *the Plain Dealer*. Wycherly again ; cf. *Apology for Heroic Poetry*, p. 182, l. 5, above.

l. 12. *on carpet ground*. Cf. *Second Miscellany*, p. 255, l. 31.

P. 86, l. 19. Virgil, *Eclogue*, 3, 26.

P. 91, l. 35. *secuit urbem*. Persius, *Sat.* i. 114.

P. 92, l. 6. *Holyday* ; above, p. 73, l. 28.

l. 19. *Stapylton*, Sir Robert, author of *The Slighted Maid* (above, vol. i. p. 209, l. 5, note), published *The first six Satyrs* of Juvenal at Oxford in 1644, and the complete version, *His Satyrs rendered in English Verse*, in 1647 ; London, 8° ; 'with seventeen designes in picture,' London, 1660, fol.

P. **93**, l. 21. *Jack Ketch.* See Macaulay's *History*, ch. 5 (execution of Monmouth).

P. **94**, l. 15. *ense rescindendum.* Virgil, *Georg.* iii. 452 :
‘ Non tamen ulla magis praesens fortuna laborum est
Quam si quis ferro potuit rescindere summum
Ulceris os : alitur vitium vivitque tegendo,’ &c.

P. **95**, l. 23. *honest Mr. Swan* : ‘ honest Mr. Sw——’ is also cited in Dennis's *Letters*, 1696, p. 65 (a letter on *Quibbling*, to Mr. —— at Will's Coffee-house in Covent-Garden). See also the *Memoirs of Scriblerus*, c. 7 : ‘ His good fortune directed him to one of the most singular endowments, whose name was Conradus Crambe, who by the father's side was related to the Crouches of Cambridge, and his mother was cousin to Mr. Swan, Gamester and Punster of the City of London.’ He is mentioned by Swift, *Remarks on Tindal*, 1708 : ‘ “ the formality of laying hand over head on a man.” A pun ; but an old one. I remember when Swan made that pun first he was severely checked for it.’ Also in *An Examination of certain Abuses, Corruptions, and Enormities in the City of Dublin*, 1732. *Spectator*, No. 61. ‘ Upon enquiry, I found my learned friend had dined that day with Mr. Swan the famous punster ; and desiring him to give me some account of Mr. Swan's conversation, he told me that he generally talked in the *Paronomasia*, that he sometimes gave in to the *Ploce*, but that in his humble opinion he shined most in the *Antanaclasis*.’ Barrow, Sermon xiv., *Against Foolish Talking and Jesting*, shows some tolerance for the figure of *Paronomasia*, and other ornaments ‘ wherein the lepid way doth consist.’

P. **97**, l. 5. *statues of the Sileni.* This is the famous comparison (*Symposium* 215 A) which is otherwise rendered by Rabelais in the *Prologue to Gargantua*, and after him quoted by Bacon in the *Advancement of Learning*, i. 3. 8 : ‘ I refer them also to that which Plato said of his master Socrates, whom he compared to the gallipots of apothecaries, which on the outside had apes and owls and antiques, but contained within sovereign and precious liquors and confections,’ &c.

P. **99**, l. 21. *Mr. Maidwell.* Lewis Maidwell, author of *The Loving Enemies*, 1680. His book of instructions for reading a course of Mathematics is referred to in a letter of Dryden's young friend, Mr. Walter Moyle.

P. **100**, l. 33. *or rather description* ; see vol. i. p. 36, l. 9 (note). The definition of Satire is given in the first book of the Dissertation of Heinsius ; p. 54 in the Elzevir of 1629.

P. **101**, l. 9. *consisting in a low familiar way of speech.* ‘ Sicut

humili ac familiari, ita acri partim ac dicaci, partim urbano ac
jocoso constans sermone.' Heinsius, *loc. cit.*

P. 101, l. 17. *grande sophos.* An oversight for the *grande aliquid*
of Persius, *Sat.* 1, 14. *grande sophos,* ' the loud *bravo,*' occurs
several times in Martial ; once in an epigram which was a household
word at one time in Westminster School ; see Dasent, *Annals of
an Eventful Life,* c. 12.

    ' Audieris cum grande sophos, dum basia captas,
       Ibis ab excusso missus in astra sago ' (4).

Also i. 50 : ' Mercetur alius grande et insanum sophos ' ;
and vi. 48 : ' Quod tam grande sophos clamat tibi turba togata,
       Non tu, Pomponi, cena diserta tua est.'

    l. 23. *pad,* saddle.

P. 102, l. 32. *underplot.* See Dedication of the *Spanish Friar,*
and of the *Third Miscellany.*

P. 103, l. 1. *Copernican system.* See above, p. 225, l. 37, note.
Sir William Temple writing *On Ancient and Modern Learning* a
few years before this, is not quite sure of the Copernican system :
' There is nothing new in Astronomy, to vie with the Ancients,
unless it be the Copernican system : nor in Physic, unless
Harvey's circulation of the blood. But whether either of these
be modern discoveries, or derived from old fountains is disputed :
nay it is so too whether they are true or no ; for though reason
may seem to favour them more than the contrary opinions,
yet sense can very hardly allow them ; and to satisfy mankind
both these must concur. But if they are true, yet these two
great discoveries have made no change in the conclusions of
Astronomy, nor in the practice of Physic, and so have been of
little use to the world, though perhaps of much honour to the
authors.'

    l. 4. *Mascardi* (Agostino). ' Cameriere d'Honore di N. Sig.
Urbano Ottavo ' ; see his *Prose Volgari,* Ven. 1630 (the Preface is
dated 1625), *Discorso Settimo : dell' Unità della Favola Dram-
matica :* a good specimen of formal criticism, and of the use of
such commonplaces as *Nature* and *Imitation* : ' the imitative arts
follow in their operation the custom of Nature ; now the custom
of Nature is at times to follow two ends, one principal and one
accessory.' *Unity* he finds to be fruitful of debate in literature :
' This is the point on which so many contests of the modern
Academies are found to turn, this the trenchant weapon of the
partisans of Tasso against Lodovico Ariosto ; under this law
Ariosto is banished, along with the other writers of Romances,
from the senate of the Epic Poets.'

    l. 6. *Il Pastor Fido.* See above, vol. i. p. 273, l. 7.

P. 105, l. 17. *Hudibras.* Dryden seems to have borne no grudge to Butler for his charges against the Heroic Play. Compare *The Hind and the Panther* :

> ' " Unpitied Hudibras, your champion friend
> Has shown how far your charities extend " :
> This lasting verse shall on his tomb be read
> " He shamed you living, and upbraids you dead." '

Compare also the well-known phrase in Dryden's letter to Laurence Hyde, Earl of Rochester (? August, 1683) : ' 'Tis enough for one age to have neglected Mr. Cowley, and starv'd Mr. Butler.'

P. 106, l. 31. *Tassoni and Boileau.* Compare Dean Lockier's account of his visit to Will's, given in Spence's *Anecdotes* : ' I was about seventeen when I first came up to town, an odd-looking boy, with short rough hair, and that sort of awkwardness which one always brings up at first out of the country with one. However, in spite of my bashfulness and appearance, I used now and then to thrust myself into Will's to have the pleasure of seeing the most celebrated wits of that time, who then resorted thither. The second time that ever I was there, Mr. Dryden was speaking of his own things, as he frequently did, especially of such as had been lately published. " If anything of mine is good," says he, " 'tis *Mac-Flecno*, and I value myself the more upon it, because it is the first piece of ridicule written in heroics." On hearing this I plucked up my spirit so far as to say in a voice but just loud enough to be heard, that *Mac-Flecno* was a very fine poem, but that I had not imagined it to be the first that ever was writ that way. On this Dryden turned short upon me, as surprised at my interposing ; asked me how long I had been a dealer in poetry, and added with a smile : " Pray, sir, what is it that you *did* imagine to have been writ so before ? " I named Boileau's *Lutrin* and Tassoni's *Secchia Rapita*, which I had read, and knew that Dryden had borrowed some strokes from each. " 'Tis true," said Dryden, " I had forgot them." A little after Dryden went out ; and in going spoke to me again, and desired me to come and see him the next day. I was highly delighted with the invitation ; went to see him accordingly, and was well acquainted with him after as long as he lived.'

ll. 31, 32. Alessandro Tassoni, of Modena, 1565–1635. The *Secchia Rapita* was published in 1622 ; translated by Perrault, *Le Seau Enlevé*, 1678. There are several editions of the Italian text printed in England ; one in 1710, with a translation by Ozell. Tassoni's critical writings are an important section of the documents for ' Ancients and Moderns,' and may have been known to Dryden (*Quisiti*, Modena, 1608 ; *Dieci Libri di Pensieri Diversi*, Roma, 1620, &c.).

P. 106, l. 33.   The *Lutrin* of Boileau was published in the 1674 edition of his works ; four cantos, along with *L'Art Poëtique* ; the fifth and sixth cantos were added in 1683.

l. 33.   Teofilo Folengo, Merlinus Cocaius, the chief of all poets in the Macaronic language, born in 1491 ; his poems were published in Venice, in 1517 and 1520 ; they are the *Zanitonella*, the *Maccaronicum*, which is *Baldus*, the *Moschœa*, or War of the Flies and Emmets, and Epigrams. He also wrote the *Orlandino per Limerno Pitocco da Mantova*, Ven. 1526 ; and the history of his life in the *Chaos del triperuno* (i. e. Merlinus, Limerno, Teofilo) *overo dialogo de le tre etadi da Teofilo Folengo da Mantoa*, Venice, 1527.   Baldus is a noble hero brought up in the cottage of a villein, where his youth is nurtured in the favourite romances, Sir Bevis, Ogier the Dane, &c. :

> ' Legerat Anchroiam, Tribisondam, Gesta Danesi,
> Antonaeque Bovum, mox tota Realea Francae
>
> .   .   .   .
>
> Vidit ut Angelicam sapiens Orlandus amavit,
> At mox ut nudo pergebat corpore mattus,
> Cui tulit Astolfus cerebrum de climate Lunae.'

So Baldus goes out on adventures, with his friendly giant Fracasse and other companions.   The *Orlando Furioso* had been published the year before, in 1516.   A translation of Folengo's work was published in Paris in 1606 : *Histoire maccaronique de Merlin Coccaie, prototype de Rabelais ; plus l'horrible bataille advenue entre les mouches et les fourmis.*

P. 107, l. 2.   *stanza of eight* ; the Italian octave, *ottava rima.*

l. 9.   *Scarron* (Paul), 1610–1660, author of *Don Japhet d'Arménie* and other dramatic versions of ' Spanish plots,' and of the *Roman Comique*, published his *Virgile Travesti* in 1648–53. It was imitated in England by Charles Cotton ; *Scarronides, or Virgile Travestie*, 1664, &c. (' a mock Poem ').

P. 108, l. 17.   *turns of words and thoughts.*   Compare the *Dedication of the Æneis*, p. 219 (speaking of the French poets), ' the turn on thoughts and words is their chief talent ; but the Epic Poem is too stately to receive those little ornaments,' &c.   And *Preface to Fables*, p. 257 : ' As for the turn of words, in which Ovid particularly excels all poets, they are sometimes a fault and sometimes a beauty. . . . Chaucer writ with more simplicity and followed Nature more closely than to use them.'   Compare also Dr. Herford's Introduction to Spenser's *Shepherd's Calendar.* Butler's *Characters, A Quibbler* (written probably about 1665) :

' There are two sorts of quibbling, the one with words and the other with sense, like the rhetorician's *figurae dictionis et figurae sententiae*—the first is already cried down, and the other as yet prevails, and is the only elegance of our modern poets, which easy judges call easiness ; but having nothing in it but easiness, and being never used by any lasting wit, will in wiser times fall to nothing of itself.'

l. 22. *Sir George Mackenzie*, of Rosehaugh (1636–1691), Lord Advocate for Scotland ; see *Wandering Willie's Tale* in *Redgauntlet* : ' the Bloody Advocate Mackenzie, who for his worldly wit and wisdom had been to the rest as a God.' His character and that of his writings have been explained by Mr. W. A. Raleigh in Sir Henry Craik's *English Prose Selections*, vol. iii. p. 261 ; and by Mr. Taylor Innes (*Studies in Scottish History*, 1892). He wrote *Aretina or the Serious Romance*, 1661 ; *Religio Stoici*, Edin., 1663 ; *Moral Gallantry, a Discourse proving that the Point of Honour obliges a Man to be Virtuous*, Edin., 1667 ; *Institutions of the Laws of Scotland*, Edin., 1684 ; and other works.

P. 109, l. 22. *Mr. Walsh.* William Walsh, 1663–1708 : ' He is known more by his familiarity with greater men than by anything done or written by himself ' (Johnson). Dryden had written a Preface for Walsh's *Dialogue concerning Women*, 1691, in which the author of the *Dialogue* is highly praised.

P. 110, l. 26. *prosodia.* Dryden explains in the *Dedication of the Æneis* that he had collected materials for an English Prosody. Compare also the Preface to *Albion and Albanius* for his interest in syllables.

PARALLEL OF POETRY AND PAINTING (1695).

P. 117, l. 19. *Bellori* (Giovanni Pietro) published his *Lives of the Painters, Sculptors*, &c. (*Vite de' Pittori*), at Rome in 1672, with a Dedication to Colbert, who was also the patron of Fresnoy's poem, *De Arte Graphica*.

P. 118, l. 13. *This Idea*, &c. ; in the original a conceit : ' questa Idea, overo Dea della Pittura.'

l. 23. *Cicero.* ' Ut igitur in formis et figuris est aliquid perfectum et excellens cuius ad excogitatam speciem imitando referuntur ea quae sub oculis ipsa cadunt, sic perfectae eloquentiae speciem animo videmus, effigiem auribus quaerimus.' *Orator* 9.

l. 30. *Proclus. Proclo nel Timeo*, i. e. Proclus in his commentary on the *Timaeus*

P. 119, l. 12. *Maximus Tyrius.* His *Discourses,* Διαλέξεις, were
edited by H. Stephanus in 1557, and by Heinsius in 1607. He
lived in the second century.

P. 119, l. 25. *Caravaggio,* &c. ' Come in questi nostri tempi
Michel Angelo da Caravaggio fù troppo naturale, dipinse i simili,
e Bamboccio i peggiori.'

l. 28. *drawn the worst likeness* ; i. e. drawn people at their
worst. In the account of *Modern Masters* appended to Dryden's
Art of Painting, p. 326, there is an account of Bamboccio :
' Pieter van Laer, commonly call'd *Bamboccio* or the *Beggar-
painter* ' (1584–1644). ' He had an admirable *Gusto* in *colouring,*
was very *judicious* in the *ordering* of his *Pieces,* nicely *just* in his
Proportions, and onely to be blam'd, for that he generally
affected to represent *Nature* in her worst *Dress,* and follow'd the
Life too *close,* in most of his Compositions.'

P. 120, l. 7. *Seneca.* The rhetorician : ' Non vidit Phidias
Iovem, fecit tamen velut tonantem, nec stetit ante oculos eius
Minerva : dignus tamen illa arte animus et concepit deos et
exhibuit.' *Controv.* x. 5. 8 ; cf. Cic. *Orat.* 9.

l. 9. Apollonius of Tyana ; his Life was written by Philostratus.

l. 14. *Alberti.* One of the great Florentine humanists of the
fifteenth century ; wrote on architecture, education, and other
branches of learning.

l. 19. *Castiglione,* Baldassarre, the author of *Il Cortigiano.*
Raphael painted his *Galatea* in 1514 for the villa of Agostino Chigi
the banker, which is now the Farnesina. Raphael's words are :
' per dipingere una bella mi bisogna veder più belle . . . ma essendo
carestia e di buoni giudici e di belle donne, io mi servo di certa idea
che mi viene alla mente. Se questa ha in sè alcuna eccellenza
d'arte, io non so : ben m' affatico d'averla.'

l. 24. *Guido Reni* ; his *St. Michael* is in one of the Chapels of
the Capuchins' church at Rome (Santa Maria della Concezione).

P. 121, l. 2. *the contrary idea.* ' Si trova anche l'idea della brut-
tezza, ma questa lascio di spiegare nel demonio ' ; i. e. ' I forbear
to render this in the picture of the Fiend.'

l. 20. *Cyllarus.* Ovid, *Metam.* xii. 393 *sq.*

l. 29. *Apelles.* ' Si Venerem Cous nusquam posuisset Apelles,'
                                Art. Amand. iii. 401.

P. 123, l. 20. *Philostratus* ; the younger.

l. 20. This Proem is quoted by Bellori, after his own Preface
to the *Lives of the Painters.*

P. 124, l. 27. *merchants* ; ' i. e. merchant vessels. The passage
seems to be so worded as to contain a sneer at the negligence of

King William's government in protecting the trade. Perhaps Dryden alluded to the misfortune of Sir Francis Wheeler, in 1693, who being sent with a convoy into the Mediterranean, was wrecked in the Bay of Gibraltar.' *Scott.*

P. 126, l. 17. *St. Catharine* ; in *Tyrannic Love.*

P. 127, l. 11. *Lentulus*, in the apocryphal *Epistle* to the Roman Senate. Fabricius, *Cod. Apoc. N. T.* t. i. p. 301.

P. 128, l. 10. *The Marquis of Normanby's opinion* ; in the *Essay on Poetry* : ' Reject that vulgar error which appears

  So fair of making perfect characters ;

  There 's no such thing in Nature, and you'll draw

  A faultless Monster, which the world ne'er saw.'

P. 129, l. 8. *Catullus* ; quoted by Dryden in the Dedication of Limberham :   ' castum esse decet pium poetam

    Ipsum ; versiculos nihil necesse est.'

l. 14. *Vita proba est.* Martial, i. 5.

P. 130, l. 2. *Annibale Caracci*, 1560–1609. His work in the Farnese Palace is described by Bellori in detail ; the Choice of Hercules (*Ercole Bivio*) at p. 33 of vol. i. of the *Vite de' Pittori.*

P. 132, l. 20. *kermis* ; a fair (Dutch).

l. 21. *snick or snee.* The subject is noted by Sir Joshua Reynolds at Amsterdam, a picture by Jan Steen in the cabinet of M. Gart (Works, ed. Malone, ii. p. 365). Compare Marvell, *The Character of Holland*, l. 96 :

' When, stagg'ring upon some land, snick and sneer,

  They try like statuaries if they can

  Carve out each other's *Athos* to a man ;

  And carve in their large bodies where they please,

  The arms of the United Provinces.'

l. 23. *Lazar.* Above, vol. i. p. 18, l. 18.

P. 133, l. 12. *Covent Garden fops.* A fop was more of a booby and less of a dandy in Dryden's time.

l. 23. *As Sir William D'Avenant observes* : ' and he that means to govern so mournfully (as it were, without any Musick in his Dominion) must lay but light burdens on his Subjects ; or else he wants the ordinary wisdom of those who, to their Beasts that are much loaden, whistle all the day to encourage their Travail ' (Preface to *Gondibert*, p. 18, in the folio).

P. 134, l. 3. *an eminent French critic.* Not identified.

P. 136, l. 20. *The principal and most important* :

' Praecipua imprimis Artisque potissima pars est

  Nosse quid in rebus Natura creavit ad Artem

  Pulchrius, idque Modum iuxta Mentemque Vetustam.'

         De Arte Graph. v. 37 sqq.

P. 138, l. 4. *Mr. Walter Moyle* (1672–1721). His writings were edited, with an account of his life, by Anthony Hammond, in 1727. ' From a set of Company of Learned and Ingenious Gentlemen, who frequented *Manwayring's Coffee-house in Fleet-street*, he fell much into the Conversation of Gentlemen at the *Grecian Coffee-house* near the Temple. . . . To be nearer the more entertaining part of the Town, he removed to *Covent-Garden*. Here it was (as Mr. Dryden declares) that *the Learning and Judgement, above his Age, which every one discovered in* Mr. Moyle, *were Proofs of those Abilities he has shewn in his Country's Service, when he was chose to serve it in the Senate, as his Father,* Sir Walter, *had done.*' A footnote here refers to Dryden's *Life of Lucian.* There are letters to Mr. Walter Moyle in Dennis's collection of *Letters,* 1696.

P. 139, l. 15. *Lopez de Vega.* Lopez is a frequent mistake for *Lope* ; the patronymic for the Christian name. Corneille, however, and generally the French before Voltaire, write accurately *'Lope.* The reference is to Lope's *Nuevo Arte de hacer Comedias* (*Obras Sueltas,* iv. p. 405), his apology for neglecting the rules, and his account of the best rules to be followed by the authors who wish to succeed with the public. ' None of them all can I reckon more barbarian than myself, since I am daring to give precepts all counter to Art, and letting myself swim with the vulgar tide, for Italy and France to call me ignorant. But what can I do, when I have written (counting the one finished this week) four hundred and eighty-three comedies, and all but six of them heinous offenders against Art ? I stand by what I have written, and recognize that though the other way were better, yet they would not have pleased as well ; for often that which breaks the rules is thereby pleasant to the taste.'

P. 140, l. 10. *similes.* See p. 202, l. 13.

P. 142, l. 9. *Another.* Lee.

l. 17. *Let every member* :
' Singula membra suo capiti conformia fiant.'
De Arte Graph. v. 126.

l. 28. *Morecraft* is the usurer in the *Scornful Lady,* whose conversion is referred to in the *Essay of Dramatic Poesy,* p. 66, l. 11 : ' Cutting,' i. e. swaggering ; a cutter is a ' roaring blade.'
' He's turn'd gallant.'
' Gallant ! '
' Ay, gallant, and is now call'd Cutting Morecraft.'
Act v. sc. 4.

' Is Pompey grown so malepert, so frampel ?
The only cutter about ladies' honours,
And his blade soonest out ? '
Wit at Several Weapons, Act iii. sc. 1.

l. 33. *The principal figure* :
    ' Prima Figurarum seu Princeps Dramatis ultro
    Prosiliat media in Tabula sub lumine primo
    Pulchrior ante alias, reliquis nec operta Figuris.'
                         De Arte Graph. v. 129.

P. 144, l. 8. *Esther*, 1689 ; written at the suggestion of Madame
de Maintenon for the pupils of her foundation of St. Cyr : ' La
célèbre maison de Saint-Cyr ayant été principalement établie pour
élever dans la piété un fort grand nombre de jeunes demoiselles
rassemblées de tous les endroits du royaume,' &c. (Racine, in
the Preface to *Esther*). Racine had begun to attract English
playwrights : Otway, *Titus and Berenice*, 1677 ; Crowne,
Andromache, 1675.

    P. 145, l. 13. *The Slighted Maid*, by Sir R. Stapylton ; see
above, vol. i. p. 209, l. 5.

    l. 30. *Venice Preserved, or a Plot Discovered*, 1682. Acted at
the Duke's Theatre.

    P. 146, l. 13. *says Aristotle. Poet.* c. 25 (p. 1460, l. 33) : οἷον καὶ
Σοφοκλῆς ἔφη αὐτὸς μὲν οἵους δεῖ ποιεῖν, Εὐριπίδην δὲ οἷοι εἰσί.

    l. 15. *drew them worse* : this case is not considered by Aris-
totle in the passage of which Dryden is thinking.

    l. 20. *that part of Œdipus* : the first and third Acts.

    l. 31. *the Gothic manner. De Arte Graph.*, l. 240 :
    ' Denique nil sapiat Gotthorum barbara trito
    Ornamenta modo, saeclorum et monstra malorum,' &c.

    P. 147, l. 11. *Du Fresnoy tells us* ; *op. cit.*, l. 137 sqq.

    l. 30. *turns of words upon the thought.* See p. 108, and note.

    l. 33. *Lena sororis. De Arte Graph.*, l. 261 :
    ' Haec quidem ut in Tabulis fallax sed grata Venustas
    Et complementum Graphidos (mirabile visu)
    Pulchra vocabatur, sed subdola Lena Sororis.'

    P. 149, l. 26. *the first verses of the Sylvæ* ; quoted by Dryden
already in the Dedication of the *Spanish Friar*.

    P. 151, l. 4. *the pencil thrown luckily*—a favourite common-
place : it appears, e. g. at the beginning of the Preface to *Ibrahim
ou 'Illustre Bassa*, 1641. The painter was Nealces.

    l. 11. *Bristol-stone* ; see vol. i, p. 227, l. 18, and note.

    l. 28. *manum de tabula.* Another commonplace, from Pliny,
Hist. Nat. xxxv. 10 : ' Protogenes curae supra modum anxiae qui
manum de tabula nesciret tollere ' ; quoted by Rapin, *Reflexions
sur la Poëtique* : ' C'est un grand défaut que de ne pouvoir finir,
dont Apelle blâmoit si fort Protogene.' *Nocere nimiam diligen-
tiam*, from the same context, is also quoted here by Rapin, in
the margin.

DEDICATION OF THE ÆNEIS (1697).

P. 154, l. 1. *A Heroic Poem, truly such.* See vol. i, p. 181, l. 6, and note.

P. 155, l. 5. *the trifling novels* ; the episodic stories in the *Orlando Furioso.* *Novel* (accented on the last syllable) had of course still the meaning of the Italian *novella,* French *nouvelle*— ' a short story generally of love.'

P. 156, ll. 10–15. [*I can think of nothing . . . Jove was born there*]. All this is left out in the third edition ; I have not been able to find a copy of the second.

P. 157, l. 9. *divinæ particulam auræ.* *Hor. Sat.* ii. 2, l. 79.

l. 33. *Corneille himself . . . was inclined to think.* The troubles of Corneille have been alluded to already, in the *Essay of Dramatic Poesy.* Compare his *Third Discourse* : ' pour moi je trouve qu'il y a des sujets si mal-aisés à renfermer en si peu de tems, que non seulement je les accorderois les vingt-quatre heures entières, mais je me servirois même de la licence que donne ce philosophe de les excéder un peu, et les pousserois sans scrupule jusqu'à trente.' See also *Corneille et la Poétique d'Aristote,* by M. Jules Lemaître.

P. 158, l. 20. *Chymical medicines* ; essences, strong medicines given in small doses ; e. g. opium, arsenic, tartar emetic.

l. 23. *Galenical decoctions* ; of simples, generally of many herbs together, in a large drench, as prescribed by the qualified physicians.

The terms belong to a controversy (more furious than any battles of the books) between the Spagirists or Paracelsians, who used chemical medicines, and the School of Paris which imposed an oath on its pupils never to use anything of the kind. I am indebted for information on this subject to Professor John Ferguson of Glasgow.

P. 159, l. 1. *orbs = orbits.*

P. 161, l. 16. *Tryphon the stationer.* Martial, iv. 72, xiii. 3, *Bibliopola Tryphon.*

l. 18. *in the* ruelle ; properly the space or ' lane' between the bed and the wall ; later, the reception of visitors at the lady's toilette ; then, generally, any party of ladies and gentlemen that pretended to wit. For the original sense, compare Chappuzeau, *Le Cercle de Femmes,* Act i. sc. 3 (about 1655) :

' Et des Cartes tout proche, auecques Campanelle,
Que ie viens de laisser ouuerts dans ma ruelle.'

For the later meaning, Sarasin, *Discours de la Tragedie* (Preface to Scudéry, *L'Amour Tyrannique*), 1639 : ' Nous sommes en un temps où tout le monde croit avoir droit de juger de la Poësie, de laquelle Aristote a fait son chef d'œuvre ; où les ruelles des femmes sont les Tribunaux des plus beaux ouvrages ; où ce qui fut autrefois la vertu de peu de personnes devient la maladie du peuple, et le vice de la multitude.'

P. 162, l. 7. *my two masters* ; Homer and Virgil.

l. 14. *your* Essay of Poetry. First published in 1682.

l. 31. *puny*, i. e. puisné, junior.

P. 164, l. 9. *Scaliger the father.* On the contrary, Scaliger in the Epistle before his *Poetice*, says : ' Nam et Horatius Artem quum inscripsit adeo sine ulla docet arte ut Satyrae propius totum opus illud esse videatur.'

l. 34. *Maevius.* The bad poet's opening line, *Fortunam Priami*, &c., was commonly attributed to Maevius. D. Heinsius quotes for this opinion the *Anticlaudianus* (i. c. 5), of Alanus de Insulis, the Universal Doctor, and supposes it derived from some old commentator—' nam unde id illi in mentem saeculo tam barbaro ? ' Cf. *Satirical Poets of the Twelfth Century*, ed. T. Wright, *Rolls Series* :

> ' Illic pannoso plebescit carmine noster
> Ennius, et Priami fortunas intonat illic
> Maevius ; in coelos audens os ponere mutum.'

The place of *Fortunam Priami* is taken in Boileau's *Art Poëtique* by the opening line of Scudéry's *Alaric* :

> ' Je chante le vainqueur des vainqueurs de la terre.'

P. 165, l. 2. *as Horace would tell you from behind*, i. e. without himself joining in the epic competition.

l. 6. *Saint Louis*, &c. See the Preface to *Juvenal*, p. 28, and note.

l. 16. *machining persons*, i. e. supernatural agents like the gods in Homer.

l. 25. *Segrais.* His Preface is the source of a good deal of this Essay of Dryden's. Jean Regnauld de Segrais (1624–1701), some time in the service of Mademoiselle de Montpensier, admitted to the circle of the Hôtel de Rambouillet before he was elected to the Academy, is perhaps best known through his association with the novels of Madame de Lafayette. *Zayde* was published under his name in 1670. There is a collection of *Segraisiana*. His *Énéide* was published in 1668.

P. 166, l. 28. *Macrobius* : in the *Saturnalia*, books v. and vi.

l. 30. *Tanneguy le Fevre*, of Saumur, ' Tanaquillus Faber ' (1615–1672), a well-known classical scholar, whom Gibbon mentions with respect, editor of Longinus, Lucretius, Aelian, Eutropius, Terence, Horace, Virgil, and others ; father of Madame Dacier, Anna Tanaquilli Fabri filia.

P. 166, l. 30. *Valois.* Dryden perhaps means the *Valesiana* (1694) *ou les Pensées critiques, historiques et morales, et les Poësies Latines de Monsieur de Valois Conseiller du Roi et Historiographe de France.* There are a few notes on Virgil in this collection ; one on discrepancies about the age of Iulus. M. de Valois (Hadrianus Valesius) was born in 1607, and died in 1692.

l. 31. *another whom I name not.* St. Évremond is probably the name which Dryden, out of respect, forbore to mention in this place. See pp. 184, 202, and notes.

P. 167, l. 30. *Persian* ; in later editions ' Assyrian or Median.'

P. 169, l. 5. *Stavo ben.* Perhaps the first appearance in England of this quotation ; repeated in the *Spectator,* No. 25.

l. 34. *Dante.* References to Dante are not frequent in this age ; there is little to note between Davenant's disrespectful mention of him in the Preface to Gondibert, and Gray's temperate appreciation. Mr. Saintsbury thinks that the interpretation of *his dantem jura Catonem,* a little further on, is due to Dante's Cato at the beginning of the *Purgatorio.* Dryden, however, in his note on the passage mentions Montaigne and not Dante as his authority.

P. 172, l. 15. *Bochartus.* His dissertation on the question ' whether Aeneas was ever in Italy,' dated ' de Caen ce 20 Decembre 1663,' is given by Segrais in his *Énéïde.*

P. 173, l. 21. *animamque in vulnere ponit. Georgic.* iv., l. 238 (*animasque . . . ponunt*) :

'   Prone to Revenge, the Bees a wrathful Race,
   When once provok'd assault th' Agressor's Face ;
   And through the purple Veins a passage find,
   There fix their Stings and leave their Souls behind.'

Dryden.

P. 174, l. 30. *Priamus.* In the first edition Atis. After ' Second Book,' the first edition reads, ' Atis then the favourite companion of Ascanius had a better right than he, though I know he was introduced by Virgil to do honour to the family from whom Julius Caesar was descended on the mother's side.' The correction is made in the third edition. I have not been able to find the reading of the second.

P. 178, l. 6. *the author of the Dauphin's* Virgil ; Ruæus (Charles de La Rue) ; his edition of Virgil appeared in 1675 ; the passage recollected by Dryden here is ' Segresius in egregia Præfatione ad Gallicam Æneidos interpretationem.'

l. 17. *Tasso.* On the relations of the two characters, Godfrey and Rinaldo, see Tasso's own views in the *Allegoria del Poema,* printed in the first editions of the *Jerusalem Delivered* (1581) ; and

Spenser's, in the Letter to Sir Walter Raleigh : ' In which I have followed all the antique Poets historicall : first Homere, who in the Persons of Agamemnon and Ulysses hath ensampled a good governour and a vertuous man, the one in his Ilias, the other in his Odysseis ; then Virgil, whose like intention was to doe in the person of Aeneas ; after him Ariosto comprised them both in his Orlando ; and lately Tasso dissevered them again, and formed both parts in two persons, namely, that part which they in Philosophy call Ethice, or vertues of a private man, coloured in his Rinaldo ; the other, named Politice, in his Godfredo.'

P. 182, l. 10. *invulnerable.* ' Dryden had forgot, what he must certainly have known, that the fiction of Achilles being invulnerable, bears date long posterior to the days of Homer. In the *Iliad* he is actually wounded.' *Scott.*

l. 11. Bernardo Tasso, father of Torquato, wrote an epic poem on Amadis of Gaul (*Amadigi*), with a continuation (*Floridante*) ; he is frequently spoken of in his son's *Discorsi.* The pathetic story how he sacrificed his fame as a learned poet to save his honour as a courtier is told by Torquato Tasso in his *Apologia*, 1585 ; it is not irrelevant in the history of the dramatic and narrative Unities : ' Know, therefore, that my father being at the Court of Spain in the service of his master, the Prince of Salerno, was persuaded by the great ones of that Court to make a poem of the fabulous story of Amadis ; which in the judgement of many, and mine particularly, is the most beautiful of all that kind, and perhaps the most wholesome ; because in sentiment and conduct it surpasses all, and in variety of incidents it yields to none, before or since composed. Having then accepted this advice, and being one who most completely understood the Art of Poetry, and especially that of Aristotle, he resolved to make a poem of one action, and framed his fable on the desperation of Amadis for the jealousy of Oriana, ending with the battle between Lisuarte and Cildadan, and many of the other more important things, befallen before or thereafter succeeding, he narrated in episodes or in digressions, as we call them. This was the design, which no master of the art could have made better or fairer. But in the end, not to lose the name of good courtier, he forbore to keep by force that of loftiest poet ; and you shall hear in what manner.

' He was reading some books of the poem to the Prince, his master ; and when he began to read, the rooms were full of gentlemen listening ; but at last they were all withdrawn ; from which thing he took argument that the Unity of Action was in itself little delightful, and not through want of art in himself ; inasmuch as

he had treated it in point of art beyond censure ; and in this he
was no whit deceived.   But perhaps he would have been content
with that which contented Antimachus of Colophon, to whom
Plato was of more account than a multitude, if the Prince had
not added his command to the general persuasion ; wherefore
he was bound to obey,
    " But with heart grieving and a darken'd brow " ;
because he knew that with the unity of the fable his poem lost
much of its perfection ' (*Prose di Torquato Tasso*, ed. Guasti,
Firenze, 1875, i. p. 319).

    P. 182, l. 28. *God-smith.*   The word is used in a different
sense in *Absalom and Achitophel* :
    ' Gods they had tried of every shape and size
      That godsmiths could produce, or priests devise.'

    l. 29. *no warluck.*   Scottish superstitions were being studied
about this time by Pepys and others ; compare Prior, *Alma* :
    ' The commentators on old Ari–
      stotle ('tis urg'd) in judgment vary ;
      They to their own conceits have brought
      The image of his general thought,
      Just as the melancholic eye
      Sees fleets and armies in the sky ;
      And to the poor apprentice ear
      The bells sound " Whittington, Lord Mayor."
      The conjurer thus explains his scheme,
      Thus spirits walk, and prophets dream ;
      North-Britons thus have *second-sight* ;
      And Germans, free from gun-shot, fight.'

    P. 184, l. 12. *a kind of St. Swithin hero.*   Cf. Perrault, *Parallèle
des Anciens et des Modernes en ce qui regarde la Poésie*, 1692 (this
is the third volume of the series of four, completed in 1696), p. 135
(L'Abbé *loquitur*) : ' Cependant puisque Virgile y a trouvé son
compte, je veux bien qu'il l'appelle Père tant qu'il luy plaira ;
mais je ne puis souffrir qu'il le fasse pleurer à tout moment. Il
pleure en voyant les tableaux qui représentent les avantures du
siége de Troye ; non seulement en jettant quelques pleurs, comme
le pouvoit permettre l'amour tendre de la patrie, mais en se
noyant le visage d'un fleuve de larmes, et en pleurant à trois
reprises sur le mesme sujet, ce qui ne convient point à une douleur
de cette nature. Il pleure en quittant Aceste, en perdant Pali-
nure, en voyant Didon dans les enfers, où cette tendresse exces-
sive ne sied point à un Heros. Mais ce qui est absolument insup-
portable, c'est la crainte qui le saisit en tous rencontres. Il tremble
de peur, et ses membres sont glacez de froid, en voyant une

tempeste. La peur le penetre jusques dans la moüelle des os, lorsqu'il voit les Dieux qu'il avoit apportez de Troye qui luy parlent la nuit. La mesme peur luy court encore dans les os, en arrachant les branches dont il dégouta du sang. Cette manière de trembler en toutes sortes d'occasions ne me semble point héroïque, ny convenir au fondateur de l'Empire Romain et au Père de tous les Cesars.'

l. 13. *One of these censors.* Dryden was thinking (with grief) of St. Évremond, *Réflexions sur nos Traducteurs*, 1673 : ' Vous remarquerez encore que toute sces lamentations commencent presque aussitôt que la tempête. Les vents soufflent impétueuse-ment, l'air s'obscurcit ; il tonne, il éclaire, les vagues deviennent grosses et furieuses ; voilà ce qui arrive dans tous les orages. Il n'y a jusque-là ni mât qui se rompe, ni voiles qui se déchirent, ni rames brisées, ni gouvernail perdu, ni ouverture par où l'eau puisse entrer dans le navire ; et c'était là du moins qu'il fallait attendre à se désoler : car il y a mille jeunes gens en Angleterre, et autant de femmes en Hollande, qui s'étonnent à peine où le héros témoigne son désespoir.'

l. 30. *Mr. Moyle* ; see p. 138, and note.

P. 186, l. 10. *Sir Robert Howard.* The old quarrel of 1668 seems to have been appeased by this time.

P. 187, l. 32. *Dr. Cudworth* (1617–1688). Author of the *True Intellectual System of the Universe*, 1678. See Dr. Tulloch's *Rational Theology in England.*

P. 189, l. 14. *his two translators.* See below, note on p. 220, l. 20.

P. 190, l. 8. *presented* ; i. e. gave him a present.

P. 191, l. 14. *Dares Phrygius.* Read Dictys Cretensis, iii. p. 15.

l. 15. *slain cowardly* ; i. e. in a cowardly manner by Achilles ; Dictys tells how Hector, with a small company of retainers, was caught in an ambush at the ford, when going to meet Penthesilea.

l. 18. *Rinaldo.* The objection that Rinaldo was not historical was made in Tasso's lifetime, and answered by him in a letter of February, 1585 : ' Di Reginaldo si fa nell' istoria menzione.'

P. 192, l. 30. *Sir Henry Wotton* : ' An ambassador is an honest man sent to lie abroad for the good of his country.' See his *Life* by Izaak Walton.

P. 193, l. 1. *One who imitates Boccalini.* Trajano Boccalini (1556–1613) began the publication of his *Ragguagli di Parnasso, News of Parnassus*, in 1612, at Venice ; the book was translated into English by Henry Cary, Earl of Monmouth, in 1656 (Adver-tisements from Parnassus in two Centuries, with the Politick Touchstone . . .). It has left some traces in English Literature,

e. g. in the story of the critic presented with the chaff for his pains in sifting (*Spectator*, No. 291), and in the more famous case of the Laconian sentenced to read the History of Guicciardini. See Mestica, *Trajano Boccalini e la letteratura critica e politica del seicento*, 1878. There were many imitators of Boccalini, but for this one it is perhaps unnecessary to make researches.

P. 194, l. 24. *splendid miracles. Speciosa miracula.* Hor., *A. P.* 144.

l. 32. *Tasso, in one of his Discourses*; i. e. in the second, *Dell' Arte Poetica*, 1587 : ' Ma sì come in Didone confuse di tanto spazio l' ordine de' tempi, per aver occasione di mescolare fra la severità dell' altre materie i piacevolissimi ragionamenti d' amore, e per assegnare un' alta ed ereditaria cagione della inimicizia fra Romani e Cartaginesi,' &c.

P. 195, l. 26. *Nec pars ulla magis. Trist.* ii. 535.

P. 197, l. 26. *so strange.* ' Mr. Malone here reads *so strong* ; but *strange* here seems to signify *alarming*, or *startling*.'—SCOTT.

P. 198, l. 15. *Quid prohibetis.* Ovid, *Metam.* vi. 349.

l. 22. *Odysseis.* The form is common, sometimes with mark of diæresis, *Odysseïs* (Dennis, *Letters*, 1695, p. 138) ; as a singular noun it goes along with *Ilias* here ; so also in Spenser's *Letter*, quoted above in the note to p. 178. The spelling *Odysses* is also found, which sometimes seems to be plural (the *Odysseys*), going along with the *Iliads*. So Hobbes, ' the Iliads and Odysses of Homer,' 1676. Sometimes, however, it is singular, as in Pope's *Essay on Homer* (1715), p. 32, ' while the *Iliad* and *Odysses* remain.'

P. 199, l. 26. *There is a kind of invention in the imitation of Raphael.* Compare p. 200, l. 5 : ' for the draughts of both were taken from the ideas they had of Nature.' This is a repetition of the views already expounded in the *Parallel of Poetry and Painting*.

P. 202, l. 1. *Another French critic, whom I will not name.* St. Évremond again, *Sur les Poëmes des Anciens*, 1685 : ' Quelquefois les comparaisons nous tirent des objets qui nous occupent le plus, par la vaine image d'un autre objet, qui fait mal à propos une diversion.' Perrault is more emphatic on the subject of *long-tailed similes* : see the *Spectator*, No. 303. But Dryden had not the same reason for showing respect to Perrault. In the *Character of M. St. Évremont* Dryden had already made his complaint openly : ' It is true that as I am a religious admirer of Virgil I could wish that he had not discovered our father's nakedness ' ; he had also made more concessions to the adversary with regard to Aeneas than he was ready to confirm in 1697.

l. 13. *similitudes . . . are not for tragedy.* See vol. i. p. 223, l. 31, and note. Similes are, however, kept by Addison in his *Cato,* at the end of almost every Act, and ' So have I seen ' remained a formula at any rate till Fielding's *Tragedy of Tragedies.*

l. 28. Perhaps meaning the allegory in *Aen.* iv. 175–188.

P. 204, l. 4. *Pontanus.* His edition of Virgil in fol., Augsburg, 1599.

l. 9. *Junius and Tremellius.* ' Commentators on the Scripture, mentioned by our author in the *Religio Laici,* where, speaking of Dickenson's translation of Père Simon's *Critical History of the Old Testament,* he calls it—

> " A treasure which if country curates buy,
> They Junius and Tremellius may defy." ' SCOTT.

Emanuel Tremellius, 1510–1580, a converted Jew of Ferrara, turned Protestant and became Professor of Hebrew at Sedan. Franciscus Junius (or Du Jon), 1545–1602, was associated with Tremellius in a Latin translation of the Bible ; he was the father of Francis Junius, the philologist, and grandfather of Isaac Vossius.

l. 35. *Ronsard. Préface sur la Franciade.* ' Le poëme héroïque, qui est tout guerrier, comprend seulement les actions d'une année entière, et semble que Virgile y ait failly, selon que luy-mesme l'escrit :

> " Annuus exactis completur mensibus orbis
> Ex quo relliquias divinique ossa parentis
> Condidimus terra."

Il y avoit desja un an passé quand il fit les jeux funèbres de son père en Sicile, et toutefois il n'aborda de long temps après en Italie.'

P. 208, l. 22. *these cant words.* Compare Ben Jonson's dissertation on the natural history of Cant (i. e. slang) in the *Staple of News,* and the Essay of Victor Hugo on the same subject in *Les Misérables.*

P. 210, l. 5. *guardian angels.* Compare the Preface to *Juvenal,* p. 34, and notes ; and *Fables,* p. 272.

l. 13. *which Tasso has not ill copied. Gerusalemme Liberata,* xviii. st. 92–97, where St. Michael shows Godfrey the heavenly host :

> ' But higher lift thy happy eyes, and view
> Where all the sacred hosts of Heaven appear,
> He look'd and saw where winged armies flew,
> Innumerable, pure, divine, and clear ;

'A battle round of squadrons three they show,
And all by threes these squadrons ranged were,
Which spreading wide in rings still wider go :
Mov'd with a stone, calm water circleth so.'
                                        FAIRFAX (st. 96).

P. 213, l. 24. *non me tua turbida.* Inaccurately quoted for
' Non me tua fervida terrent Dicta ferox.' *Aen.* xii. 894–5.

P. 214, l. 35. *ornari res ipsa negat.* Manilius, iii. 39 (Malone's
reference).

P. 215, l. 17. *Cæsura.* Here used for elision of vowels ;
synalepha in *Third Miscellany.*

P. 217, l. 14. *nobis non licet esse tam disertis.* Again. See
p. 103, l. 9.

l. 25. *Dic, quibus in terris* ; Eclogue 3, 106.

l. 31. *Though deep, yet clear,* &c. This couplet was no longer
left unnoticed, after Dryden's quotation of it. It had even to be
put in the *Index* of things too often repeated :

> ' If Anna's happy reign you praise,
> Pray not a word of halcyon days :
> Nor let my votaries show their skill
> In aping lines from *Cooper's Hill* ;
> For know, I cannot bear to hear,
> The mimicry of *deep, yet clear.*'
>   Swift, *Apollo's Edict,* 1720.

This poem of Swift's, by the way, is another proof of the influence
of Boccalini ; it is ' occasioned by *News from Parnassus.*'

P. 218, l. 25. *Formerly the French . . . had but five feet.* Dryden
probably judged hastily, from the decasyllabic verse of the
Franciade, that the Alexandrine was not of long standing in
French poetry :

> ' Charles, mon Prince, enflez-moy le courage ;
> En vostre honneur j'entrepren cet ouvrage ;
> Soyez mon guide et gardez d'abysmer
> Ma nef, qui flotte en si profonde mer.'

P. 219, l. 6. *The turn on thoughts and words.* Above, p. 108,
l. 17.

l. 23. *The want of genius.* ' Although the ordinary genius of
the *French* appears indifferent enough, it is certain that those
who distinguish themselves amongst us, are capable of producing
the finest things,' &c. (*Some Observations upon the Taste and
Judgment of the French,* in the volume of St. Évremond's *Miscellaneous Essays,* for which Dryden wrote the Introduction, 1692 ;
Œuvres, iv. p. 205.) Compare also another passage of St. Évremond about the want of depth in French imaginative work : ' En

effet nous nous contentons des premières images que nous donnent les objets ; et pour nous arrêter aux simples dehors, l'apparent presque toujours nous tient lieu du vrai et le facile du naturel ' (St. Évremond, *De la Comédie anglaise*, 1677 : see vol. i. p. xv.).

P. 220, l. 7. *Non fù si santo*, &c. *Orlando Furioso* xxxv. st. 26, from the discourse of St. John the Evangelist to Astolpho in the Heaven of the Moon.

l. 20. *the two brothers.* ' Robert et Antoine le Chevalier d'Agneaux, frères, de Vire en Normandie,' 1582 : new edition, 1607, with sonnets by Vauquelin de la Fresnaye : already referred to, p. 189, l. 19.

l. 21. *Hannibal Caro.* See above, vol. i. p. 256, l. 19, and vol. ii. p. 29, l. 34.

l. 25. *Le Clerc.* Jean Le Clerc (1657–1736) in *Bibliothèque Universelle et Historique*, t. ix. p. 219 (*de l'Année* 1688) : *Essai de Critique, où l'on tâche de montrer en quoi consiste la Poësie des Hébreux.*

l. 27. *arrant.* Common in the sense of *genuine, thoroughgoing.*

P. 221, l. 7. *the white* ; the middle of the target.

l. 10. *Doctor Morelli.* ' Dr. Henry Morelli, one of the College of Physicians in our author's time ; whose name appears among the Subscribers to the scheme for a publick Dispensary in 1696.' *Malone.*

l. 22. *Sorti Pater æquus utrique. Aen.* x. 450 : ' " My father will be able to bear either extreme of fortune " ; an answer to Turnus' speech, v. 443 ' (Cuperem ipse parens spectator adesset). *Conington.*

P. 222, l. 3. *Sic ait* ; *ibid.* v. 473. Conington refers to Dryden here, and disapproves of Ruæus. Waller translated *Aen.* iv. 437–583.

l. 26. *Sir John Denham, Mr. Waller, and Mr. Cowley.* Denham did the Second Book (*The Destruction of Troy, an Essay on the Second Book of Virgil's Æneis*, 1636) ; also a free version of the *Passion of Dido.* Cowley, the Second *Georgic* from v. 458.

P. 223, l. 10. *in a former dissertation* ; i. e. in the *Parallel of Poetry and Painting*, p. 147.

l. 30. *These are mob readers.* ' Mob ' was not yet quite established in 1692 ; ' mob, *as they call them*,' Preface to *Cleomenes.* Two years before in *Don Sebastian* it is the *mobile* (Act i. sc. 1 ; Act iii. sc. 3. ' 'Tis a laudable commotion ; the voice of the *mobile* is the voice of Heaven ').

P. 224, l. 12. *like the Mançanares.* From Bouhours' *Entretiens d'Ariste et d'Eugène : II. La Langue Françoise.* ' Pour moy je

n'entends jamais ces mots et ces expressions de la langue Castillane, que je ne me souvienne du Mançanares. On diroit à en-
tendre ce grand mot que la rivière de Madrid est le plus grand
fleuve du monde : et cependant ce n'est qu'un petit ruisseau, qui
est le plus souvent à sec ; et qui, si nous en croyons un Poëte
Castillan, ne mérite pas d'avoir un pont. Je me souviens des vers
Espagnols, et vous ne serez peut-estre pas fasché de les apprendre
en passant :

> " Duelete dessa puente, Mançanares,
> Mira que dize por ti la gente,
> Que no eres rio para media puente,
> Y que ella es puente para treinta mares."

Luis de Góngora.

Voilà ce que c'est que le Mançanares, et voilà aussi à peu près ce
que c'est que la langue Castillane.'

P. 224, l. 22. *Owen's Epigrams.* See above, note on p. 27, l. 25.

l. 25. *a bladdered greatness.* See vol. i. p. 247, l. 11 : ' swelling
puffy style.'

P. 225, l. 3. *as a wit said formerly.* Lord Rochester ; see p. 258.

l. 24. *imagination only.* Imagination has been degraded in
meaning since Dryden explained its functions in the account of
Annus Mirabilis ; what here is called Imagination is there called
Fancy, or Invention and Fancy.

l. 28. *Marini's* Adone. Published at Paris in 1623, with a
Preface (in French) by Chapelain : *L'Adone, poema del Cavalier
Marino.* The poem has been fully described by Mr. J. A. Sy-
monds in his *Renaissance in Italy.* Marino was known to English
poets, though his influence has been unduly exaggerated. He is
seen at his best in Crashaw's version from his poem on the
Slaughter of the Innocents. In the *Guerre di Parnaso,* 1643, by
Scipione Herrico, ' one who imitates Boccalini,' Marino is the
leader of a revolt against Aristotle and Apollo.

P. 226, l. 11. *Dampier.* His *Voyages* came out in this year : *A
New Voyage round the World.* Dampier is speaking of Quito, in
the year 1684 : ' I know no place where Gold is found but what is
very unhealthy.'

l. 28. *Mr. Creech.* See vol. i. p. 264, l. 19.

P. 227, l. 5. *Philarchus, I remember, taxes Balzac.* More accurately *Phyllarchus i. q. dux foliorum,* with an equivoque ' Head of
a house of *Feuillants* ' : according to the *Segraisiana,* Balzac's
sagacity at once discerned in this name the Feuillant his adversary. See for the whole controversy Emile Roy, *De Ioan. Lud.
Guezio Balzacio contra Dom. Ioan. Gulonium disputante,* 1892.
Phyllarchus was Jean Goulu de St. François ; his criticism of

Balzac's style appeared in 1627, *Lettres de Phyllarque à Ariste où il est traicté de l'éloquence françoise* ; a second Part in 1628. Balzac in these Letters is *Narcisse*. Dryden refers to a passage in Letter xxi : ' Le mesme Quintilian enseigne que la suitte de plusieurs monosyllabes est vicieuse, d'autant qu'elle fait sauteller le discours entrecoupé de petites particules et le rend comme raboteux : et que partant il faut esviter la continuation des petits mots comme aussi par raison contraire on doit fuir l'entresuitte des parolles qui sont longues, à cause qu'elles apportent une pesanteur des-agréable à la prononciation. Voyons si Narcisse n'a point encores péché contre cette reigle. Il parle de la sorte en la mesme Letre [*en la Letre* 20 *du* 4 *livre*]. Qui est-ce qui peut dire cela de soy ? Où sont ceux qui se sont tenus fermes, &c. ? Ariste, tu peux remarquer la suitte de quinze petits mots dont les treize sont monosyllabes ; ce qui montre ou qu'il est ignorant des préceptes de la Rhétorique, ou qu'il y a des reigles qui sont particulières à luy, et incognues à tous les Orateurs.'

P. 229, l. 1. *a Pindaric* ; i. e. an Alexandrine.

l. 5. *Chapman has followed him.* Triplets in Chapman's *Odyssey*, e. g. i. 399, iv. 27, v. 361, vi. 351.

l. 7. *Mr. Cowley.* Cf. Johnson's *Life of Cowley* : ' Cowley was, I believe, the first poet that mingled Alexandrines at pleasure with the common heroick of ten syllables, and from him Dryden borrowed the practice whether ornamental or licentious.' ' Of triplets in his *Davideis* he makes no use, and perhaps did not at first think them allowable ; but he appears afterwards to have changed his mind, for in the verses on the government of Cromwell he inserts them liberally with great happiness.'

P. 230, l. 10. *Staff*, i. e. *stave, stanza.* See note in vol. i. on p. 12, l. 35 : Davenant's views in the Preface to *Gondibert.*

P. 231, l. 19. *the excuse of Boccace.* In the Epilogue to the *Decameron* (*Conclusione dell' autore*) : ' che maestro alcun non si truova da Dio in fuori, che ogni cosa faccia bene e compiutamente. E Carlo Magno che fu il primo facitore de' paladini non ne seppe tanti creare, che esso di lor soli potesse fare hoste.'

P. 232, l. 14. *hammered money, for want of milled.* Compare Letter xvii. in Scott's *Dryden* (to Tonson ; Feb. 1696 ?) on the difficulties about the currency : ' I shall lose enough by your bill upon Mr. Knight ; for after having taken it all in silver, and not in half-crowns neither, but shillings and sixpences, none of the money will go ; for which reason I have sent it all back again, and as the less loss will receive it in guinneys at 29 shillings each.' And again May 26 (Letter xviii), ' Sir Ro. Howard writt me word, that if I cou'd make any advantage by being paid in clipp'd money, he would change it in the Exchequer.' See Macaulay, *History of England*, c. xxi. 1, where Dryden's phrase is quoted from this Essay.

P. 233, l. 8. for *Cupid* read *Ascanius* :

> ' Lull'd in her Lap, amidst a Train of Loves
> She gently bears him to her blissful Groves :
> Then with a wreath of Myrtle crouns his Head,
> And softly lays him in a flow'ry Bed.'

l. 21. *quisquis studet.* Hor. *Od.* iv. 2, 1.

l. 22. *Aude, hospes. Aen.* viii. 364.

P. 235, l. 6. *The late Earl of Lauderdale.* Richard Maitland (1653–1695), fourth Earl, sent over his translation from Paris, where he was living doubly exiled, outlawed in England, and not received at St. Germain's by reason of his opposition to the extreme Catholic policy of King James. His work was published in 1737.

l. 30. *Two other worthy friends of mine.* Dr. Knightly Chetwood and Mr. Addison. Dr. Chetwood wrote the *Life of Virgil*, and the Preface to the *Pastorals* ; see Dryden's letter to Tonson, No. xxvi. in Scott's edition : ' I have also this day written to Mr. Chetwood, and let him know that the book is immediately goeing to the press again. My opinion is that the printer shou'd begin with the first *Pastoral*, and print on to the end of the *Georgiques*, or farther if occasion be, till Dr. Chetwood corrects his *Preface*, which he writes me word is printed very false.' Addison wrote the Preface to the *Georgics*.

P. 236, l. 12. *why I writ not always in the proper terms.* See Introduction to *Annus Mirabilis*, and compare Warton on Dante, *History of English Poetry*, cxlix : ' We are surprised that a poet should write one hundred cantos on Hell, Paradise, and Purgatory. But this prolixity is partly owing to the want of art and method ; and is common to all early compositions, in which everything is related circumstantially and without rejection, and not in those general terms which are used by modern writers.'

l. 23. *the four preliminary lines* :

> ' Ille ego qui quondam gracili modulatus avena
> Carmen et egressus silvis vicina coegi
> Ut quamvis avido parerent arva colono
> Gratum opus agricolis at nunc horrentia Martis.'

l. 19. *Tucca and Varius.* The story being that these editors ' retrenched ' the four opening lines, leaving *Arma virumque* at the head of the first book.

P. 238, l. 28. *A Sixth Pastoral (Silenus)*, translated by Lord Roscommon ; *Pharmaceutria* (the Eighth Pastoral).

l. 29. *Orpheus*, ' being a Translation out of the Fourth Book of Virgil's *Georgic* ' by Lord Mulgrave, referred to already, p. 222.

P. **239**, l. 3. *Erichthonius*. Virgil, *Georg.* iii. 113 :

' Primus Erichthonius currus et quattuor ausus
    Iungere equos, rapidusque rotis insistere victor.'

l. 20. *your noble kinsman the Earl of Dorset*. ' Their mothers were half-sisters, being both daughters of Lionel Cranfield, Earl of Middlesex.' SCOTT.

POSTSCRIPT TO THE ÆNEIS.

P. **242**, l. 25. *The present Earl of Peterborough*. The friend of Pope and Swift, the hero of the war of the Spanish succession, ' Mordanto.'

l. 34. *Sir William Trumball* ; to whom Pope's first Pastoral is dedicated ; died 1716.

P. **243**, l. 15. *Fabrini* : printed at Venice, 1623.

l. 18. *Sir William Bowyer*. Mentioned in a note on the Second *Georgic* : ' Nature has conspired with Art to make the garden at Denham Court of Sir William's own plantation one of the most delicious spots of ground in England ; it contains not above five acres (just the compass of Alcinous's garden, described in the *Odysses*),' &c.

l. 27. *Earl of Exeter*. John Cecil, fifth Earl, a Nonjuror. The village of Dryden's birth is Aldwinkle in Northamptonshire.

P. **244**, l. 1. *William Walsh*. See Pope's note on his First *Pastoral*, where this remark of Dryden's is quoted ; and the Epistle to Dr. Arbuthnot.

l. 20. *part of the Third Georgic*. Mr. Malone conjectures the concealed translator may have been Lord Lansdowne, author of the poem which precedes that translation in the *Miscellanies*. SCOTT.

l. 27. *After his Bees*. Alluding to a translation of the Third Book of the *Georgics*, exclusive of the story of Aristæus, which appeared in the third volume of the *Miscellanies* ; by the famous Addison, then of Queen's College, Oxford. SCOTT.

l. 32. *Dr. Guibbons*. The same of whom Dryden elsewhere says :

' Guibbons but guesses, nor is sure to save.' SCOTT.

l. 32. *Dr. Hobbs*. Also an eminent physician of the time, ridiculed, in the *Dispensary*, under the title of Guiacum. SCOTT.

l. 35. *The only one of them*. Blackmore.

PREFACE TO FABLES (1700).

P. 246, l. 10. *a certain nobleman.* The Duke of Buckingham.

l. 18. *the speeches of Ajax and Ulysses.* See i. p. 223.

l. 19. *balk.* Cf. *Dedication of the Georgics,* ' if I *balked* this opportunity.'

l. 20. *Fifteenth Book.* ' Of the Pythagorean Philosophy.'

P. 247, l. 4. *the Hunting of the Boar.* Meleager and Atalanta from the Eighth Book.

l. 5. *Cinyras and Myrrha,* from the Tenth ; *Baucis and Philemon* from the Eighth.

l. 11. *Sandys.* See above.

l. 20. *Spenser more than once insinuates that the soul of Chaucer was transfused into his body. Faery Queene,* iv. 2, 34 :

' Then pardon O most sacred happie spirit !
That I thy labours lost may thus revive,
And steale from thee the meede of thy due merit,
That none durst ever whilest thou wast alive,
And being dead in vaine yet many strive :
Ne dare I like ; but through infusion sweete
Of thine own spirit which doth in me survive,
I follow here the footing of thy feete,
That with thy meaning so I may the rather meete.'

ll. 26–28. Fairfax's *Tasso* was published in 1600. *Godfrey of Bulloigne, or the Recovery of Jerusalem.* One of the stanzas is quoted above in a note on p. 210, l. 13.

P. 248, l. 23. *octave rhyme.* The stanza was used, in French, by Thibaut, King of Navarre, in the previous century, and before Boccaccio, in Italian, by the author of the *Cantare di Fiorio e Biancifiore.* But Boccaccio was the first author to give the octave its rank as the Italian ' measure for heroic verse ' (p. 107).

P. 249, l. 2. *our learned Mr. Rymer.* From the severity of the *Third Miscellany* (1693), Dryden had returned to his more gentle opinion of Rymer, ' an excellent critic ' as he is called in the *Vindication of the Duke of Guise* (1683).

l. 3. *from the Provençal.* See Rymer on the ' Provencial Poetry ' in his *Short View of Tragedy.* ' This *Provencial* was the first of the modern languages that yielded and chim'd in with the musick and sweetness of ryme ; which making its way by *Savoy* to *Monferat,* the *Italians* thence began to file their *volgare,* and to set their verses all after the Chimes of *Provence.* Our Intermarriages and our Dominions thereabouts brought us much sooner acquainted with their Tongue and Poetry ; and they with us that would write verse, as King *Richard, Savery de Mauleon,* and *Rob. Grostead*, finding the English stubborn and unwieldy, fell readily to that of *Provence*, as more glib, and lighter on the Tongue. But they who attempted verse in English, down till *Chaucers* time, made an heavy pudder, and are always miserably put to 't for a word to clink : which commonly fall so awkard and unexpectedly as dropping from the Clouds by some Machine or Miracle. *Chaucer* found an Herculean labour on his Hands; and did perform to Admiration. He seizes all Provencal, French, or Latin that came in his way, gives them a new garb and livery, and mingles them amongst our English: turns out English, gowty, or superannuated, to place in their room the foreigners, fit for service, train'd and accustomed to Poetical Discipline. But tho' the Italian reformation was begun and finished well nigh at the same time by *Boccace, Dante*, and *Petrarch*, our language retain'd something of the churl ; something of the Stiff and Gothish did stick upon it, till long after *Chaucer*. *Chaucer* threw in Latin, French, Provencial, and other Languages, like new Stum to raise a Fermentation ; in Queen *Elizabeth's* time it grew fine, but came not to an Head and Spirit, did not shine and sparkle till Mr. *Waller* set it a running.' This is the passage of literary history summed up in Rymer's table of contents in the following remarkable terms : ' Chaucer *refin'd our English. Which in perfection by* Waller.' Rymer knew something about Provençal poetry, and something about Chaucer, and through Dryden and Pope has made it a matter of traditional belief that Chaucer belongs, in some way or other, to ' the Provençal School.' Dryden seems not to have distinguished between Provençal and old French.

l. 31. *the other harmony of prose* ; a reminiscence of Aristotle, *Poet.* c. iv. τῆς λεκτικῆς ἀρμονίας.

P. 250, l. 19. *dead-colouring.* See vol. i. p. 109, l. 7.

l. 26. *staved* ; like contraband hogsheads.

P. 251, l. 9. *a religious lawyer.* Jeremy Collier.

P. 252, l. 24. *Mr. Hobbes.* ' *The Iliads and Odysses of Homer.* Translated out of Greek into English by Thomas Hobbes of Malmesbury, with a large Preface concerning the Virtues of an Heroic Poem written by the Translator,' 1676.

l. 31. *now the words are the colouring.* See p. 147, and p. 223.

P. 253, l. 14. *Choleric*, &c. Dryden had before him the *locus classicus* on humours, in the *Nun's Priest's Tale* (the Cock and the Fox).

l. 34. *Longinus*, c. 12 καὶ ὁ μὲν ἡμέτερος διὰ τὸ μετὰ βίας ἕκαστα ἔτι δέ τάχους ῥώμης δεινότητος οἷον καίειν τε ἅμα καὶ διαρπάζειν σκηπτῷ τινι παρεικάζοιτ' ἂν ἢ κεραυνῷ, ὁ δὲ Κικέρων ὡς ἀμφιλαφής τις ἐμπρησμὸς οἶμαι πάντη νέμεται καὶ ἀνειλεῖται, κ.τ.λ.

P. 254, l. 6. *the violent playing of a new machine.* Dryden's memory had misplaced the Dream of Agamemnon, which in the Second Book comes *before* the Catalogue of the Ships.

l. 26. *philology.* Includes all studies connected with literature.

P. 255, l. 5. *the invention of Petrarch.* What Petrarch sent to Boccaccio was a Latin version of Boccaccio's story of Griseldá in the *Decameron,* accompanied by a letter : there is an English translation of the letter in Robinson and Rolfe's Essay on *Petrarch,* 1898. Petrarch made his translation in the year 1373.

l. 8. *by a Lombard author.* See *Troilus and Cressida* above, vol. i. p. 203, l. 14.

P. 256, l. 32. *John Littlewit* : at the beginning of Ben Jonson's *Bartholomew Fair* ; not quite as in Dryden's quotation : ' A pretty conceit and worth the finding ! I have such luck to spin out such fine things still, and like a silk-worm, out of myself.'

P. 257, l. 17. *the turn of words.* See p. 108, l. 17, and note.

P. 258, l. 5. *one of our late great poets.* Cowley ; see above, p. 108, and compare the judgement of the *Battle of the Books* on Cowley : ' — one half lay panting on the ground to be trod in pieces by the horses feet ; the other half was borne by the frighted steed through the field. This Venus took, washed it seven times in ambrosia, then struck it thrice with a sprig of amarant ; upon which the leather grew round and soft, and the leaves turned into feathers, and being gilded before, continued gilded still ; so it became a dove, and she harnessed it to her chariot.' Compare Dryden's reference in the Dedication of *Aurengzebe* : ' — his master Epicurus and my better master Cowley.'

l. 27. for *Catullus* read *Martial* :
     ' Occurrit tibi nemo quod libenter
     Quod quocunque venis, fuga es et ingens
     Circa te Ligurine solitudo :
     Quid sit scire cupis : nimis poeta es.' iii. 44.

l. 30. *auribus istius temporis accommodata* : ' auribus iudicum accommodata.' Tac. *Orat.* c. 21.

P. 259, l. 2. *he who published the last edition of him.* ' Thomas Speght's edition of Chaucer was published in 1597 and 1602. The Preface contains the passage which Dryden alludes to : " And for his (Chaucer's) verses, although, in divers places, they seem to us to stand of unequal measures, yet a skilful reader, who can scan them in their nature, shall find it otherwise. And if a verse, here and there, fal out a syllable shorter or longer than another, 1 rather aret it to the negligence and rape of Adam Scrivener (that

I may speake as Chaucer doth), than to any unconning or oversight in the author : for how fearful he was to have his works
miswritten, or his vearse mismeasured, may appeare in the end
of his fift booke of *Troylus and Creseide,* where he writeth
thus :

> ' And for there is so great diversitie
> In English, and in writing of our tongue,
> So pray I God that none miswrite thee,
> Ne thee mismetre for defaut of tongue.'

By his hasty and inconsiderate contradiction of honest Speght's
panegyric, Dryden has exposed himself to be censured for pro-
nouncing rashly upon a subject with which he was but imperfectly acquainted. The learned Tyrwhitt has supported Speght's
position with equal pains and success, and plainly proves that the
apparent inequalities of the rhyme of Chaucer arise chiefly from
the change in pronunciation since his time, particularly from
a number of words being now pronounced as one syllable, which
in those days were prolonged into two, or as two syllables, which
were anciently three. These researches, in the words of Ellis,
" have proved what Dryden denied, viz., that Chaucer's versification, wherever his genuine text is preserved, was uniformly
correct, although the harmony of his lines has, in many cases,
been obliterated by the changes that have taken place in the mode
of accenting our language." *Specimens of the Early English Poets,*
vol. i. p. 209.' Scott.

l. 20. *a Harrington.* Sir John Harington's *Orlando Furioso
in English Heroical Verse* appeared in 1591.

P. 260, l. 12. *the tale of Piers Plowman,* i. e. the *Ploughman's
Tale,* printed at the end of the *Canterbury Tales* ; written by the
author of the *Ploughman's Creed.* See Skeat, *Chaucerian and other
Pieces* ; *Supplement to the Works of Geoffrey Chaucer.*

P. 261, l. 21. *Dr. Drake.* James Drake wrote an answer to
Collier. *The Ancient and Modern Stages Reviewed, or Mr. Collier's
View of the Immorality and Profaneness of the Stage set in a True
Light,* 1699.

l. 27. *prior læsit.* Terence, *Eunuchus prol.* 4 :

> ' Tum siquis est qui dictum in se inclementius
> Existumabit esse, sic existumet
> Responsum non dictum esse quia laesit prior.'

P. 262, l. 15. *Baptista Porta* ; the famous Italian physiogno-
mist.

P. 263, l. 16. *Wife of Bath, in the Prologue to her Tale* ;
modernized by Pope.

P. 264, l. 34. *The late Earl of Leicester.* Philip, third Earl, to whom *Don Sebastian* is dedicated ; brother of Algernon Sidney. He died in 1697.

P. 267, l. 17. *some old Saxon friends.* The study of early English and the cognate dialects was making great progress at this time, through the industry of George Hickes, Edward Thwaites, and other scholars ; Dryden was probably thinking also of Rymer.

l. 30. *their grandam gold.* Compare *The Wild Gallant*, iv. 1 : ' now I think on 't, Frances has one hundred and twenty pieces of old grandam-and-aunt gold left her, that she would never let me touch.'

P. 268, l. 13. *into the old Provençal* : as before, Dryden does not distinguish Provençal from old French.

P. 269, ll. 25–33. Dryden did not know Boccaccio's *Teseide*, the immediate original of the *Knight's Tale.*

P. 270, l. 33. *M——* : Milbourne.

l. 33. *B——* : ' the City Bard or Knight Physician,' Sir Richard Blackmore.

P. 272, l: 5. *his* Arthurs : *Prince Arthur* and *King Arthur*, Blackmore's *Epics*, published in 1695 and 1697.

l. 8. *the Guardian Angels of Kingdoms.* See Preface to *Juvenal*, p. 34.

l. 11. *the whirl-bats of Eryx. Aen.* v. 400.

l. 17. *Mr. Collier.* Jeremy Collier, 1650–1726, a non-juring clergyman, wrote, besides his *Short View of the Immorality and Profaneness of the Stage*, 1698, an *Historical Dictionary*, 1701–1721, from which a remark on Shakespeare is quoted by Mr. Browning :, ' His genius was jocular but, when disposed, he could be very serious.' Collier had found fault with Dryden's want of religion : ' The Author of *Don Sebastian* strikes at the *Bishops* through the sides of the *Mufti*, and borrows the Name of the Turk to make the Christians ridiculous.' ' In *Cleomenes* Cassandra rails against Religion at the Altar, and in the midst of a publick Solemnity :

" *Accurs'd be thou, Grass-eating fodder'd God !*
Accurs'd thy Temple, more accurs'd thy Priests ! " '

P. 273, l. 24. *the battle of Senneph* (Senef), Aug. 11, 1674, when Condé fell on the rear-guard of the Prince of Orange, then re-treating between Charleroi and Mons. The battle had been described by Sir William Temple in his *Memoirs of what passed in Christendom from* 1672 *to* 1679.

APPENDIX A

A SHORT HISTORY OF CRITICISM FROM THE TRANSLATOR'S PREFACE TO *MIXT ESSAYS WRITTEN ORIGINALLY IN FRENCH BY THE SIEUR DE SAINT EVREMONT*, 1685.

AFTER the Italians the *French* took fire, and began to sublime and purifie themselves upon the rising of that glorious Minister *Cardinal Richlieu*, who founded the *Royal Academy*, and having muster'd the best Wits together, employ'd them in reforming the Stage, the Language, and Manners of his Country. *L'Abbé Hedelin* undertook the Theater, of which he published the most perfect Treatise yet extant ; and if the *Cardinal* had liv'd some years longer, he would have carried it much higher, and even contended with *Athens*, and *Rome* themselves. *Malherbe, Corneille, Chapelain, Moliere, Boileau, Fontaine*, and *Rapin*, have cultivated, and exalted the Subject. The Learned *Chanoine* of *St. Geneviéve* R. P. le *Bossu*, hath given us the best *Idea*, and most exact Model of *Epick* Poem. The *Dutch* and *Germans* (as though frozen up) have produced little in this kind ; yet we must confess that *Grotius, Heinsius, Scaliger* and *Vossius* were Learned Criticks. Some of the *English* have indeed rais'd their Pens, and soar'd as high as any of the *Italians*, or *French* ; yet Criticism came but very lately in fashion amongst us ; without doubt *Ben Johnson* had a large stock of Critical Learning ; *Spencer* had studied *Homer*, and *Virgil*, and *Tasso*, yet he was misled, and debauched by *Ariosto*, as Mr. *Rymer* judiciously observes ; *Davenant* gives some stroaks of great Learning and Judgment, yet he is for unbeaten Tracks, new Ways, and undiscover'd Seas ; *Cowley* was a great Master of the *Antients*, and had the true *Genius* and Character of a Poet ; yet this nicety and boldness of Criticism was a stranger all this time to our Climate ; Mr. *Rymer* and Mr. *Dryden* have begun to launch out into it, and indeed they have been very fortunate Adventurers. The Earls of R. and M. and Mr. W. have given some fine touches ; Mr. *Drydens Criticks* are generally quaint and solid, his Prefaces doth as often correct and improve my Judgment, as his Verses doth Charm my Fancy ; he is every-where Sweet, Elegant, and Sublime ; the *Poet* and *Critick* were seldom both so Conspicuous and Illustrious in one man as in him, except *Rapin*. Mr. *Rymer* in his incomparable Preface to *Rapin*, and in his Reflections upon some late *Tragedies*, hath given sufficient proofs that he hath studied and understands *Aristotle* and *Horace*, *Homer*, and *Virgil*, besides the *Wits* of all Countries and Ages ; so that we may justly number him in the first rank of *Criticks*, as having a most accomplish'd *Idea* of Poetry and the Stage.

APPENDIX B

AUTHORITIES, CRITICAL AND HISTORICAL

BELJAME, *Le Public et les Hommes de Lettres en Angleterre.*
1883.

BLOUNT, *De Re Poetica*, 1694.

BOSSU, *Traité du Poëme épique.* 1675.

BOUHOURS, *Les Entretiens d'Ariste et d'Eugène.* 1671.

BREITINGER, *Les Unités d'Aristote avant le Cid de Corneille.*
1879.

BUTCHER, *Aristotle's Theory of Poetry and Fine Art.* 1897.

BUTLER, Samuel, *The Genuine Remains in Verse and Prose.*
1759.

CAMPBELL, Lewis, *Greek Tragedy.* 1891.

CHAPELAIN, Preface to *L'Adone* of Marino. 1622.

—— Preface to *La Pucelle.* 1656.

CHAPPUZEAU, *Le Théâtre Français.* 1674.

COLLINS, J. Churton, *Essays and Studies.* 1895.

CORNEILLE, *Le Théâtre de P. Corneille*, 3 volumes, 8º, 1660,
containing the three Discourses and the *Examens* :—
[Vol. i. *Discours de l'Utilité et des Parties du Poëme
dramatique.*
Vol. ii. *Discours de la Tragedie et des moyens de la
traiter selon le vraysemblable ou le necessaire.*
Vol. iii. *Discours des trois Unitez d'Action, de Jour et
de Lieu.*]

DACIER, *Preface sur les Satires d'Horace.* 1687.

D'AUBIGNAC (HÉDELIN), *La Pratique du Théâtre.* 1657.

DAVENANT, Preface to *Gondibert.* 1651.

DENNIS, *Select Works.* 1718.

ELTON, O., *The Augustan Ages.* 1899.

FOURNEL, *Le Théâtre au xviie Siècle ; La Comédie.* 1892.

GARNETT, R., *The Age of Dryden.* 1895.

GOSSE, *From Shakespeare to Pope.* 1885.

HAMELIUS, *Die Kritik in der Englischen Literatur des* 17. *und* 18. *Jahrhunderts.* 1897.

JOHNSON, *Lives of the Poets.* 1779–1781.

JUSSERAND, *Shakespeare en France sous l'Ancien Régime.* 1898.

LA MESNARDIÈRE, *La Poétique.* 1640.

LEMAITRE, *Corneille et la Poétique d'Aristote.* 1888.

MALONE, *Critical and Miscellaneous Prose Works of John Dryden.* 1800.

PERRAULT, *Parallèle des Anciens et des Modernes.* 1688–1696.

PETIT DE JULLEVILLE, *Le Théâtre en France.* 1889.
—— (edited by), *Histoire de la Langue et de la Littérature française.* 1896–1900.

RAPIN, *Œuvres diverses du R. P. R. Rapin.* Amsterdam. 1686.

RIGAL, *Alexandre Hardy et le Théâtre français à la fin du xvie et au commencement du xviie Siècle.* 1889.

RYMER, *The Tragedies of the Last Age Considered and Examined by the Practice of the Ancients.* 1678.
—— *A Short View of Tragedy.* 1693.

SAINT-ÉVREMOND, *Œuvres,* ed. Des Maizeaux. 1705.

SAINTSBURY, *Dryden* [' English Men of Letters ']. 1881.

SARASIN, *Discours de la Tragédie.* 1639.

SCALIGER, J. C., *Poetices libri septem.* 1561.

SCOTT, *Life of Dryden,* in his edition of Dryden's *Works.* 1808.

SCUDÉRY, Preface to *Ibrahim ou l'illustre Bassa.* 1641.
—— Preface to *Alaric.* 1654.

SETTLE, *Notes and Observations on the Empress of Morocco revised.* 1674.

VAUGHAN, C. E., *English Literary Criticism.* 1896.

WESELMANN, *Dryden als Kritiker.* 1893.

INDEX

THE END.